MEDIEVAL INDIA 1

MEDIEVAL INDIA 1

Researches in the History of India 1200–1750

Edited by
IRFAN HABIB

CENTRE OF ADVANCED STUDY IN HISTORY
Aligarh Muslim University

OXFORD
UNIVERSITY PRESS

OXFORD
UNIVERSITY PRESS

Oxford University Press is a department of the University of Oxford.
It furthers the University's objective of excellence in research, scholarship,
and education by publishing worldwide. Oxford is a registered trademark of
Oxford University Press in the UK and in certain other countries

Published in India by
Oxford University Press
22 Workspace, 2nd Floor, 1/22 Asaf Ali Road, New Delhi 110002, India

First Edition published in 1992
Oxford India Paperbacks 1999
36th impression 2022

ISBN-13: 978-0-19-564658-0
ISBN-10: 0-19-564658-4

Phototypeset at All India Press, Pondicherry 605 001
Printed in India by Replika Press Pvt. Ltd.

Contents

Prefatory Note

The present collection of essays on Medieval India seeks to bring within a single volume the fruits of some of the recent researches on Medieval India, and includes a study of a document, and reviews. The new series is a successor to the *Medieval India Quarterly* (5 volumes, 1950–63) and *Medieval India—a Miscellany* (4 volumes, 1969–75), issued successively under the editorship of Professors S. A. Rashid, S. Nurul Hasan, and K. A. Nizami and the undersigned. It is hoped that, though not claiming to be an annual periodical, the volumes of the present series will appear annually.

While almost all the papers and reviews in this volume are from authors who had worked, or are working, at Aligarh, it is not our intention to confine future contributions only to those who fall under this category. The widest definition of Medieval India would be adopted in terms of time and scope, so as to embrace any historical theme pertaining to any portion of the millennium preceding 1800, and to any region of South Asia.

The Centre is grateful to the Oxford University Press for their willingness to undertake this enterprise on its behalf. Suggestions for improvement will be most welcome, and I should like to thank in advance all those who care to make them.

IRFAN HABIB

1

Formation of the Sultanate Ruling Class of the Thirteenth Century

IRFAN HABIB

The Delhi Sultanate was based on a political system which appears to have been different in many essential particulars from the 'feudalism' of the states which it supplanted. This was due partly to the administrative mechanism, revolving around the *iqṭā'*, or transferable revenue-assignment, and partly to the character of its ruling class. A number of problems relating to the formation and subsequent changes in the composition of the Sultanate ruling class, however, seem to stand in need of elucidation. That would, of course, be a large task. The present paper is restricted to a study of the genesis and early history of the class, covering the last years of the twelfth and the larger part of the thirteenth century.

Since the Sultanate was created as a result of the Ghorian conquests, our study must naturally begin with the ruling groups in the kingdom of Ghor.[1] Our main source for Ghor as much as for the early Sultanate is the *Ṭabaqāt-i Nāṣirī*, whose author, Minhāj Sirāj, had grown up in that region.[2]

The core principality of Ghor corresponded largely to the modern Afghan province of that name, which contains the mountainous district (*jibal*) described by Minhāj. But it probably

[1] C.E. Bosworth in his article, 'The Early Islamic History of Ghūr', *Central Asiatic Journal*, VI (1961), assembles much useful information from varied sources; but he stops just short of the period with which we are concerned.

[2] Minhāj Sirāj's own remarks, *Ṭabāqāt-i Nāṣirī*, ed. 'Abdu'l Ḥaī Ḥabībī, Kabul, 1342, I, pp. 318–19. See also the information on the author's family and early career collected by Ḥabībī in Vol. II (Kabul, 1343), pp. 230–48; and Raverty (tr.), *Tabaḳāt-i Nāṣirī*, London, 1881, pp. xix–xxv. In our references *TN* stands for Ḥabībī's ed. of *Ṭabāqāt-i Nāṣirī*.

also included a large part of modern Oruzgān, as it contains the town of Tamurān.[3] The population of the region was largely sedentary, and had apparently been so since ancient times.[4] It was, in spite of its isolation owing to geographical barriers, a part of the Iranian zone, with practically no identifiable Turkic influences. The descent of the inhabitants was traced to 'Arab tribes' who were reputedly settled here by a son of the Perso-Arab emperor Ẓaḥḥāk, himself fleeing from the Iranian hero Afrīdūn.[5] Some local survivals of the Rustam legend also existed.[6]

The ruling dynasty was called Shansabānī. The tribe (*qabīla*) next in importance was that of the Shīshānī, from which military notables (*pahalwāns*) were drawn.[7] The Kharmīl was yet another clan, contributing *pahalwāns* and, in course of time, *maliks* or nobles.[8]

As the kingdom of Ghor expanded in the twelfth century, especially under 'Alā'auddīn Jahān Soz (1149–61), some other elements were brought into the Ghorian ruling class. The most significant of these entrants were those drawn from the region or race of Khalj. In view of their subsequent role in the political history of India these deserve more than passing notice.

An early statement (by Istakharī, *c.* 930) is to the effect that the Khalj were settled, of old, 'behind' Ghor, and, being originally Turks, were 'cattle breeders of Turkish appearance, dress and language'.[9] From this and other statements in certain later sources, it has been widely accepted by modern scholars that the Khalaj or Khalj were Turks, though Minorsky does suggest a confusion with the Khalakh in certain authorities.[10] Bosworth speaks freely of them as 'Khalaj Turk nomads' even in the eleventh century.[11] This is not the place to enter into a debate on the real or fancied Turkish origins of the Khalj. (In fact, the correct name seems to be Khalich, which would further discount any possible relationship with

[3] *TN*, I, pp. 328–9, for both the mountains and Tamurān.

[4] Bosworth, *Central Asiatic Journal*, VI, p. 118, also p. 133 *n*.

[5] *TN*, I, pp. 320–3.

[6] Ibid., p. 328.

[7] Ibid., pp. 325–7.

[8] Ibid., pp. 341–2.

[9] Quoted by V. Minorsky, 'The Turkish Dialect of the Khalaj', *BSO(A)S*, X, 2 (1940), p. 430. Cf. Le Strange, *Lands of the Eastern Caliphate*, Cambridge, 1930, p. 346.

[10] Minorsky, *BSO(A)S*, X, 2, pp. 426–34, esp. p. 431.

[11] C.E. Bosworth, *The Ghaznavides*, Edinburgh, 1963, p. 155. See also pp. 35–6, 206.

Minorsky's Turkish K̲h̲alj dialect).[12] What is more relevant is that in India in the thirteenth century no one spoke of them as Turks; and that by then they had been closely associated with the principality of G̲h̲or, on the borders of which they had been settled (as witness Istak̲h̲arī) for centuries.

From an interesting passage at the beginning of Minhāj's biographical notice of Ḥusāmuddīn 'Iwaẓ K̲h̲aljī, later to be Sultan of Bengal (1211–27), it is obvious that the K̲h̲alj formed not a military clan, but were ordinary folk: 'Iwaẓ K̲h̲aljī was going to a village taking some load on an ass, when he met and fed some dervishes. He is said to have belonged to the K̲h̲alj of the Garmser (Plains District) of G̲h̲or, the village being near Wālisht̲ān, a town stated to be within G̲h̲or.[13] Similarly, Bak̲h̲tyār K̲h̲aljī is said to have been a K̲h̲alj of 'G̲h̲or and the district of Garmser'.[14] This district of Garmser was probably the Helmand valley in modern Oruzgān, since it simultaneously bordered upon G̲h̲or, Zamīndāwar and G̲h̲aznīn.[15]

The K̲h̲alj appear first in the political history of G̲h̲or, when, along with G̲h̲azz and Turkish soldiers, they deserted 'Alā'uddīn Jahān Soz (1149–61) in a battle with the Saljuqid Sultan Sanjar's troops.[16] Despite this rather questionable conduct, their chiefs still formed a recognized segment of the ruling class of the G̲h̲or kingdom. Thus, when in 1206 Mu'izzuddīn's nephew, G̲h̲ayāṣuddīn Maḥmūd, marched to claim the throne of G̲h̲or, 'the *umarā*'

---

[12] *Satī* inscriptions in Devanāgarī, belonging to the 15th century, give the name of the K̲h̲aljī dynasty of Malwa as 'Khilchī' and 'Khalchī' (A. Cunningham, *Archaeological Survey Reports*, X, 90; XXI, 171–2). Two towns, apparently named after the K̲h̲aljīs, and written K̲h̲aljipur in the *Ā'īn-i Akbarī*, are actually called Kilchipur and Khilchipur (Irfan Habib, *Atlas of the Mughal Empire*, Delhi, 1982, Sheets 6A (26+ 76+) and 8A (24+ 76+)). There is no reason why 'j' should change into 'ch' in Indian pronunciation. There is evidence from Afghanistan too which is worth considering. 'Abdu'l Ḥamīd Lāhorī, *Pādshāhnāma*, Bib. Ind., Calcutta, 1866–72, I, pp. 61–2, gives a list of major forts in the Qandahār province. One of these was Bust, and Lāhorī shows K̲h̲alj as one of its dependent places. This is in the area of our K̲h̲alj. The name of the place, however, is not pronounced K̲h̲alj, but K̲h̲alich, located at 31°32 N, 64°15 E in Ludwig Adamec's *Historical and Political Gazetteer of Afghanistan*, II, Garz, 1973, p. 154. Clearly the fact that 'j' and 'ch' are not distinguished in Arabic writing, has been responsible for the conversion of the name K̲h̲alich or K̲h̲ilich into the K̲h̲alj of the scholarly world. Since the latter is now so well established, it would be churlish to insist on a restoration of the true spelling; neither, however, should the wrong spelling be made the basis for tracing any Turkish associations.

[13] *TN*, I, p. 435. For Wālisht̲ān as a town of G̲h̲or, see *TN*, II, pp. 327–8.

[14] *TN*, I, p. 422.   [15] See ibid., pp. 373, 396.   [16] Ibid., p. 373.

(nobles, commanders) of the Khalj of Garmser joined him with their numerous troops; and the *umarā'* of Ghor, all of them, came to receive him.'[17] Clearly the Khalj formed the population of a region now included within the Kingdom of Ghor and, as such, contributed their share of both its soldiers and commanders. Their association with the Ghorians continued long after their arrival in India.[18]

II

The Ghorians occupied Ghaznīn (1173–4); and with that capital of the great Maḥmūd as his headquarters, Shihābuddīn (Mu'izzudīn) began to organize expeditions into India. It was natural that his armies should, in the beginning, consist largely of the Ghorians and the Khalj. When he occupied Tabarhinda (Bhatinda), 1,200 men of Tūlak, a town of Ghor, were assigned to its garrison.[19] In the first battle of Tarāin (1191), Shihābuddīn was rescued by a Khalj youth, whereafter 'the group of *umara*', the Ghorian soldiers (lit. youth) and the notables' gathered around the Sultan.[20]

The major appointments also went to the Ghorian notables.

[17] Ibid.

[18] The founder of the Khalji dynasty in Mālwa, Maḥmūd Shāh (1436–69) traced his descent, from his grandmother's side, to the Sultans of Ghor. As for the Khaljīs, they now seemed to have opted for a Mongol origin, from Qilij (Qilich) Khan, said to be a son-in-law of Chengiz Khan! (Shahāb Ḥakīm, *Ma'āṣir-i Maḥmūd Shāhī*, ed. Nurul Hasan Ansari, Delhi, n.d., pp. 8–9). But then the Ghorian prince 'Alā'uddīn Jahān Soz too was thought to be a Mongol by Shaikh Naṣīruddīn (*c.*1354) (*Khairu-l Majālis*, ed. K.A. Nizami, pp. 86–7). The Hazāras, who inhabit much of the territory which once contained the Khalj, also claim Mongol origin (Abū'l Faẓl, *Ā'īn-i Akbarī*, Bib. Ind., I, p. 593).

[19] *TN*, I, pp. 398–9. For the annexation of Tūlak to Ghor, see ibid., p. 348–9. It is within the modern province of Ghor.

[20] Ibid., p. 399. Firishta gives an alternative (but surely later) version ascribed to '*Zainu'l Ma'āṣir*' to the effect that Shihābuddīn was saved by his Turkish slaves. He also says that Shihābuddīn showed much annoyance with the conduct of 'the nobles of Ghor, Khalj and Khurāsān' (*Tārikh-i Firishta*, Nawal Kishore, Kanpur, 1874, I, 57). The alternative version becomes significant in the light of the rivalry and conflict that subsequently developed between the free-born Tāzīks or Tājīks (Ghorians, Khalj, etc.), and the Turkish slave-officers in the Ghorian empire and Delhi Sultanate. Incidentally, the site of the battle can be roughly located by the fact that Minhāj (*TN*, I, 456) describes an incident as taking place 'in the vicinity of Manṣūrpūr and Tarāin'; elsewhere (II, 66), he refers to the territory of 'Sunām and Manṣūrpūr'. Manṣūrpūr was shown in the old *Indian Atlas* sheets (No. 48), but was replaced by Chintanwala in the Quarter-Inch Maps. It was still a *pargana*-headquarters in Akbar's time, in the *sarkār* of Sāmāna. See Habib, *Atlas of the Mughal Empire*, Sheet 4A (28+ 76+). Firishta's placing of Tarā'in at Tirāwrī (p. 57) near Thānesar has little to recommend it.

After the occupation of Multān (1179–80), *Sipah-sālār* 'Alī Karmākh was made the *Wālī* (Governor) of Multan; on Lahore being occupied (1186), he was given charge of it.[21] The Karmākhs apparently belonged to the Shīshānī tribe of Ghor.[22] The fort of Siālkot, seized in 1184–5, was placed under Ḥusain Kharmīl, who bore as we have seen a Ghorian name. Malik Ziā'uddīn, the *qāẓī* of Tūlak, was given charge of the fort of Tabarhinda.[23] No Turk, free or slave, is mentioned as holding any territory in India until after the second battle of Tarāin (1192).

.But after the second battle of Tarāin, the situation changed very considerably. Except for the Khaljī seizure of Bihar and Bengal, the Ghorian commanders seem increasingly to play a secondary role in further conquests. Most of these took place under Shihābuddīn's Turkish slave, Quṭbuddīn Aibak, placed at Ghurām and then Delhi.[24] When in 1194 Shihābuddīn came to invade the Gahaḍvāla kingdom, the leadership of the vanguard was shared between the Ghorian commander, 'Izzuddīn Ḥusain Kharmīl, and Quṭbuddin Aibak.[24a] When Shihābuddīn sent reinforcements to assist Aibak in his raid on Gujarāt in 1196, these were led by four officers, two of whom can be identified as Ghorians and two as Turks.[25]

The conquered areas in India were now placed practically entirely under Shihābuddīn's slaves. The Ghorian governor of Lahore, 'Alī Karmākh, is no longer heard of; and 'Izzuddīn Ḥusain Kharmīl was transferred to Gurzawān in northern Afghanistan.[26] Undoubtedly, some Ghorian notables continued to hold *iqṭā*'s (transferable territorial fiscal assignments) in India. Nuṣratuddīn Sālārī was the commandant of Hānsī in 1193; and Bahā'uddīn Muḥammad, 'Governor (*Wālī*) of Sangwān(?)', and his brothers held *iqṭa*'s in the region of Multān in 1205.[27]

[21] *TN*, I, p. 398.

[22] Cf. *TN*, I, p. 327.

[23] Ibid., pp. 398–400. The *qāẓī* was a kinsman of Minhāj from his mother's side.

[24] Ibid., pp. 401, 407.

[24a] Ibid., p. 417.

[25] *Tāju'l Ma'āṣir*, transcript from Asafiya MS in the Department of History, Aligarh Muslim University, pp. 408–9. Unless otherwise specified, all references will henceforth be to the transcript. I assume from their names that Asaduddīn Arsalān Qilīj and Sharfuddīn Muḥammad Chirak were Turks. Nāṣiruddīn Ḥusain is probably identical with Malik Nāṣiruddīn Ḥusain *Amīr-i Shikār* (*TN*, I, pp. 381–2, 405, 413); and 'Izzuddīn, son of Muwayyiduddīn Bahanj (?) was probably the son of the Shīshānī notable, Muwayyiduddīn Fatḥ (MS var. Banj) Karmākh (*TN*, I, p. 327). Elliot reads 'Balkh' for 'Bahanj' in *Tāju'l Ma'āṣir* (Elliot and Dowson, *History of India, as told by its own Historians*, II, p. 229).

[26] *TN*, I, p. 402.

[27] *Tāju'l Ma'aṣir*, pp. 138, 473.

On the other hand, Quṭbuddīn Aibak rose quickly to acquire the status of Shihābuddīn's viceroy in India.[28] He apparently held charge of Lahore as well, since in 1205–6 he went to assist his master in operations in the Salt Range.[29] His zone of authority extended to the extreme east. One of his subordinates, Ḥusāmuddīn Ughalbak, first governor of Kol and then of Awadh, was a Turk to judge from his second name.[30] So also, though with less certainty, was Hizabruddīn Hasan Arnab, *muqṭi'* of Badāūn and then of Mahoba.[31]. Bahā'uddīn Ṭughril, a senior (*qadīm*) Turkish slave of Shihābuddīn, was posted at Thankar (near Bayana) in 1196, independently of Aibak.[32] Some time before 1204, the important charge of Multān and Uchh was held by Nāṣiruddīn Aitam.[33] Aitam or Aitamar seems a Turkish name, and there was a later namesake of his who was a slave of Bahā'uddīn Ṭughril.[34] When the earlier Aitam died at the battle of Andkhud (1204), the charge of Multān and Uchh was transferred to Nāṣiruddīn Qubācha, a Turkish slave of Shihābuddīn.[35] Finally, the road from Ghaznin to India was controlled by Shihābuddīn's leading slave, Tājuddīn Yildūz, who held the *iqṭā'* of Kurramān (upper Kurram valley).[36]

The removal of Ghorian commanders from India and their widespread, almost total, replacement by Shihābuddīn's Turkish slaves during the last fifteen years of his reign needs explanation. The main reason was quite possibly the incapacity of the political structure of Ghor to serve as a framework for empire. The classic device for centralization in Islamic states at this time was the *iqṭā'*. But the Ghorian polity was based upon the clan and family system. The *pahalwāns* (military commanders) were mostly Shīshānīs; the kingdom as it expanded was divided up among hereditary apanages of members of the Shansabānī family. So arose the Shansabānī dynasty of Bāmyān.[37] Sultan Ghayāṣuddīn (1163–1203)

[28] This is quite obvious from Ḥasan Niẓāmī's preface to *Tāju'l Ma'āṣir*, written in 1205 (p. 3). Cf. Elliot and Dowson, II, pp. 208–9.

[29] See the long account in *Tāju'l Ma'āṣir*, pp. 467–512; *TN*, I, p. 443.

[30] *Tāju'l Ma'āṣir*, p. 325; *TN*, I, p. 423. See also Hodivala, *Studies in Indo-Muslim History*, com. on Elliot and Dowson, II, p. 222.

[31] *TN*, I, p. 422; *Tāju'l Ma'āṣir*, p. 460.

[32] *Tāju'l Ma'āṣir*, pp. 375–7; *TN*, I, p. 421. His title Alp Arsalān suggests Saljūqid antecedents.

[33] *TN*, I, p. 419. [34] Ibid., pp. 446, 451; II, pp. 7–8. [35] Ibid., I, p. 419.

[36] *Tāju'l Ma'āṣir*, pp. 213–14; TN, I, p. 411.

[37] *TN*, I, pp. 384–92.

himself gave over Ghaznīn to his brother Shihābuddīn as a permanent charge, from 1173–4 onwards. All areas that Shihābuddīn conquered from his own headquarters were governed by him without any interference from the Sultan. But Shihābuddīn must have become familiar at Ghaznīn with the traditions of the empire of which that city had been the capital. The attraction of collecting a corps of expensively trained slaves to make his writ run and his treasures and territories safe from clannish co-sharers must have seemed irresistible. He accordingly collected, by purchasing, some thousands of Turkish slaves (*bandagān-i Turk*), whom he is said to have regarded as his own children.[38] Shihābuddīn seems to have distinguished quite clearly between his Indian dominions, which he regarded as his personal territories, and the parent kingdom of Ghor, of which he became Sultan in 1203. He did not send any of his slaves to govern any district in his ancestral dominions, which remained under the control of the princes and nobles of Ghor.[39] On the other hand, so sharply had the Ghorian nobility been excluded from his own 'Ghaznavide' dominions that the fact that he now took 'some *mulūk* and *umarā'* of Ghor' to Ghaznīn is especially recorded.[40]

The attempted exclusion of the Ghorian and related nobility from the Indian conquests, however useful for establishing royal authority, had its disadvantages. The first stemmed from the fact that the Turks could only provide commanders and élite guards. The ranks of the army had to be recruited from the people of Ghor and the Khalj. Only a small fraction of the 120,000 horsemen (*bargustuwān*) (undoubtedly an inflated figure), whom Shihābuddīn is said to have mustered in the field of Tarāin in 1192, could have been Turks.[41] But so long as the troops were so largely non-Turkish, it would still be possible for power to pass into the hands of non-Turkish military men. The Khaljī conquerors of Bengal provided an illustration of how the possibility could become a fact.

Characteristically, Muhammad Bakhtyār Khaljī came from amongst the 'tribes' of Ghor and Garmser to enrol as a soldier at Ghaznīn. On being rejected by the officials of the Inspection Department (*dīwān-i 'arẓ*) there, he came to Delhi, to be again

[38] Ibid., pp. 410–11. [39] Ibid., p. 401. [40] Ibid.

[41] Ibid., p. 400. The author himself obtained the report from a person from Tūlak (and so a Ghorian), who was present at the battle.

similarly rejected. He then sought employment with the *muqṯi'* of Badāūn, who assigned him a salary (*mawājib*). From there he went to Awadh, having by now acquired 'a good horse and weapons'. After he had rendered good service, he was given two places (not satisfactorily identified) in *iqṯā'*. As the report of his exploits spread, 'all the K͟halj from Hindustān' joined him.[42] People like 'Iwaẓ K͟haljī even came from the K͟halj homeland to take service with him.[43] With an army so collected and consisting practically entirely of K͟haljīs,[44] he conquered Bihar and Bengal, which he ruled in the capacity of an autonomous potentate. He thus created a separate K͟haljī dominion in India, which lasted till 1227.

It was natural that the sudden rise of the Turkish slaves should draw the hostility of the old G͟horian and K͟halj nobles and commanders, who felt that the Indian conquests too belonged of right to them. Imitating Shihābuddīn, Muḥammad Bak͟htyār K͟haljī left one 'Turkish slave' of his and one K͟haljī *amīr* (commander) to guard a crucial bridge on the borders of Kāmrūp; the two quarrelled with each other and abandoned the bridge, bringing disaster to the entire army.[45] Upon the death of Shihābuddīn (or Mu'izzuddīn, to give him the royal title he adopted in 1203), the hostility between the two groups, hitherto latent, broke out into the open.

III

Shihābuddīn died on 15 March 1206, while returning from the Salt Range to Ghaznīn.[46] The Ghorian *amīr*s in the dead Sultan's army supported one candidate for the throne, while another was favoured by the 'Turkish *malik*s and *amīr*s, who were the slaves of the Sultan.' The latter seized the treasury. In a subsequent battle near G͟haznīn, 'the *umarā'* of G͟hor and the great *malik*s' were slaughtered by the 'Turkish army' (*lashkar-i Turk*), led by Tājuddīn Yildūz.[47] While Yildūz seized G͟haznīn, the entire Indian dominions

[42] These particulars are given in *TN*, I, pp. 422–3. Of the two places given him in *iqṯā'* one (written Siholī, Bhiyūlī) could be Bhuili, a *pargana*-headquarters in *sarkār* Chunār in the time of the *Ā'īn* (see Habib, *Atlas of the Mughal Empire*, Sheet 8A, 25+ 83+).

[43] *TN*, I, pp. 422–3, 435.

[44] Thus, when in 1208 Bak͟htyār K͟haljī returned from his unsuccessful expedition into the Himalayas, all the dead that he left behind are said to have been K͟haljīs (*TN*, I, p. 431).

[45] Ibid., pp. 428, 430.

[46] Ibid., pp. 403–4.

[47] Ibid., pp. 390, 408–9.

of Shihābuddīn passed into the hands of Quṯbuddin Aibak.[48] This undoubtedly represented an unalloyed triumph for the Turkish *amīrs*.

The unity of the Turkish *amīrs* was, however, subject to continuous internal disruption. Yildūz and his son-in-law Aibak fought out a short war.[49] When Aibak died in 1210, there was a brutal conflict between two groups of Turks for the inheritance. Iltutmish, from the Ilbarī tribe of the Turks, a slave of Aibak and *muqṯi'* of Badāūn, seized Delhi, to set himself up as Sultan:

> As the *Quṯbī* Turks and *amīrs* gathered from all directions at Delhi, some of the *Mu'izzī* Turks and *amīrs* gathered to oppose them, and pursued the path of enmity. They left Delhi, and assembling in the environs; began a rebellion and insurrection.

They were, however, defeated; and Iltutmish, the 'mystic prince', ordered all of them beheaded.[50]

It may be noted that the term Mu'izzī signified the slaves of Shihābuddīn (Mu'izzuddīn) and Quṯbi those of Quṯbuddīn Aibak. Quite obviously Aibak's Turkish slaves were as determined to destroy the slaves of Aibak's master, as the latter had been to drive out the old Ghorian nobility. In time, the leading Mu'izzī slaves, Yildūz and Qabācha, who had established their own sultanates, one in Ghaznīn and the other in Multān, Uchh and Sind, also met their doom at the hands of Iltutmish. Yildūz was eliminated in 1215–16, and the struggle with Qubācha ended with his fall in 1227.[51] In Bengal the Khaljī regime too was destroyed the same year.[52]

Iltutmish can be considered the real founder of the Delhi Sultanate. If there was a time at the beginning when he needed his fellow Quṯbī slave officers to save him, he succeeded soon enough in placing himself well above his peers. He did so, first of all, by creating his own corps of Turkish slaves. This fact, owing to

[48] 'From Purshūr to the ocean and from Sīwistān (in Sind) to the mountains of (bordering upon) China' (*Tāju'l Ma'āṣir*, pp. 530–1).

[49] *TN*, I, pp. 412–14.

[50] Ibid., p. 444. This passage has been most confusingly rendered by Raverty, I, p. 600, as well as in Elliot and Dowson, II, p. 323. The struggle is also described in the *Tāju'l Ma'āṣir* (Elliot and Dowson, II, p. 237. The Asafiya MS lacks this portion).

[51] *TN*, I, pp. 413, 420–1. Qubācha committed suicide rather than surrender to Iltutmish.

[52] Ibid., pp. 436–7, 453–4.

Minhāj's long biographical notices of twenty-five of these slaves (Shamsī *maliks*), and Baranī's vivid account of their emergence, is quite well recognized,[53] even if it has not yet received adequately detailed analysis. Secondly—an aspect on which equal emphasis has not, perhaps, been laid—he collected a large number of Tāzīk or Persian-speaking officers, including scions of the Gh̲or–Kh̲alj nobility.

Iltutmish collected his slaves by purchase from all sources, from professional slave-merchants who dealt in war captives and other slaves,[54] as well as from private owners.[55] The slave marts of Bag̲h̲dād and Egypt were especially filled in those times by captives sold by the Mongols.[56] Most of these came from non-Muslim tribes, so that the fact that a slave was Muslim-born (*Musalmān-zāda*) is especially recorded.[57] Of the twenty-five 'Shamsī' slaves whose biographical notices are given by him, Minhāj gives the regional or tribal origins of nineteen.[58] The largest number (six) are Qipchāq, the Turkish tribe of the steppes extending from north of the Jaxartes to the Volga. Next in number (five) are the Qara K̲h̲itā of Sinkiang, the 'Black Chinese', who had defeated Shihābuddīn at Andk̲h̲ud. There are three Rūmīs, i.e. either Saljūqs or Greeks. Three again are Ilbarīs, a tribe in Turkistān (Iltutmish's own) said to consist of 10,000 families.[59] One slave was a Turk of Georgia (Turk-i Garjī), and another a native of K̲h̲wārizm (Khiva). The only non-Turk among the twenty-five slaves is one Hindu K̲h̲ān, who is said to have originally belonged to Mathura.[60]

In selecting his twenty-five Shamsī *maliks* for biographical treatment, Minhāj has not been guided only by the positions they held under Iltutmish. In fact as many as fourteen are not known to

[53] Cf. for example, K. A. Nizami in *Comprehensive History of India*, V, ed. M. Habib and K. A. Nizami, Delhi, 1970, pp. 232–3.

[54] *TN*, II, pp. 9, 41, etc.

[55] Ibid., pp. 5,7, 45, etc.

[56] Ibid., pp. 33–4, 45, 48.

[57] Ibid., p. 24: The slave in question was a 'Rūmī', i.e. probably a Saljuq.

[58] For the biographical notices see *TN*, II, pp. 1–89.

[59] Ibid., pp. 43, 45, 47–8.

[60] Ibid., p. 18. The title Hindū K̲h̲an, although pointing strongly to an Indian origin, is not conclusive since the name 'Hindū' is also found among Turks, Hindū meaning black and so an alternative to the Turkish word *qara*, popular in Turkish names. But 'Mahur' (not properly identified in Raverty, I, p. 744 *n.*) is decisive, for 'Mahur' in Persian writing with the dots dropped, is really Mathur or Mathurā; it thrice appears coupled with Mahāvan in *TN*, II, pp. 11, 44, 62.

have held any important office under that Sultan. They are noticed by Minhāj mainly on account of the power and position acquired by them after their master's death. It is also possible that some who were important under Iltutmish have been ignored. With all these limitations, Minhāj's information is still of some help in indicating the position Iltutmish's slaves had acquired by the time of his death.[61]

At least three or four of these slaves had risen to be of such status that Iltutmish gave them the title 'Khān'.[62] This title is not found attached to the name of any Ghorian noble or slave of Shihābuddīn. Its award was thus an innovation; and the inspiration for it came surely from the fact that the Mongols, who had recently succeeded in establishing a world empire, called their sovereign Khan or Qā'ān. Before Iltutmish's successors greatly devalued it, the title therefore was extraordinarily exalted.[63]

The substance of power and wealth was, of course, represented not by titles but by the *iqṭā*'s or revenue and military charges. These changed hands, and Minhāj often records how one man was transferred from one *iqṭā* to another. It is possible to prepare from his statements the following list of *iqṭā*'s held by the Shamsī *malik*s at the time of the death of Iltutmish:

[61] *All* the 25 'Shamsī' *malik*s whose biographies are given by Minhāj were actually purchased by Iltutmish. Even when some slaves are designated 'Mu'izzī' or 'Bahā'ī', after the names of their earlier masters (Mu'izzuddīn and Bahā'uddīn Ṭughril), the author tells us that Iltutmish purchased them from their subsequent masters (*TN*, II, pp. 5,7). This detail is not available in only one case (ibid., p. 10). There does not seem, therefore, much room for the doubt raised by K. A. Nizami in *Comprehensive History*, V, pp. 233–4, that some of Minhāj's 'Shamsī' *malik*s were really slaves 'inherited' by Iltutmish from his predecessors. Qutlugh Khan, a prominent Turkish noble under Iltutmish, was not included by Minhāj among the 'Shamsī *malik*s', because he was not a Shamsī slave at all.

[62] Tāju'ddīn Sanjar Kazlak Khān died in 1231–2 (*TN*, II, 5) and must, therefore, have been given this title by Iltutmish. References to the conferment of the title on Kabīr Khān and Qarāqash Khān are explicit; Iltutmish did so some time after 1228 (ibid., pp. 5, 20). A fourth 'Khān' was a Turk, Aibak, given the title of Avar Khān, possibly by Iltutmish (ibid., p. 13). Other slaves, e.g. Nāṣiruddīn Aitmār, Saifuddīn Aibak-i Uchh, Saifuddīn Aibak Yaghāntut, and Nuṣratuddīn Tā'isī, who died in Iltutmish's time or shortly afterwards, were not granted this title (see their biographical notices, ibid., pp. 7–13).

[63] The Mongols naturally disapproved of this presumption at Delhi in respect of the title of their Emperor. Much gratification was felt (at Delhi) when Hulāgū allowed Balban's title, Ulugh Khān, to be pronounced in his presence (*TN*, II, pp. 85–6).

Iqṭā'	*Wālī Muqṭi'*	*Reference*
Multān	Qarāqash Khān Aitagīn	*TN*, II, 20
Uchh	Saifuddīn Aibak-i Uchh	Ibid., 8
Kūchāt and Nandana (Salt Range)	Ikhtiyāruddīn Aitigīn	Ibid., 22
Palwal	Kabīr Khān	Ibid., 6
Bayāna (with command of Gwalior)	Nuṣratuddīn Tā'isī	Ibid., 10–11
Baran	'Izzuddīn Balban	Ibid., 36
Bihār	'Izzuddīn Tughān Khān Ṭughril	Ibid., 13

The important *iqṭā'* of Lakhnautī or Bengal was held by Awar Khān Aibak, who is expressly said to be a Turk, though he might not have been a slave of the Sultan.[64]

However, Iltutmish's Turkish slaves are not known to have occupied a single of the highest central or court offices at his death, however large the territories they held in *iqṭā'*. This should help us to realize that the free-born element in Iltutmish's nobility was by no means inconsiderable. Minhāj gives at the end of his account of Iltutmish's reign a list of twenty of his leading nobles (*mulūk*).[65] Of these, three belong to his list of Shamsī *maliks*; three others were also slave-officers since they bear the designation, 'Bahā'ī' and 'Nāṣirī' indicating the names of their original masters (Bahā'uddīn Ṭughril and Nāṣiruddīn Qubācha). Another noble is called Turk. As against these seven, there are three Ghorians,[66] two Khaljīs, and a native of Kūlāb (Tajikistan)—eight in all who can definitely be styled free men. Of the remaining five, none has a Turkish name; and they too could well have been free-born.

Coming to offices and *iqṭā'*s, Niẓāmu'l Mulk Muḥammad Junaidī was the *Wazīr* of Iltutmish at the time of his death.[67] He had led the Sultan's army against Qubācha in 1226–7.[68] He was

[64] *TN*, II, p. 13. [65] Ibid., I, pp. 450–2.

[66] One of these, 'Izzuddīn Muḥammad Shāh Mahdī, is apparently the same as 'Izzuddīn Sālārī. His name, listed among Sultan Nāṣiruddīn Maḥmud's nobles, is given as 'Izzuddīn Muḥammad Sālārī Mahdī (*TN*, I, p. 476). For the likelihood of his belonging to Ghor see the following paragraph in our main text. The other two Ghorians are designated *Malik-i Ghor*.

[67] *TN*, I, pp. 446–7, 456.

[68] *Tāju'l Ma'āṣir*, Elliot and Dowson, II, p. 242; *TN*, I, pp. 446–7.

undoubtedly a Tāzīk.[69] The office of *Dabīr o Mushrif-i Mamālik* (Chief of the Secretariat and Finance Departments) was held by Tāju'l Mulk Maḥmūd, the victim of a massacre of Tāzīk functionaries soon after Iltutmish's death.[70] According to a rather late account, two other important central offices, *Wakīl-i dar* and *Bārbak*, both concerned with the court, were held by 'Izzuddīn Sālārī and Quṭbuddin Ḥasan G͟horī.[71] To both these persons, tradition assigned a very high status under Iltutmish.[72] There is no explicit statement that 'Izzuddīn belonged to G͟hor; but his clan 'Sālār' appears to be the same as that of a commandant of Hānsī in the very early years of the G͟horian conquests.[73] 'Izzuddīn himself was *Amīr-i ḥājib* (Lord Chamberlain) in 1227 and was sent against Nasīruddīn Qubācha.[74] Quṭbuddīn Ḥasan was a leading notable of G͟hor, probably a member of the Shansabānī family. He took a vigorous part in the unsuccessful resistance to the Mongol invasion of G͟hor (1220–3), and then fled to India.[75]

Among the *muqṭi*'s, at Iltutmish's death, Malik Alā'uddin Jānī, 'a prince of Turkistān',[76] held the important charge of Lahore, 'the seat of the (Ghaznavide) K͟husrau Malik', in succession to the Sultan's eldest living son.[77] Earlier, he had been assigned the *iqṭā*' of Bihar and then of Bengal (Lakhnautī).[78] Saifuddīn Kūchī, who held the *iqṭā*' of Hansi, was also probably free-born;[79] and the *iqṭā*' of Badāūn was held by 'Izzuddīn Sālārī.[80]

From the point of view of Iltutmish himself, the fact that leading nobles of the kingdom of G͟hor should swear fealty to him, a slave of a slave of a G͟horian ruler, was an important factor in establishing his moral authority. On the other hand, the Mongol invasions left

[69] His son was a victim of the massacre of the Tāzīk officials in 1236 (*TN*, I, p. 456). A hostile tradition, doubtless of Turkish-slave origin, alleged that he was descended of a weaver (Baranī, *Tārīk͟h-i Fīrūzshāhī*, Bib. Ind., p. 39).

[70] *TN*, I, p. 456. [71] Barani, p. 39. [72] Ibid., p. 37.

[73] *Tāju'l Ma'āṣir*, p. 138, says Nuṣratuddīn Sālārī held Hānsī in 1194.

[74] *TN*, I, pp. 446–7; II, p. 4.

[75] Ibid., I, pp. 132–41. 'Iṣāmī, *Futūḥu-s Salāṭīn*, ed. Usha, Madras, 1948, pp. 127–8, writing in 1350, says that his ancestor Fak͟hru'l Mulk 'Iṣāmī, minister at the court of a King of Baghdad (!), migrated to India, and became the *wazīr* of Iltutmish. No such person is mentioned by Minhāj, though one 'Iṣāmī is mentioned among the court officers of Balban by Baranī, p. 36.

[76] *TN*, I, p. 452. [77] Ibid., pp. 454–5.

[78] Ibid., pp. 438, 448; II, p. 9.

[79] Ibid., p. 456. [80] Ibid., p. 455.

the surviving Ghor nobility little choice in the matter. In 1222 and 1223, the *maliks* of Ghor fled in large numbers to Qubācha, who received them hospitably.[81] Iltutmish pursued a similar policy, and Minhāj's praise of him as a provider of refuge to those who had abandoned their homes in 'Ajam, owing to the incursions of the 'Mongol Infidels', is not pure hyperbole.[82] Minhāj was himself such an immigrant from Ghor, characteristically joining Qubācha and receiving an office from him at Uchh (1227),[83] and then going over to Iltutmish's camp on the very day the latter arrived outside that city a few months later.[84] Immigrants came from other regions as well; and Fīrūz Shāh Iltutmish, 'Prince of Khwārizm', and Malik Jānī, 'Prince of Turkistān', were probably only the highest among a number of fugitives granted offices by Iltutmish.[85]

It is possible that soldiers also emigrated in large bodies to India. The 'Khalj, Turkmāns and Ghorīs' formed the soldiery of the Khwārizmians in Afghanistan during the Mongol invasion.[86] Their defeat in 1221–2 led to large-scale migrations into India: such, for example, was that of the Khalj soldiery into Sind in 1226, which was in the nature of an invasion.[87] A large number of individual soldiers dispersed by the Mongols must have fled to India and sought service here. The armies of the Delhi Sultans and their nobles are thus likely to have continued to retain a very large Ghor-Khalj, i.e. non-Turkish, component. Its presence must always have been a source of strength to the free and non-Turk elements in the ruling class.

Iltutmish accordingly presided over a nobility in which his own corps of Turkish slaves, who held a large number of *iqṭā*'s, and the free-born immigrants, who occupied high offices at the court and also held some *iqṭā*'s, were almost evenly matched. The ruling class could appear as a coalition of two quite different groups, the Turks and the Tāzīks. As Minhāj would say, in a poem at the time of Nāṣiruddīn Maḥmūd's accession (1246):

[81] Ibid., p. 420.
[82] Ibid., p. 441.
[83] Ibid., p. 420.
[84] Ibid., p. 447.
[85] Ibid., p. 452.
[86] Atā Malik Juwaynī, *Tārīkh-i Jahān Gushā*, II, London, 1916, pp. 192–8. *TN*, II, p. 117, describes the very same army as consisting of 'Turks, Ghorian *amirs*, Tājīks, Khalj and Ghazz'.
[87] *TN*, I, p. 420.

Everywhere are the Turk and the Tājīk (Tāzīk) servants of his court. The pagan Hindu is obedient to his orders.[88]

Since this assumption of twin racial elements in the nobility occurs elsewhere too in Minhāj, as we shall see, some clarification of the distinction made between Turk and Tāzīk may be necessary. While practically all the slaves of the Sultan were Turks, there were free-born persons too of Turkish origin or speech, such as Malik Jānī or Fīrūz Iltutmish. As far as the Tāzīks or Tājīks, men of Persian speech,[89] are concerned, all of them appear to have been free-born and so constituted the bulk of the free-born section of the ruling class. There is also the very strong probability that the highly Persianized nobles of the Khwārizmian court felt more at home with the Tāzīks than with the neo-Muslim Turkish slaves. For all practical purposes, therefore, the division between Turk and Tāzīk corresponded with the one between slave or ex-slave and the free-born.

IV

During the three decades that followed Iltutmish's death in 1236, important changes occurred in the distribution of power within the Sultanate ruling class. Baranī, writing about a hundred years later, offers us an interpretation of these changes, which, without much apology, may be reproduced here:

During the reign of Sultan Shamsuddīn (Iltutmish), as a result of the fear of massacre and chastisement by the accursed Mongol, Chengīz Khān, *malik*s and *amīr*s of fame, who had been chiefs and commanders for years, and numerous *wazīr*s and notables, came to Iltutmish's court. It was as a result of the presence of such unrivalled *malik*s and such *wazīr*s and notables...that Iltutmish's court rivalled that of (Sultans) Maḥmūd and Sanjar, and acquired great prestige. After Iltutmish's death (however), the Forty Turkish Slaves (*Bandagān-i Turk-i Chihalgānī*) were able to fulfil their ambitions. Iltutmish's successors did not behave as princes must and should, and could not carry out the duties of a King—and after Prophethood, there is no greater or more precious function than that of a King. As a result of the ascendancy of Iltutmish's Turkish Slaves (*Bandagān-i Turk-i Shamsī*), all those nobles and

[88] Ibid., p. 473. The other spelling 'Tāzīk' also occurs here in MSS as noted by the editor.

[89] The editor of *TN*, II, pp. 384–7, *n*., has some interesting comments on this word.

sons of nobles, who for generations had been *malik*s and sons of *malik*s, and *wazīr*s and sons of *wazīr*s, were destroyed under various pretexts during the period of Iltutmish's successors, who did not have any inkling of the world and the way to rule it. After the destruction of those chiefs and commanders, Iltutmish's Slaves rose and became K͟hāns, and every one of them established a new court and (insignia of) pomp (for himself).... People of that time were witnesses to the fact that until nobles and generals do not fall from their positions, the vain and the purchased (slaves) do not rise and become chiefs and generals. Since Iltutmish's Slaves were, all of them, of one master, and all the Forty Slaves had obtained greatness all at once, one did not bow to or obey another, and in (obtaining) *iqṭā*'s, army, greatness and honour, everyone demanded equality and parity.... As a result of the incompetence of Iltutmish's successors and the dominance of the Slaves of Iltutmish, no majesty attached any longer to the office of the Sovereign.[90]

There is no doubt that in spite of Baranī's tendency to use more words than strictly necessary, this passage contains a striking depiction of the nature of political change in the Sultanate between 1236 and 1266. One cannot but notice in passing that even the statement that all the Forty Slaves 'became K͟hans' is historically accurate. As we have seen, the award of the title was an innovation of Iltutmish's last years, and was as yet sparingly awarded. But the 'Shamsī' *malik*s who survived him and whose biographies are given by Minhāj are all accorded the title of K͟han, with just a few exceptions.[91] Nor is it necessary to cavil at the number forty.[92] One might as well protest at references to the Two Hundred Families that once reputedly controlled France. What Baranī—or rather the tradition he was drawing upon—implied was that the number of the principal Shamsī Slaves was quite limited. This is corroborated by Minhāj's detailed narrative, where those Slaves who played a prominent role or held important *iqṭā*'s number twenty-five (or rather twenty, if we omit those who died before or within a short period of time after the death of Iltutmish), whose biographical notices he furnishes.

[90] Baranī, pp. 26–8.

[91] The exceptions are Saifuddīn Aibak-i Uchh, Nuṣratuddīn Tā'isī, Ik͟htiyāruddīn Altūniya, Ik͟htiyāruddīn Aitigīn, Badruddīn Sangar Rūmī, Tājuddīn Sanjar Qutlug͟h, and Saifuddīn Arkalī Dādbak. Of these the first three died within five or six years of Iltutmish's death. The number of those given the title of K͟hān is sixteen. Two others without the title of K͟hān predeceased Iltutmish.

[92] At the same time one need not go as far as Wolsey Haig who speaks of 'a college of forty' of 'the leading Turks' (*Cambridge History of India*, III, p. 62).

In the *Ṭabaqāt-i Nāṣirī* of Minhāj Sirāj we also possess a uniquely detailed history of this phase, coming down to 1260. It gives us a narrative without any explicit interpretation. But it is astonishing how the facts Minhāj supplies corroborate Baranī in almost every particular. One feels either that Baranī had closely read Minhāj Sirāj and then evolved his brilliant insights—insights that many subsequent historians failed to obtain[93]—or that he had access to an independent tradition existing perhaps within the bureaucracy, which conveyed to him the essence of the factional struggles of that period.

Minhāj, as a panegyrist of Ulugh K͟hān Balban, a Shamsī slave, was undoubtedly in a difficult position when it came to describing the partial destruction of the free-born nobility. Minhāj himself was a Tāzīk, and practically a native of G͟hor.[94] He manages to supply us the essential facts, while concealing—not always quite successfully—his own sympathies.

Immediately after Iltutmish's death, a number of *muqṭi*'s refused to accept his successor, Ruknuddīn Fīrūz. It is interesting that of the four rebel nobles, only one (Kabīr K͟hān) was a Shamsī slave; the other three ('Izzuddīn Sālārī, 'Alāuddīn Jānī and Saifuddīn Kūchī) were Tāzīks. They were joined by Niẓāmu'l Mulk Junaidī, the *wazīr*, the leading Tāzīk functionary. The conflict soon took a 'racial' form; 'The Turkish *amīr*s and the Sultan's slaves' rose at the Sultan's camp and carried out a massacre of Tāzīk officials (*kārdārān*). The names of seven victims are given, and these included the *dabīr o mushrif-i mamālik* and the *wazīr*'s son.[95] The Turkish *amīr*s then marched to Delhi and placed Iltutmish's daughter, Raẓiya, on the throne as Sultan. Quite obviously, Iltutmish's death had opened the question of 'succession' in more than one sense. A major issue undoubtedly was whether the free-born or Tāzīk nobles could retain their previous influence; and

[93] No one reading Yahyā's *Tārīk͟h-i Mubārakshāhī*, whose author drew directly on Minhāj, would, for example, obtain the view that Baranī offers. Some modern narrators have not gone any further. The simple fact of the ascendancy of the Turkish slaves is indeed accepted by all, but mainly it seems on the basis of Baranī.

[94] Minhāj Sirāj's ancestors belonged to Jūzjān, not G͟hor, and the family later migrated to G͟haznīn; but he himself was brought up in G͟hor. The editor, *TN*, II, pp. 223–49, brings together all that is known, from references in *TN*, about the author's family and his life till his arrival in India.

[95] *TN*, I, pp. 455–6.

they suffered a great setback. Junaidī, Kūchī and Malik Jānī were killed; only 'Izzuddīn Sālārī, significantly in company with Kabīr Khān, was able to make his peace.[96]

Subsequently, Raẓiya's successor Mu'izzuddīn Bahrām was overthrown (1242) by 'the *amīrs* and Turks'.[97] Soon afterwards the Tāzīk *wazīr* Muhazzibuddīn, who had engineered this coup, was killed in a 'tumult' (*ghūgha*) by 'the King's Turks' (*Turkān-i Sulṭānī*), for he had attempted to take away 'all offices' from the Turkish nobles (*umarā'-i Turk*).[98]

The death of Quṭbuddīn Ḥasan in June 1255 represented apparently the climax of the supremacy of the Turkish *maliks*. Quṭbuddīn was a Ghorian notable of great reputation and had enjoyed high office since the time of Iltutmish. In 1242 he became *Nā'ib-i Mulk*, holding thereby the highest office available to a noble.[99] It is possible that he was removed in October 1249 to make room for Balban; but he was probably restored to the office upon Balban's own dismissal in 1253, as a result of a great schism within the Turkish nobility.[100] Quṭbuddīn Ḥasan played some part in achieving a reconciliation between Balban and his opponents.[101] This did not, however, save him. Although he was still *Nā'ib-i Mulk*, he was imprisoned and killed because he conveyed to the Sultan something that was not to Balban's liking.[102] The event made a deep impression. 'Iṣāmī writes of it at some length,[103] without, however, suggesting any racial element involved in the event. But an anecdote recorded in Shaikh Niẓāmuddīn's conversations (1311) refers to this murder with the seeming intent of highlighting the wonder in a wealthy Turk going out of his way to recognize and help an impecunious local scholar at such a time.[104]

Baranī in the passage we have quoted also brings out the inherent contradiction between the dominance of a corps of élite slaves and the functioning of a despotism based on some hierarchical order. Internal tensions among the slaves were thus inevitable. Alliances were rapidly formed only to be soon abandoned.

[96] Ibid., pp. 458–9.
[97] Ibid., pp. 466–7.
[98] Ibid., p. 469; II, pp. 27, 42.
[99] Ibid., I, p. 468.
[100] Ibid., II, pp. 486–7.
[101] Ibid., I, p. 68.
[102] Ibid., p. 489. It is to Minhāj's credit that he does not ignore such episodes.
[103] 'Iṣāmī, pp. 159–61.
[104] *Fawā'idul Fu'ād*, ed. Latif Malik, Lahore, 1966, pp. 112–14. The date of the particular conversation is 30 May 1311.

The quick succession of Sultans, one deposed after the other, was quite obviously owing to this basic cause. The rapid rise of Ulugh Khān Balban (who did not hold any important office at the death of Iltutmish) to the position of *Nā'ib-i Mulk* in 1249 soon provoked serious opposition to him. Although the Indian slave, 'Imāduddīn Raiḥān, was alleged to have played a major role in instigating the conspiracy of 1253, the principal leaders were Kishlū Khān 'Izzuddīn Balban and Qutlugh Khān. Kishlū Khān was perhaps the seniormost Shamsī *malik* at the time, and in 1242 had status enough to proclaim himself Sultan for a brief period.[105] His father-in-law, Qutlugh Khān was the second husband of Malika Jahān, the reigning Sultan's mother.[106] It seems that he was the son of Malik Jānī (the 'Prince of Turkistan'),[107] and his status perhaps explains the marriage with the royal widow. He was, therefore, a free-born noble, though a Turk, not a Tāzīk. It is also admitted by Minhāj that there was 'a group of Turks (*jamā'at-i Atrāk*) in whom some hostility to Ulugh Khan Mu'azzam (Balban) was ingrained', and who were, therefore, 'Imāduddīn Raiḥān's natural accomplices.[108]

It may be mentioned in passing that the Mongol presence on India's north-west was also a factor intensifying the divisions. When Ulugh Khān Balban was dismissed in 1253, the rival prince he supported, Jalāluddīn, and his own cousin, Sher Khān, made their way to the distant court of Mangū (Monk-ke), the Great Khān of the Mongols. They even succeeded in obtaining military assistance from that quarter.[109] 'Izzuddīn Balban, upon his own discomfiture, similarly sent a letter of submission to Hulāgū in Iran

[105] *TN*, I, p. 468; II, p. 36.

[106] Ibid., I, p. 489; II, p. 64.

[107] Ibid., II, p. 35, makes this statement, which Raverty, II, p. 769 *n.*, strongly doubts. It is, however, possible to reconstruct a consistent biography if the two persons, Qutlugh Khān and Jalāluddīn Qutlugh (MS vars. Khalj, Qilīj) Khān Mas'ūd Jānī are regarded as identical. In the list of Nāsiruddīn Maḥmūd's nobles, the latter (Jalāluddīn Khalj Khān Malik Jānī') is given a place, but not the former (*TN*, I, p. 476). He is there designated *Malik* of Awadh and Lakhnautī; and we know that Qutlugh Khān, the husband of Malika Jahān, was appointed to Awadh in 1255 (*TN*, I, p. 489); and Qutlugh (Qilīj) Khān is said to have been appointed to Lakhnautī in 1258 (*TN*, II, p. 78), the very time 'Malik Jalāluddīn Mas'ūd Shāh Malik Jānī' is said to have been appointed to the same position (*TN*, I, p. 495).

[108] *TN*, II, p. 68.

[109] Ibid., p. 44, for Sher Khān; *Tārīkh-i Waṣṣāf*, Bombay, AH 1264, p. 310, for Jalāluddīn, and the army sent for his assistance under Shālī Bahādur.

(1256–65) and ultimately himself paid a visit to Hulāgū's court. Henceforth he was safe in Multān as a vassal of the Mongols.[110] Thus the Mongols offered protection first to one faction, then to another. Had the Mongol (Īl-Khānid) power not been shaken subsequently by the Nigudaris in Afghanistan, they might have interfered even further in the internal affairs of the Sultanate.

Yet in spite of the tribulations which the Sultanate suffered during the thirty years following Iltutmish's death, the fact that it was able still to retain some kind of unity, and indeed even survived at all, is a matter for reflection. *Iqṭā*'s continued to be transferred, as Moreland has noted;[111] and when a governor of Bengal declared himself Sultan, and rebelled, Minhāj records what appears to have been genuine indignation among all those who counted.[112] It seems that in spite of the great cleavage between the Turks and Tāzīks, and the slave and the free-born, the concept of a 'composite' ruling class still existed. Minhāj goes out of his way to praise Balban's brother Kishlī Khān, *Mīr-i Ḥājib* (Chamberlain), for 'his kindness and favours to the Turkish *malik*s, Tājīk notables and Khalj *amīrs*'.[113] The Tāzīks and Khalj were thus still recognized as important elements in the nobility.

In a curious way, the basic unity between the Turks and Tāzīks was manifested in a common hostility to outsiders. When Raẓiya (1236–40) promoted Jamāluddīn Yāqūt, 'the Abyssinian (Ḥabashī)' to the post of *Amīr-i Akhur* (Master of Horse), this caused disaffection among 'all the *malik*s and *amīrs*, Turk, Ghorian and Tājīk'.[114] Similarly, when Balban regrouped his forces to move against the Sultan's court in 1254, this was justified on the grounds of an intolerable situation: 'The servants and *malik*s of the Court were all either Turks of pure lineage or Tāzīks of select birth; and (yet) 'Imāduddīn (Raiḥān) who was a eunuch of the tribes of Hindustān was now issuing orders to (such) nobles of high

[110] *TN*, II, pp. 38–40.

[111] *Agrarian System of Moslem India*, reprint, Allahabad, p. 218.

[112] 'Among all the people of Hindūstān, scholars and commanders and Muslims and Hindus' (*TN*, II, p. 32). Raverty (II, p. 764 *n.*) draws attention to this reference to Hindus as suggesting that their views too commanded attention.

[113] *TN*, II, p. 46.

[114] Ibid., pp. 22–3. See also *TN*, I, pp. 460–1, where those who rose against Yāqūt are described simply as 'Turkish nobles' (*umarā'-i Turk*).

status.'[115] The nobility was still considered the preserve of certain strata, especially Turkish slaves and G͟horian and K͟halj elements. This was the basis too of the policy of restricting offices to persons of 'high birth' which Baranī repeatedly and at length ascribes to Balban.[116] The Turks were often out to curb and even eliminate leading Tāzīks; this they had done after Iltutmish and tried to do also in 1289–90 after Balban's death, when the targeted victims were the leading K͟haljī nobles and commanders.[117] But the G͟horians and the K͟halj still belonged to the 'club'. To that extent, the K͟haljīs who seized power in 1290 were no upstarts, but representatives of a long-established (and, as we have seen, pre-Turkish) segment of the ruling class. In immediate terms, their seizure of power, with Jalāluddīn K͟haljī as Sultan, seemed to signify not only a K͟halj triumph over the Turks, as contemporaries saw it,[118] but a G͟horian restoration. In the end, however, it was to prove much more than a negation of negation: under 'Alāuddīn K͟haljī (1296–1316) the 'club' itself was swept away; and, faced with the unending, baffling changes in the composition of the Sultanate nobility that now ensued, Barani could only look back with nostalgia to bygone days, when, though murder and poison stalked the corridors of power, birth was still king.[119]

[115] *TN*, II, p. 66. [116] Baranī, pp. 36–9.

[117] 'Iṣāmī, pp. 203–4; Baranī, pp. 194–5.

[118] 'Fate folded up the carpet of the Turk's authority, wherever the K͟haljī encountered him. Aye, such are the ways of rapid-moving Fortune, that it does not favour one race (*qaum*) all the time' ('Iṣāmī, p. 206). Baranī, p. 173, says the same thing, but in prose: 'From the date of the death of Sultan Mu'izzuddīn (Kaiqubad) the country came out of the hands of the house of the Turks and fell into those of the race (*aṣl*) of the K͟haljīs.'

[119] See Irfan Habib, 'Baranī's Theory of the History of the Delhi Sultanate', *Indian Historical Review*, VII, Nos. 1–2, pp. 107–10, for an interpretation of Baranī's views on the instability of the Sultanate nobility after Balban.

2

Social Mobility in the Delhi Sultanate

IQTIDAR HUSAIN SIDDIQUI

The treatment by modern historians of the Delhi Sultanate has often been confined to rather narrow concerns, such as the chronology of important battles or the centralising efforts of individual sultans. At best there has been an analysis of the nature of kingship under individual sultans or dynasties, concerned, for example, with how far the sultans were able to suppress factions within the ruling élites. Adequate attention does not seem to have been paid to any analysis of the patterns of political behaviour of successive sultans and the socio-economic changes accompanying changes in state policies and royal institutions. Undoubtedly, part of the limitation of modern research has been due to the paucity of evidence in conventional historical sources.

Recently, attention has been drawn to hagiographic literature, epigraphic material, and literary works that supplement the meagre information available in historical works about socio-economic conditions in India during pre-Mughal times. The odd bits pieced together from the chronicles, supplemented by explorations of other source material, may hopefully enable us to reconstruct a fuller portrait of the society of the Delhi Sultanate than hitherto.

The aim of this paper is to analyse the scattered evidence contained in miscellaneous sources about social mobility under the Delhi Sultanate. We will briefly refer to demographic mobility as well; however, the meagre source material discourages us from investigating it in detail.

Factors for Mobility

With the foundation of the Sultanate in north India about the beginning of the thirteenth century, considerable changes took place in the socio-political life of the country. The multi-state system that had evolved after Harsha gave way to a centralized political organization, enabling the country to acquire political identity in the course of time. The old cities took on the form of cosmopolitan urban centres; while in the newly-founded towns and cities artisans and craftsmen, considered low-caste in the Hindu social system, could now live in their huts even in the vicinity of the quarters owned by members of the ruling élite.[1] This process of urbanization, started under the Sultans, soon led to social mobility among craftsmen in the urban centres.

The artisans and other working people appear to have prospered as the new socio-political system provided them with work in the expanding towns.[2] Further, the outlying border territories were linked to the centre by means of highways along which *thānas*[3] (police posts) were established to ensure the safety of merchant caravans. Foreign merchants who came in caravans over the land routes with merchandise for sale in India returned loaded with Indian products. This boost in trade encouraged diversity in tastes and suggested ideas for the modification and improvement of old and indigenous crafts.[4]

Several factors induced a large number of people to migrate from Central Asia just after the establishment of Turkish rule in Delhi, while the conquest of large territories and the need to consolidate their rule led the Sultans to welcome the immigrants to India. Attracted by the opportunities in the newly-established Sultanate, people from the region of Ghaznin seem to have turned to India in large numbers in order to seek their fortunes. This seems to have been the case with the Khaljis and the Afghans, both of whom are reported to have lived at the level of bare subsistence in their ancestral lands.[5] The Khaljis who had served in the army of

[1] 'Iṣāmī, *Futūḥ-us Salāṭīn*, ed. A.S. Usha, Madras, 1948, pp. 105–6, for the tanners' huts located in the vicinity of the royal palace.

[2] Ibid., pp. 114–15.

[3] See Ẓiāuddīn Baranī, *Tārīkh-i Fīrūz Shāhī*, Calcutta, 1862, pp. 57–9.

[4] Ibn Baṭṭuṭa, *Travels*, Eng. tr. H. Gibb, Cambridge, 1971, III, pp. 547, 550, 584, 602, etc.; Baranī, p. 365; *Futūḥ-us Salāṭīn*, p. 114. 'Iṣāmī alludes to the presence of Chinese painters in Delhi. Quite possibly these painters were brought to Delhi as slaves for sale, since foreign merchants brought slaves trained in various arts and crafts.

[5] See Minhāj-i Sirāj al-Jūzjānī, *Ṭabaqāt-i Nāṣirī*, ed. Abdul Ha'i Habibi, Kabul, 1342 Shamsi, I, pp. 426–7, 435, for the poverty-stricken Khaljī emigrants. Cf. Iqtidar Husain Siddiqui, 'The Afghans and Their Emergence in India as Ruling Elite during the Delhi Sultanate Period', *Central Asiatic Journal*, Wiesbaden, 1982, Vol. 26, Nos. 3–4, pp. 241–61; 246–50.

the rulers of Ghaznīn as *sawārs* (horsemen) and petty officers[6] established themselves rapidly and emerged as a new social group within the first decade of their arrival.[7] Unlike the Khaljis, the Afghan immigrants from the tribal lands took longer to gain positions of influence and authority in state service. Strangely enough, the Afghans lagged behind even the Hindu converts to Islam in this regard, for soon the sons of neo-Muslims were able to raise themselves socially, as will be discussed subsequently.

The condemnation by Minhāj-i Sirāj[8] and Ẓiāuddīn Baranī of Indian converts to Islam, or those who were descended from the early converts, suggests that these had started competing with members of the aristocratic families of early immigrants from Central Asia and other Islamic countries, for posts in state service. Advocating that the Sultans employ people with aristocratic backgrounds, Baranī advises that the children of low-born converts to Islam should not be admitted into *madrasahs* because this education would qualify them for government jobs. Further, he implies that only noble families had been chosen by God to rule mankind, and that their existence was necessary for the maintenance of justice and stability in society.[9] He is also full of praise for Sultan G͟hiyāṣuddīn Balban for his considering noble birth a prerequisite for state service, citing the case of a certain Kamāl Mahiyār whom the nobles took to the Sultan as a candidate for the *K͟hwājgī* (post of accountant) of Amroha district. The Sultan rejected him because his father had been a low-caste convert to Islam.[10] It is interesting to note that Sultan Balban's son, Prince Muḥammad, who held the trans-Sutlej territories under his charge, valued knowledge and talent more than anything else, and noble birth reputedly had of itself no significance for him.[11]

Balban's immediate successor, his grandson, Sultan Kaiqubād (1287–90), also seems to have had no prejudice against people on the grounds of birth, for Baranī includes Kamāl Mahiyār's son in the list of the high nobles of his reign.[12] In fact, the social

[6] *Ṭabaqāt-i Nāṣirī*, I, p. 399.

[7] Iqtidar Husain Siddiqui, 'The Nobility Under the Khalji Sultans', *Islamic Culture*, Hyderabad, January 1963.

[8] *Ṭabaqāt-i Nāṣirī*, I, p. 489; II, pp. 69–70.

[9] Ẓiāuddīn Baranī, *Fatāwā-i Jahāndārī*, Eng. tr. Afsar Begum and Muhammad Habib, *Medieval India Quarterly*, Aligarh, 1958, Nos. 3–4, p. 172.

[10] Baranī, p. 36. [11] Ibid., p. 68. [12] Ibid., p. 126.

stratification that had resulted from the political domination of Muslim immigrant families, which monopolised key positions both in the civil and military administration, could not last long. The progress of learning, expansion and consolidation of the central authority, cultural influences such as those of the *ṣūfī*s (Muslim mystics), and the employment of skilled craftsmen in the royal *kārkhāna*s, paved the way for the rise of people from unprivileged families in society. The consolidation and expansion of the Sultan's authority in the provinces created the need for a large number of educated people to carry on administrative work. The old aristocratic families could no longer supply sufficient officers to meet these needs.

With the advent of the Khaljis in Delhi, far-reaching changes took place in state policies with regard to the recruitment of officers. The Khalji Sultans had no pretensions to noble lineage or past glory. During their period, the doors of official opportunity were thrown open to all, and race, birth and even creed ceased to be all-important criteria.[13] Under Sultan Jalāluddīn Khaljī (killed, 1296), a Hindu chief who belonged to the Mandahar tribe was honoured with the post of *Vakīl-i dar* (minister charged with the responsibility of arranging ceremonies at court).[14] Sultan 'Alāuddīn Khaljī (1296–1316) continued and even extended the policies of his uncle. Dividing 'Alāuddīn Khaljī's reign into three phases, Baranī says that the last phase was dominated by low-born officers. 'The last part of 'Alāuddīn's reign,' says he, 'lasted for four or five years. In these years the Sultan remained unwell, and the whole administration was conducted by Malik Nāib [Kāfūr]. All the important posts were held by indecent and low-born persons.... With the ascendancy of low-born *shiqqdār*s and officers, the whole administration was disturbed and people suffered.'[15]

Even ministerial posts of a religious and quasi-religious nature, such as those of the chief *qāẓī* (chief justice), called *Quzzāt-i Mamālik*, and *Ṣadr-us Ṣudūr* (minister for theological affairs), called *Ṣadr-i Jahān*, could be entrusted to the charge of those educated people who had no claim to noble descent, although these posts had been the exclusive privilege of the members of certain old respectable families of Shaikhs and Saiyids. Criticizing Sultan

[13] Cf. Siddiqui, 'Nobility under the Khalji Sultans', p. 55.

[14] Baranī, pp. 336–7, 194–5.

[15] Ibid., pp. 336–7.

'Alāuddīn Khaljī's policy with regard to the appointment of officers, Baranī suggests that the offices of *Quzzāt* and *Ṣadr-i Jahān* could only be held by...learned men belonging to certain noble families who commanded respect in the country for their piety and learning. Sultan 'Alāuddīn Khaljī had followed this tradition in the beginning of his reign; Qazi Ṣadruddīn 'Ārif, the father of Dāūd Malik and grandson of the daughter of *Ṣadr-i Jahān* Minhāj Juzjānī (author of the *Ṭabaqāt-i Nāṣirī*) was given joint charge of both offices. The office of *Quzzāt* and *Ṣadr-i Jahān* acquired lustre and prestige thereby. Even if the incumbent was not considered a distinguished scholar, yet, being a capable man of noble family, he commanded respect and discharged his duties properly. He was succeeded by Qāẓī Jalāluddīn Livalji in the office of chief *qāẓī* and Maulana Ziāuddīn of Bayāna as *Ṣadr-i Jahān*. The latter had served as *qāẓī-i lashkar* (*qāẓī* in the army). Since both of them lacked high family status, the departments lost much of their influence and prestige. Baranī says, 'During the last phase of Sultan 'Alāuddīn's reign, the *Quzzat* of the empire that was in every way an important and lofty position and for which no one but the member of a well-established family of noble descent, traditionally known for learning and religiosity could be considered fit, was entrusted to *Malik-ut-Tujjar* (Chief of the Merchants), Hamiduddīn Multani. The latter had served in the royal household as *Pardahdār* (incharge of curtains) and *Kulīddār* (Keeper of the Keys). Any mention of this *Malik-ut-Tujjār* (Hamīd Multānī) is not worthy of space in history. Nobody had courage to point out [to the Sultan] that only education and knowledge were not sufficient grounds for appointment to this position.'[16] It is of interest that Shaikh Naṣīruddīn *Chirāgh-i Dehli*, the contemporary Chishtī, had a different and better opinion of the same minister's good qualities. Ḥamīduddīn is said to have been helpful to scholars and other deserving persons as *Ṣadr*, and to have performed the functions of chief justice with honesty and integrity.[17] In short, the spread of education helped to undermine the social barriers created by Muslim immigrant families in the early days of the Delhi Sultanate.

It is also noteworthy that elevation of members of unprivileged families and slaves to high positions in the army and administration

[16] Ibid., pp. 351–2.

[17] Ḥamīd Qalandar, *Khair u'l Majālis*, ed. K.A. Nizami, Aligarh, 1959, pp. 88, 241.

created conditions favourable for the entry of others of the same class. For example, the appointment of Khusrau Khān Parwarī as the *Nāib-i Sultanat* under Sultan Qutbuddīn Mubārak Shāh Khaljī (1317–20) paved the way for the short-lived ascendancy of the Hindu Parwarīs of Gujarat at the imperial court.[18] Though the murder of Sultan Mubārak Shāh Khaljī by the Parwarīs brought about their downfall, no reaction seems to have occurred against the appointment of Hindus and low-caste people to government posts. Sultan Ghiyāṣuddīn Tughluq Shāh came to power with the slogan of punishing Khusrau Khān and his supporters, and so made use of the obvious advantage in condemning the religious affiliations of the Parwarīs. Yet he himself already had Hindu Khokkars as officers and *sawār*s in his service in his *iqtā*ʿ of Depalpur. They supported him in his struggle for the throne of Delhi against Khusrau Khān.[19]

The most important period in this respect, marked by a remarkable example of upward mobility in the nobility, was the reign of Sultan Muḥammad bin Tughluq (1325–51). Both Ibn Baṭṭuta and Barani mention many low-born persons whom Sultan Muḥammad bin Tughluq raised to important positions in the empire. The nature of the officers and the posts assigned to them indicates that many of them were educated people. Ibn Baṭṭūta's reference to Ratan, a Hindu, who was a barber by caste, is of great significance. Despite his lowly origin, Ratan was a scholar of mathematics. Impressed by his knowledge and competence, the Sultan appointed him *wālī* (governor) of the *vilāyat* of Sind with permission to have drums and flags, a privilege accorded only to prominent nobles.[20] The following passage in the *Tārīkh-i Fīrūz Shāhī* shows how social mobility resulted from the Sultan's attitude: 'Najīb, the musician of obscure origin was so much honoured that he superseded in position and status many of the [old] nobles. He was assigned the charge of Gujarat, Multan and Badaun [territories perhaps held in succession]. Like him, 'Azīz Khummār and his brother were favoured. Firoz, the barber, Mankah, the cook, Mas'ūd Khummār (liquor-brewer), Ladhā, the gardener, and many other base and mean people were elevated to important posts and assigned *iqṭā*ʿs.

[18] Baranī, p. 409.

[19] Amīr Khusrau, *Tughluq Nāma*, Aurangabad, 1938, lines 2, 522, p. 131.

[20] Ibn Battuta, III, p. 599.

Shaikh Bābū, son of Nayak, the weaver, was made a royal associate and thus the scoundrel became an influential man in society. Pīrā *Māli* [gardener], who was the meanest and most ignoble person in India, was honoured with the charge of the *dīwān-i wizārat* and raised in this way over and above the *malik*s, nobles, *wālī*s and *muqta*s.[21] Kishan Bāzran of Indrī who was mean of the meanest got the governorship of Awadh. Maqbal, the slave of Aḥmad Ayāz, was entrusted with the governorship of Gujarat, an office meant for high nobles and prominent ministers, although he possessed no qualities outwardly or inwardly.'[22] 'Iṣāmī would have us believe that the Sultan favoured Hindus because he was the enemy of Islam, and, therefore, subjected Muslims everywhere to tyranny.[23]

Of the low-born nobles mentioned by Baranī, Ibn Baṯṯūta also mentions a few, showing how much they had risen because of the Sultan's regard for their competence. 'Azīz Khammar held successively the governorships of Amroha and Malwa, while Maqbal ruled over Gujarat as the *nāib* (deputy) of the *Wazīr*, Khwāja Jahān. 'Azīz is described as a man of violent temper[24] but Maqbal had no such shortcoming. Ibn Baṯṯuta found him a cultured and hospitable person.[25]

It will not be out of place to discuss here the role of a few cities, the growth of which were marked by social mobility. The cities had definite social and economic functions to perform. We shall analyse the relevant evidence about the port city of Cambay and the metropolitan city of Delhi in some detail: Cambay underwent a complete transformation after its annexation to the Sultanate in 1300, while the latter developed into a centre of international culture during the reign of Sultan Iltutmish (1210–1336).

[21] The spelling *muqṭi'* is preferable to *muqṭ*, the last short vowel being not, of course, indicated in the texts.

[22] Baranī, pp. 505–6.

[23] *Futūḥ-us Salāṭīn*, p. 515.

[24] Ibn Baṯṯūṭa, II, p. 762.

[25] Ibn Baṯṯūṭa mentions Malik Maqbal first in his account of the rebellion of Jalāl Afghān and then in his account of his visit to Cambay on the way to China. In Cambay he enjoyed his hospitality as Governor. Since Gibb's volume comes to a close before Ibn Baṯṯūṭa left for the Deccan, we have to utilize the Urdu translation as well for information about the cities in the Deccan and Gujarat. Agha Mahdi Husain's translation of Ibn Baṯṯūṭa's account of India seems to be faulty at places. Ibn Baṯṯūṭa (Eng. tr.), III, p. 730; *'Ajāib-ul Asfār* (Urdu tr.), Maulvi Muhammad Husain, second edition, Islamabad, 1983, II, pp. 280–1.

Prior to its conquest by the Delhi army, the port city of Cambay was part of the kingdom of Gujarat. It was largely inhabited by artisans and workers, with small pockets of Muslim traders, Zoroastrians of Iranian origin and members of the Hindu business community and aristocracy. Qāẓī Sadiduddīn Muḥammad 'Awfī, the Bukhara-born immigrant who landed in Cambay in 1220, furnishes useful information about the life and conditions there under the rule of the Rāi (Raja) of Gujarat. He was astonished to see that the Rāi not only granted religious freedom to Muslims and Zoroastrians but also went out of his way to protect them. However, he called Cambay a city of extremely poor and miserable Indians.[26] Unlike the generality of the city's inhabitants, the Hindu traders of Gujarat were so rich that they are reported by the same writer to have invested their capital in Ghaznin. One of them, Salbhir, had invested one hundred million *balutras*[27] (a silver coin) in Ghaznin.[28] Incidentally, Shaikh Niẓāmuddīn Auliyā corroborates this when he praises the Hindu traders of pre-Muslim Gujarat for their fair dealing, in contrast to those of Muslim merchants from Lahore during the first half of the thirteenth century.[29]

It is noteworthy that the final conquest of Gujarat and its annexation to the Sultanate of Delhi in 1304–5[30] led to the emergence of Cambay as an emporium of international trade and

[26] Sadiduddīn Muhammad Awfī, *Javami'-ul Hikāyāt-wa Livāmi' ul Rivāyāt*, ed. Muhammad Nizamu'ddin, Hyderabad, 1965, I, Part 2, pp. 255–6.

[27] The Sanskrit works refer to this silver coin, which was in circulation in Gujarat during the Chalukya period, as Parutha. Ch. Dashratha Sharma, 'Coins in the Kharataragachh pattarah', *Journal of the Numismatic Society of North India*, XXII, 1960, pp. 196–201.

[28] *Javāmi'-ul Ḥikāyāt*, I, Part 2, pp. 304–5. The third volume of the work has been edited and published in Iran; the fourth volume still remains unpublished.

[29] Mīr Ḥasan Sijzī, *Fawāid ul Fu'ād*, Kanpur, pp. 116–17.

[30] It is wrongly held that Gujarat was annexed by Sultan 'Alā'uddīn Khaljī in 1299 after it had been plundered by the army commanded by Ulugh Khan and Nuṣrat Khān. As a matter of fact the Sultan sent the expedition in 1299 only for plunder. The details furnished by Baranī in this regard show that on the entry of the Delhi army into Nahalwarah, the local ruler, Rāi Karan fled away, but his wife, Kamla Devi, his treasures and elephants were seized by Ulugh Khan. Then the entire region up to Somnāth was ravaged. In Cambay the rich Muslim merchants were also divested of their wealth. He also tells us that both generals returned loaded with the spoils of war to Delhi. The Mongols mutinied on the way because they were forced to surrender the booty for the royal treasury. Baranı does not mention that a governor was appointed by the Sultan to hold Gujarat for him at this time (Baranī, pp. 251–2).

commerce. Many foreign merchants engaged in the overseas trade settled at Cambay and carried on trade inside India as well as with foreign countries. All this gave a fillip to the overseas trade of the Delhi Sultanate, and brought prosperity to artisans and workers in Cambay, which according to Ibn Baṯṯūṯa, was the finest city in the Sultanate. The merchants who are reported to have settled there had their establishments in countries ranging from Central Asia to Egypt.[31] Their beautiful fortress-like mansions and the adjacent mosques constructed in the styles of different countries of the Middle East held a great fascination for the visitor. The merchants are also reported to have vied with one another in having their mansions and mosques constructed on a grand scale.[32]

It needs to be pointed out that with a view to creating conditions favourable for the progress of trade and the growth of commerce, the Sultans entrusted the administration of Cambay to a leading merchant. If any merchant came to Delhi, he was honoured at the royal court and treated as a state guest during his stay in the capital.[33] The first merchant to be entrusted with the government of Cambay was Malik-ut Tujjār Pirwīz from Gāzrūn (Iran).[34] After he was murdered by robbers in Gujarat, Malik-ut Tujjār Tājuddīn al-Kawlāmī was appointed Governor of Cambay. He carried on

---

Unlike Baranī, 'Iṣāmī mentions two expeditions sent by the Sultan to Gujarat at two different times. The first was a raid, and a few years later Gujarat was finally conquered and annexed to the Delhi Sultanate (1304–5). Alap Khan, the Sultan's brother-in-law, was appointed its first governor. Dewal Rānī, the daughter of Rāi Karan, was captured at this time (*Futūḥ-us Ṣalāṯīn*, pp. 287–8).

'Iṣāmī's account is corroborated by Amīr Khusrau, the court poet of Sultan Ala'uddin Khalji. In his *mathnavī*, *'Dewal Rānī-o Khiẓr Khān'*, he describes both expeditions. He tells us that Kawnla Dī (Rānī Kamala Devī) who had been married by the Sultan in 1299, requested her new husband to ask the Rāi of Gujarāt to send princess Dewal Devī, her daughter, to Delhi, to be married to Prince Khiẓr Khān. The Rāi was first asked to send his daughter and then Gujarat was invaded a second time. Dewal Rānī was captured and Gujarat annexed to the Sultanate. Alap Khān was ordered to proceed to Gujarat and govern it (Amīr Khusrau, *Dewal Rānī Khiẓr Khān*, Aligarh, 1917, pp. 81–7).

The Gujarat chronicles also show that the date of Gujarat's annexation to the Delhi Sultanate is 1304–5 and not 1299. See S.C. Misra, *The Rise of Muslim Power in Gujarāt*, second edition, New Delhi, 1982, pp. 63–4.

[31] Ibn Baṯṯūṯa, III, pp. 730, 733.

[32] *'Ajāib-ul Asfār*, II, pp. 280–1.

[33] Ibn Baṯṯūṯa, III, p. 733.

[34] Ibid.

trade with different countries of Africa and Asia, and built a beautiful college in Egypt. He came to Delhi from 'the lands of the Turks' with magnificent gifts, including slaves. camels, merchandise, weapons and woven stuffs. 'The Sultan was highly delighted with his action and gave him twelve laks, though it is said that the value of his gift was no more than one lak, and appointed him to the government of the city of Kanbāya [Cambay]. ...from Cambay al-Kawlāmī sent vessels to the towns of Mulaibār, the island of Sailān [Sri Lanka] and elsewhere, and valuable articles and gifts came to him in these vessels and he became enormously wealthy.'[35] Likewise, Shihābuddīn Gāzrūnī, a merchant from Iran, was given several times the value of the gift that he had brought from his country.[36]

Some of the foreign merchants established charitable endowments at Cambay. For instance, Khwāja Isḥāq established a *khānqāh* (hospice) where travellers were served free food and the poor and destitute given money daily. His wealth increased, in spite of the expenditure incurred on maintenance of the *khānqāh*.[37] In short, Cambay became a city of great prosperity for merchants, and of modest well-being for all.

Many Ṣūfī saints also came from foreign countries and settled in Cambay. Qāẓī Naẓīr, who had arrived from Diyar Bakr, lived in extreme poverty, confined to a cell in the Jama' Mosque: people came to listen to his exhortations.[38] Shaikh 'Alī Ḥaidarī Qalandar's *khānqāh* also attracted a large number of visitors daily, including foreign merchants. Every visitor offered him gifts in kind and cash. Sea traders used to take vows to give large sums to him and on arriving at Cambay they would go first of all to pay him their respects.[39]

Fourteenth-century Indo-Persian writers add to the information provided by Ibn Baṭṭūṭa about Cambay. 'Iṣāmī informs us that in addition to the lofty buildings, every mansion possessed an inner stronghold for protection against rebels or other refractory elements.[40] References in Baranī's *Tārīkh-i Fīrūz Shāhī* similarly tend to suggest that Cambay had become the principal port for the import

[35] Ibid., III, p. 734.

[36] Ibid., p. 673.

[37] *Ajaib-ul Asfar*, II, p. 231.

[38] Ibid.

[39] Ibn Baṭṭūṭa, III, pp. 705–6.

[40] 'Iṣāmī, *Futūḥ-us Salāṭīn*, ed. A.S. Usha, pp. 108, 509–10.

of foreign products and war-horses for the royal court at Delhi.[41] Another fourteenth-century writer, 'Ain-ul Mulk Māhrū, who visited Cambay in connection with some official work during the reign of Sultan Muḥammad bin Tughluq, called it Shahr-i Mu'aẓẓam ('a great city') having all around it high and large buildings, surrounded by beautiful gardens.[42] It may be noted that the extent of Cambay's prosperity impressed Barbosa,[43] one of the early European travellers.

As regards the metropolitan city of Delhi, contemporary sources naturally provide us with much greater information than they do for Cambay. Before its conquest by Quṭbuddīn Aibak, Delhi was a mere local military headquarters.[44] It developed into a magnificent city after Iltutmish made it his capital in 1210. It received large numbers of immigrants from Central Asia and Persia, who were driven hither by the Mongol invasions. Among these refugees were many celebrities of the Persian-speaking world. As a result, Delhi became the repository of the best of Islamic culture that had developed in Persia, Khurasan and Central Asia. Early thirteenth-century writers refer briefly to the exodus of people from foreign countries;[45] the later historian, 'Iṣāmī, however, gives a graphic description of the categories to which these foreigners belonged: 'Many genuine descendants of the Prophet arrived there from Arabia, many artisans from Khurāsān, many painters from the country of China, many *'ulama* [learned men], born in Bukhārā, many saints and devotees from every quarter [of the world]. There also came craftsmen of every kind and every country,.... many experts knowledgeable in precious gems, innumerable jewel

[41] Baranī, pp. 507–8, 516, for the overseas trade of Cambay.

[42] *Inshā-i Māhrū*, ed. Shaikh Abdur Rashid, Lahore, 1965, p. 133.

[43] *The Book of Durarte Barbosa*, tr. Mansel Longworth Dames, London, 1918, I, pp. 112, 120, 140.

[44] *Futūḥ-us Salāṭin*, p. 108, lines 7 and 8.

[45] A contemporary poet, who left Bukhārā for India and was attached to the court of Iltutmish, says: '[People] sought refuge [at your court] against the tyranny perpetrated by the infidels of China [Mongols]' (*Qaṣīda* contained in Bihamad Khānī, *Tārīkh-i Muḥammadī*, MS British Library, London, Or. 134, f. 345 b). Minhāj-i Sirāj states: 'This city through the number of grants and unbounded munificence of that pious monarch (Iltutmish) became the retreat and the resting place for the learned, the virtuous and the excellent of the various parts of the world.' He goes on to state that everyone who fled from the tyranny of the Mongols and sought refuge in India was helped by the Sultan (*Ṭabaqāt-i Nāṣirī*, pp. 440–1).

merchants, philosophers and physicians of the Greek school. In that happy city they gathered like moths around a burning candle.'[46]

Again, 'Iṣāmī refers to the immigrants from foreign lands and also from different parts of India settling in Delhi and other cities and towns when he praises Sultan 'Alāuddīn K͟haljī's concern for The welfare of the people: 'Anyone who arrived from "two 'Irāqs" [Iraq and Persia], Sind and Arabia to this "garden of happiness" [India], developed so much predilection for it that he hardly even remembered his native land. World-travellers, who did not stay at any place even for a month, settled down in India overcome by its charm.'[47]

'Iṣāmī aslo supplies valuable information about the large population, the numerous artisans adept in different crafts, and the supply of essential as well as luxury goods in plenty in the bazars of Delhi.[48] According to him, Delhi had become the largest of the cities of India during Alāuddīn K͟haljī's time. None of its quarters would look empty of people even if a hundred divisions were raised there and sent out. Many of its scientists and men of arts and learning had acquired fame in foreign countries.[49] Baranī corroborates this in his praise of the progress of arts and crafts in Delhi during the K͟haljī period. In Baranī's opinion, only the achievements of the nobly born or men of aristocratic background were to be recorded in history, and yet he was constrained to mention the artisans of Delhi for their skills. Indeed, he glows with pride while claiming that Delhi's artisans had excelled the master craftsmen of foreign countries in manufacturing weapons, garments, rosaries, etc.[50]

Of the important institutions of foreign origin,[51] the *kārk͟hānas* (workshops and store-houses) and *madrasas* (schools and colleges) that contributed greatly to social mobility in urban centres, deserve mention. The *kārk͟hānas* seem to have been established in Delhi just after the founding of the Sultanate. Baranī refers to them in his account of Sultan Balban's reign (1266–87).[52] Nobles posted in the

[46] *Futūḥ-us Salāṯīn*, pp. 114–15.

[47] Ibid., pp. 504–5.

[48] Ibid., p. 452.

[49] Ibid., pp. 445–6.

[50] Baranī, p. 365.

[51] *Javāmi'-ul Ḥikāyāt* Vol. 2, Part III (Iran, 1353 Shamsi), pp. 467–8, for its Central Asian origin.

[52] Baranī, pp. 50, 60.

provinces as governors also maintained *kārkhānas*,[53] and efforts were made to employ master craftsmen to work there. The author of the *Masālik-ul Abṣār* was informed about a *kārkhāna* maintained by Sultan Muḥammad bin Tughluq in Delhi wherein 4,000 skilled workers were employed to work. They wove and embroidered silk cloth. This *kārkhāna* supplied different kinds of cloth used in making robes of honour and other garments. The robes were distributed among the officers of the State twice a year. The Sultan used to distribute 2,00,000 suits of cloth, one half of it in the winter and the remainder in summer.[54] His successor, Fīrūz Shāh (1351–88), is said to have surpassed his predecessors in maintaining large *kārkhānas* in Delhi, numbering thirty-six in all. Goldsmiths, gem-cutters, perfumers, artisans skilled at making different types of weapons and armour, were all employed in large numbers. Master craftsmen trained thousands of slave boys in different crafts.[55] Many slaves trained in the *kārkhānas* attained important positions. They took active part in the politics of the Delhi Sultanate and ultimately emerged as a powerful group after the death of Sultan Fīrūz Shāh in 1388. Towards the close of the fourteenth century, Malik-ush Sharq Khwāja Jahān (founder of the Sharqi kingdom of Jaunpur) was Fīrūz Shāh's slave and had been assigned, at the beginning of his career, the duty of a water-bearer.[56]

Like the *kārkhānas*, educational institutions maintained or aided by the state greatly increased social mobility in Delhi. In Delhi there seems to have been a strong local school system leading to higher seats of learning, such as *Madrasa-i Mu'izzi*.[57] The *Madrasa-i Nāṣirī*,[58] and later the *Madrasa-i Fīrūz Shāhī*,[59] were staffed with reputed scholars, and these institutions seem to have admitted

[53] Ibid., p. 92.

[54] Shihāb u'ddīn al-'Umarī, *Masālik-ul Absār-fī Mamālik-ul Amṣār*, Iqtidar Husain Siddiqui, *A Fourteenth Century Arab Account of India Under Sultan Muhammad bin Tughluq*, Aligarh, 1971, p. 39.

[55] Shams Sirāj Afīf, *Tārīkh-i Firoz Shāhī*, Calcutta, 1891, pp. 270–2, 307.

[56] Shaikh Kabir Batini, *Afsāna-i Shāhān*, MS British Library, London, Add. 24, 409, f. 90b.

[57] The *Madrassa-i-Mu'izzī* was the oldest college in Delhi, founded after its conquest by Quṭbu'ddīn Aibak. Cf. Ḥasan Sijzi, *Fawāid-ul Fuād*, p. 23.

[58] It was founded by Sultan Iltutmish and named after his eldest son, Nāṣiruddīn Maḥmūd (*Ṭabaqāt-i Nāsirī*, I, p. 460).

[59] See K.A. Nizami, 'A Medieval Indian Madrasah', *Studies in Medieval History and Culture*, Allahabad, 1966, pp. 73, 79, for details.

students belonging to different strata of society. The number of schools (also called *madrasas*) increased in Delhi with the expansion of old cities and the foundation of new ones. By the time of Sultan Muḥammad bin Tughluq (1325–51), the number had increased to one thousand in Delhi alone.[60]

The *Madrasa-i Fīrūz Shāhī*, founded by Sultan Fīrūz Shah (1351–88), was housed in large double-storied buildings, and provided its students with board and instruction free of cost. The fame of its teachers drew visiting scholars from far and near;[61] these visitors were served, along with the inmates, different varieties of food at state expense.[62]

It is possible that education spread through the *madrasas* was responsible for a certain amount of social tension in Delhi and other cities. The few details furnished by Baranī and 'Iṣāmī of the rebellion by Ḥājī Maulā (a liberated slave) in Delhi in 1301 show how resentful people belonging to the lower cadres of state service had become over the inequitable distribution of state patronage. Ḥājī Maulā, who served in Ritol[63] as *Shahna* (police inspector), decided to take advantage of the situation; he came to Delhi, won over soldiers and others and led a revolt against 'Alāuddīn Khaljī. Tirmizī, the *Kotwāl* of the old city, was treacherously killed and the royal stables, treasury and the armoury were seized. The entire force of the *kotwālī* men (*kotwālīyān*), the *lashkar* (soldiery) and the *khalq* (commoners) rallied around Ḥājī Maulā.[64] 'Iṣāmī's condemnation of them as *mard-i kammāya* (penniless fellows) suggests their plebeian background.[65] Similarly Ḥāji Maulā's selection of an 'Alavī (descendant of 'Alī, the fourth Caliph of Islam) as

[60] Siddiqui (tr.), *India Under Sultan Muhammad bin Tughluq*, p. 36.

[61] Baranī, p. 563.

[62] Nizami, 'A Medieval Indian Madrasah', pp. 77–8.

[63] The printed text of Baranī's *Tārīkh-i Fīrūz Shāhī* mentions Ritol as Ritank but the manuscript copy of the first recension, released by its author in the 4th year of Firuz Shah's reign, correctly mentions the place as Ritol (district Meerut, U.P.). The first recension was revised by Baranī in the 6th year of Fīrūz Shah's reign. In the revised recension, the didactic element becomes preponderant in the author's approach to the history of the Delhi Sultans. Hence the qualitative difference in them. The copies of the first recension are available in manuscript in the Raza Library, Rampur, and the Bodleian Library, Oxford. See *Tārīkh-i Fīrūz Shāhī*, MS Raza Library, Rampur, Cat. No. 1846, f. 106 b.

[64] Baranī (printed text), pp. 279–80.

[65] 'Iṣāmī, p. 277.

king, suggests that the rebels wanted a different kind of state. Ḥājī Maulā's rebellion was brutally suppressed.[66]

It was the fear of antagonising public opinion in Delhi that served as a check on the Sultans from time to time. The transfer of population from Delhi to Daulatabad in 1327 did not take place only on account of Sultan Muḥammad bin Tug͟hluq's desire to develop the newly-founded city of Daulatābād in the Deccan into a leading centre of Muslim culture. He wanted to get rid of Delhi's population before he began to pursue his radical policies and religious goals.[67] Both 'Iṣāmī and Ibn Baṭṭūṭa corroborate each other when they say that the Sultan did not trust the people of Delhi and forcibly shifted them to Daulatābād by way of punishment.[68] The relevant evidence contained in Baranī's account of G͟hiyāṣuddīn Tug͟hluq's reign clearly indicates that people in Delhi were hostile to the Sultan for his niggardliness in distributing money among people even on occasions of social significance.[69] It is also true to say that Delhi was never abandoned as the first capital and after the evacuation of the entire population, people were brought from the neighbouring towns and cities to inhabit the empty city. Obviously many of these newcomers in Delhi, whom Iṣami dubs rustic fellows having no cultural background, got the opportunity to take to professions or even occupy posts that previously they could not have hoped to do.[70] In this way social

[66] Baranī, pp. 279–80.

[67] The evidence available in Baranī's first recension calls for a reappraisal of the history of the so-called transfer of the capital under Sultan Muhammad bin Tughluq. In this recension Baranī informs us that first the Sultan sent the wives, children and other dependents of the nobles in Delhi, along with his mother, to Daulatabad. Soon afterwards he ordered the Saiyids, *mashāik͟h* (ṣūfī saints), *'ulamā* and other notables (of Delhi) to be brought to Daulatabad. All of them left the city (Delhi) with their dependents. In the third phase, after the rebellion of Kishlū K͟hān had been quelled, the entire population of Delhi was shifted to Daulatabad. Thus Baranī corroborates 'Iṣāmī and Ibn Baṭṭūṭa regarding the evacuation of the old population of Delhi (*Tārīk͟h-i Fīrūz Shāhī*, MS. Raza Library, Rampur, Cat. No. 1846, f. 106 b; Bodleian Library MS 173, Elliot, 353, f. 192 a).

[68] 'Iṣāmī states that the Sultan had doubts about the loyalty of the citizens of Delhi and, therefore, he ordered people to migrate to Daulatabad. Others were then brought from neighbouring places to fill the vacant city. He remarks: This was like replacing nightingales and parrots with crows and ravens (*Futūḥ-us Salāṭīn*, p. 446. Cf. Ibn Baṭṭūṭa, Eng. tr., III, pp. 707–8).

[69] Baranī, pp. 434, 436–7.

[70] *Futūḥ-us Salāṭīn*, pp. 707–8.

mobility in the largest city of the Sultanate increased further.

The main reason for the transfer of population from Delhi to Daulatābād was the Sultan's fear of popular opposition to his state and religious policies—people who lived in provincial cities and towns were thought to be more docile. The important outcome of this measure was that Daulatābād received large numbers of the old capital's citizenry and it soon began to rival Delhi.

Ibn Baṯṯūṭa's description of Daulatābād shows that its rise to being the second metropolitan city of the empire benefited the Deccan. The establishment of *kārkhānas* and other institutions, cultural as well as political, led to social mobility. Daulatābād soon compared with Delhi in both size and grandeur.[71] However, it ceased to be a place of any importance when the founder of the Bahmani dynasty shifted the capital to Gulbarga, again for political reasons. In Daulatābād, the Afghans and other supporters of Makh Afghān, antagonistic to the Bahmani Sultan, were quite powerful. Soon Gulbarga replaced Daulatabad as a seat of culture.[72]

Social Groups

The emergence of the Afghans, Kalāls (liquor-brewers), Jains, Khatris and Kambos of the Panjab as prominent communities during the period of the Delhi Sultanate also provides us with insights into the social processes at work. The Afghans, who seem to have settled in large numbers in the frontier region to the north-west of Panjab long before their conversion to Islam and the annexation of their homeland by Sultan Maḥmūd of Ghaznin, were a tribal people much given to plunder. They began to enter the fold of Islam during the reign of Sultan Maḥmūd (998–1030), and by the close of the twelfth century almost all the Afghan tribes seem to have become Muslims. The only reference to their presence in Delhi contained in the *Ṭabaqāt-i Nāṣirī* is indicative of the fact that they were known for their ferocity and rustic ways. They served the nobles as soldiers till the second half of the thirteenth century.[73] Their lack of culture and sophistication apparently retarded their

[71] *'Ajā'ib-ul Asfār*, Vol. 2, p. .

[72] *Futūḥ-us Salāṭīn*, pp. 558–9, 570.

[73] Siddiqui, 'The Afghans during the Delhi Sultanate Period', *Central Asiatic Journal*, 1982, Vol. 26, Nos. 3–4, Wiesbaden, pp. 242–3.

upward mobility; in India they took a long time to acquire culture, but then at last began to improve their position in state service.

During the reign of Sultan G͟hiyāṣuddīn Balban, a new generation of Afghans, brought up in the environment of the Delhi Sultanate, came on the scene. Sultan Balban entrusted them with the charge of newly-established *thānas* (police posts) around Delhi and other territories, and in the provincial armies also the number of Afghan soldiers had considerably increased.[74] This improvement in their position seems to have encouraged them to impart education to their children. As a result, the Afghans rose to the status of high nobles during the reign of Alā'uddīn K͟haljī.

Amīr K͟husrau, who mentions the Afghans as uncultured people not fit to reside in the midst of civilized people in his *diwān*, *Tuḥfat-ul Sig͟har*,[75] had to change his tune in the reign of Alā'uddīn K͟haljī. As the Afg͟hāns got used to aristocratic ways and competed with members of the old aristocratic families, Amīr K͟husrau now simply called them boastful persons bereft of excellence.[76] K͟husrau, being an aristocrat opposed to change, was clearly not free from prejudice against Afghans and others who had risen from below, for the details furnished by Ibn Baṭṭūṭa, 'Iṣāmī and Baranī about the Afghan nobles of their time, show that by then many of them had become cultured aristocrats and commanded respect in society for their services to the Empire.

During the Tug͟hluq period their number increased considerably, and they held important administrative posts in every province. By the time Sultan Muḥammad bin Tug͟hluq came to the throne, the Afghans had emerged as a new social group in the Sultanate. In Multan, Gujarat and the Deccan, they became so powerful that some of them began to aspire to kingship. Even the suppression of their rebellions against Sultan Muḥammad bin Tug͟hluq in different provinces did not weaken their strength in India, and they continued to hold important *iqṭā*'s and posts in the Delhi Sultanate as well as the regional kingdoms that arose after Timur's sack of Delhi in 1398.[77] Mention may be made of Malik K͟hurram Nuhānī (Afghan), who was the first Afghan to found an independent

[74] Barani, pp. 57–9.

[75] Amir Khusrau, *Tuhfat-ul Sig͟har*, cited by Wahid Mirza, *The Life and Works of Amir Khusrau*, Calcutta, 1939, pp. 51–2.

[76] *Ā'īna-i Sikandarī*, ed. Muhammad Said Farooqi, 1917, lines 29–30, p. 37.

[77] *Central Asiatic Journal*, 1982, Vol. 26, Nos. 3–4, pp. 253–6.

principality, that of Jalore in Rajasthan, in the beginning of the fifteenth century. His descendants continued to rule over it till the next century.[78]

The Kalāls (liquor-brewers) seem to have prospered particularly because of the introduction of liquor distillation, which is mentioned by Baranī. He describes them as *khumārs* (wine-makers) and *'araqīs* (distillers). Later medieval writers refer to them by their Hindustani caste name, 'Kalāl'. The wealth and prosperity acquired by members of the caste seems to have led some of them to embrace Islam. Information is provided by Ibn Baṭṭūṭa and Baranī about 'Azīz Khumār, his brother, Najīb, and Mas'ūd Khumār. This tends to suggest that they had abandoned their hereditary profession and were educated Muslims who acquired prominent positions through merit. Though 'Azīz Khumār was notorious for his harsh dealings with people, he enjoyed the confidence of Sultan Muḥammad bin Tughluq, who first appointed him controller of revenue in the territorial unit of Amroha,[79] and later governor of Malwa.[80]

Traditions which seventeenth-century writers incorporated in their works about the origin of the founders of the regional dynasties of Nagaur and Gujarat in the beginning of the fifteenth century not only shed light on the social mobility of low-caste converts to Islam but also hint that close contact with the Muslim élites could have attracted some Hindus towards Islam. According to these traditions, Ẓafar Khān, founder of the Sultanate of Gujarat and his brother, Shams Khān Dandanī (who founded the principality of Nagaur) were the sons of Saharan, a member of the Kalāl caste. According to Shaikh Kabīr Bāṭinī, Saharan married his sister to Fīrūz Shāh, and this marriage was followed by the family's conversion to Islam. Saharan and his brothers were honoured with high ranks and titles.[81]

[78] Cf. M.S. Commissariat, *A History of Gujarat*, Bombay, 1983, I, pp. 50–2.

[79] Ibn Baṭṭūṭa, Eng. tr. Gibb, *The Travels of Ibn Baṭṭūṭa*, III, p. 762.

[80] Baranī, pp. 501–2.

[81] *Afsānah-i Shāhān*, MS British Library, London, Add. 24, 409, ff. 90b–91a. The early official historians of Gujarat are silent on the origin of Ẓafar Khān. Sikandar bin Manjhū is the first Gujarati historian to deny the validity of the traditions about his low origin. He corroborates Shaikh Kabīr in so far as the details of the marriage with Fīrūz Shah are concerned but twists the facts about Saharan's social background. According to him, an ancestor of Saharan was expelled from the Khatri caste because of his weakness for wine. Since then the family had been fond of wine and its members were called Nāyak (Sikandar bin Manjhū, *Mirāt-i Sikandarī*, Bombay, AH 1308, p. 566.)

Our sources for other regions also show that alcoholic drinks were much in demand in every city.[82] Certain members of the ruling classes cultivated a taste for liquor. Liquor-sellers and manufacturers were still predominantly Hindus who acquired aristocratic habits on account of their prosperity. An inscription dated 24 February 1436 mentions Bhola Maharaj Khumar who spent money on the construction of a step-well in Jahtra for the benefit of the people at large.[83]

In the kingdom of Malwa, certain Kalāls are said to have changed over to other trades. Mushtāqī in his narrative of the love-affair between Sultan Nāṣir Shāh Khaljī and a Kalāl girl says that her family traded in utensils. It is said that Nāṣir Shāh became enamoured of the girl, and, when approached, the girl's mother gave her to the Sultan in marriage. In the case of this family also the matrimonial alliance paved the way for the rise of its members to a rank in the nobility. The brothers of the girl were assigned titles, ranks and *iqṭā*'s.[84]

Like the liquor-brewers, the Jains, a community of merchants and tradesmen, moved upward socially. The Jains are reported to have attained high positions in the Sultan's service from the reign of Sultan Alā'uddīn Khaljī. For instance, Pheru Jain, an expert gemmologist, was appointed superintendent of the royal mint in Delhi by Sultan Ala'uddīn Khaljī. He retained his position till the reign of Sultan Muḥammad bin Tughluq, and had so much influence that he could recommend men of his community to the Sultan.[85] Samar Singh Jain held an important position during the reign of Sultan Quṭbu'ddīn Mubārak Shāh Khaljī.[86] In the provinces of Gujarat and Nagaur as well, Jains rose in the social hierarchy under the patronage of Muslim governors. Sultan Muḥammad bin Tughluq (1325–51) went out of his way to befriend the Jain community along with other non-Muslims. The traditions set by the fourteenth-century Sultans in conferring favours on the Jains seem to have been followed by the regional Sultans and chiefs who rose into prominence after the dissolution

[82] Rizqullāh Mushtāqī, *Waqi'āt-i Mushtāqī*, MS British Library, London, No. Add. 11, 633, ff. 81a–b.

[83] *Epigraphia Indica, Arabic and Persian Supplement*, 1953–4, pp. 39–40.

[84] *Wāqi'āt-i Mushtāqī*, ff. 81a–b.

[85] Cf. *Thakura Pheru's Rayana Parikha*, ed., tr. S.R. Sarma, Aligarh, 1984, pp. 3–12 (Introduction).

[86] (Agha) Mahdi Husain, *Tughluq Dynasty*, New Delhi, reprint 1976, pp. 315–16, 363–4.

of the Delhi Sultanate in the fifteenth century, as will be discussed presently.

The Kambos originally belonged to a Hindu caste of the Panjab and were mostly peasants.[87] In Multan they embraced Islam under the influence of the Suhrawardī saints; their association with Shaikh Bahā'uddīn Zakariyā of Multan led to their descendants being seized with a passion for learning.[88]

A document in the *Inshā-i Māhrū*, a fourteenth-century collection of epistles, reflects the social mobility owing to which people once belonging to the lower strata of society could manoeuvre for position through what may be termed as their ability to create a nuisance. By the time of Sultan Fīrūz Shāh the Kambos of Multan had become so influential that they could intervene with the governor and could even approach the royal court and be heard by the Sultan.[89] They emerged as an influential group in the fifteenth century. In 1443, they supported Shaikh Yūsuf Qureshī, a descendant of Shaikh Bahā'uddīn Zakariyā, and declared him Sultan of Multan.[90] By now many of the Kambos of Multan had distinguished themselves as *ulamā* (scholars) and *mashāikh* (ṣūfī saints). One of the eminent Suhrawardī sūfīs, Shaikh Samāuddīn Kambo, became the patron saint of the Lodi dynasty in Delhi;[91] Shaikh Samāuddin Kambo's son-in-law, Shaikh Jamālī, was elevated to the status of poet laureate at the court of Sultan Sikandar Lodī,[92] and many other Kambos occupied important ranks and positions in the Lodi Empire.[93] One of the ministers of Sher Shāh Sūr was Imādul Mulk Kambo, who headed the department of *Amīr-i 'Āriẕ*.[94]

Like the Kambos of Multan, the Khatris, who resided mostly in

[87] William Crooke, *The Tribes and Castes of North-Western India*, reprint, Delhi, 1975, pp. 118–21.

[88] Shaikh Farīd Bhakharī, *Zakhīrat-ul Khawānīn*, ed. S. Moin-ul Haque, Karachi, I, p. 148.

[89] 'Ain-ul Mulk Māhrū, *Inshā-i Māhrū*, ed. Sh. Abdur Rashid, Lahore, 1965, Letter 29, pp. 65–7.

[90] Niẓāmu'ddīn Aḥmad, *Ṭabaqāt-i Akbarī*, III, p. 53.

[91] Shaikh Jamālī, *Siyar-ul 'Ārifīn*, p. 177; also Ahmad Khan, *Shajrah-i Suhraward*, MS Raza Library, Rampur, ff. 15b–17a.

[92] Ni'mat u'llah Harevi, *Tārīkh-i Khān-i Jahānī*, ed. Imam al-Din, Dacca, 1960, I, pp. 225–7.

[93] See Iqtidar Husain Siddiqui, 'The Composition of the Nobility Under the Lodi Sultans', *Medieval India—A Miscellany*, Aligarh, 1977, Vol. 4, pp. 20, 23, 62, for Kambo nobles under the Lodi Sultans.

[94] Iqtidar Husain Siddiqui, *Mughal Relations with the Indian Ruling Elite—16th Century*, New Delhi, 1983, p. 94.

the Panjab and Delhi, also appear to have emerged as an important new social group in the Sultanate during the fourteenth century. Having acquired proficiency in accountancy and arithmetic, they were employed in the revenue department. Many of them went to the provinces as finance officers along with the governors. When Sultan Muḥammad Shāh II appointed Ẓafar Khān and Dilāwar Khān Ghorī as governors of Gujarat and Malwa respectively between 1391 and 1392, both took their Khatri *dīwān*s with them. Their sons and relations also gained important positions through their influence at the provincial courts. Upon the decay of the Delhi Sultanate, the Khatri nobles began to play an important role both in Gujarat and Malwa.[95] Most prominent among the Khatri nobles in Gujarat were Malik Shāhpidar Khatrī, Jīvan Khatrī and Rāī Dās Khatrī. They were among the trusted nobles of Sultan Muẓaffar Shāh, founder of the Gujarat kingdom.[96]

In the Sultanate of Delhi the revenue department was also heavily manned by Khatri officials. Under Khiẓr Khān Saiyid and his successor, Sultan Mubārak Shāh, the Khatris enjoyed high positions at Delhi.[97] Similarly, they supervised the financial administration at the Centre and in the provinces during the Lodi period. Babur was surprised to see that all revenue officials were Hindus.[98] Hindu domination of the revenue department seems to have caused resentment among the Muslim land grantees, for they were not expected to show any leniency in collecting state revenues at the time of harvest. For this reason, Shaikh 'Abdu'l Quddūs Gangohī, a prominent Chishtī saint, suggests in a letter to Babur that Hindus should not be entrusted with the work of collecting revenue.[99]

Social mobility increased in certain regions under the provincial rulers after the dissolution of the Delhi Sultanate in 1398. Local rulers took a keen interest in the economic development of their kingdoms and cemented their relations with the local people by constructing large tanks, step-wells and other buildings of public utility.[100] In the fifteenth century, under the fostering care of its

[95] Shaikh Kabīr Bāṭinī, *Afsānah-i Shāhān*, ff. 33a–b.

[96] *Mirāt-i Sikandarī*, p. 22.

[97] Cf. Yahya Sirhindī, *Tārikh-i Mubārak Shāhī*, Calcutta, 1931, p. 234.

[98] *Bāburnāma*, Eng. tr. A. Beveridge, II, p. 518.

[99] *Maktūbāt-i Quddūsī*, Delhi, AH 1287. Letter to Babur, pp. 53–6.

[100] Cf. Z. A. Desai, 'Inscriptions of the Khanazads of Nagaur', *Epigraphia Indica, Arabic and Persian Supplement*, 1970, Calcutta, 1975, pp. 16–20.

rulers, Nagaur developed from a small town into an important centre of learning and commerce.[101] Its fame attracted people from distant parts who were patronised by the local rulers. The evidence in the contemporary literature shows that the Chishti ṣūfīs of Nagaur were also responsible for increasing social mobility. They admitted disciples (*murīds*) from different strata of the society and many of them were able to rise in social status because of their association with the *dargāh* of Shaikh Ḥamīduddīn Nāgaurī, a thirteenth-century Chishtī ṣūfī of great eminence.[102]

Mention should be made of Shaikh Ḥusain Nāgauri Chishtī, who flourished during the fifteenth century, and whose disciples included nobles, traders and even untouchables. One of his non-Muslim *murīd*s, a sweeper who had converted to Islam, performed religious exercises under his master's guidance and turned into a devout ṣūfī. Later on, many traditions developed about his spiritual powers.[103] Rich people brought him gifts and sought his blessings. He would undoubtedly otherwise have lived and died an untouchable. Indeed, the activities of genuine ṣūfīs often led to social mobility in the cities and towns; their *khānqāh*s served as seats of learning because lectures were delivered daily on the religious sciences followed by discussions relating to literary and spiritual matters. Often, unlettered people were seized with a passion for learning and serving mankind. Another advantage they offered was that the poor *murīd*s of an eminent ṣūfī could get help from the richer *murīd*s of the same *pīr*. Many disciples of Shaikh Husain Nāgaurī were members of the ruling élite in different regions. Ahmad Khān Lodī Sārang Khānī, governor of Jaunpur under Sikandar Lodī, was one of his *murīd*s,[104] as was Sultan Ghiyāṣuddīn Khaljī, who is said to have offered him great treasure on his visit to Mandu. The Shaikh spent some part of it on constructing buildings at Ajmer and Nagaur; the remainder was given away to the poor.[105]

[101] Cf. M.A. Chaghtai, 'Nagaur: A Forgotten Kingdom', *Bulletin of the Deccan College and Research Institute*, Poona, Vol. II, nos. 1–2, 1940, pp. 166–83.

[102] Anonymous, *Ṣudūr-us Ṣudūr*, MS Habib Ganj Collection, Maulana Azad Library, Aligarh, folios unmarked.

[103] Abdul Haque Muhadith, *Akhbār-ul Akhyār*, p. 209.

[104] *Wāqi'āt-i Mushtāqī*, f. 36b.

[105] 'Abdul Ḥaq Muḥaddiṣ Dahlavī, *Akhbār-ul Akhyār*, Delhi, p. 255; Shaikh Ruknu'ddīn, *Laṭā'if-i Quddūsī*, Delhi, AD 1311, pp. 57–8, for the low-caste *murīd*s of Shaikh 'Abdul Quddūs of Gangoh (d. 1535).

Like Shaikh Ḥusain Nāgaurī, other ṣūfī saints also admitted low-caste people into the circle of their *murīds*. Some of them belonged to the weavers' or dyers' communities and gained prestige as dervishes.[106]

The improvement of trade and commerce in the principality of Nagaur also deserves attention. Situated along the trade route linking Gujarat with Delhi and other centres in north India, Nagaur was frequently visited by merchant caravans. The details Mushtāqī gives about Miān Maḥmūd Farmalī's career show that Nagaur had become famous for its trade in war horses of good breed, weapons, and fine cloth.[107] This trade seems to have given a boost to indigenous crafts as well.

Epigraphical sources indicate that among the business communities of Nagaur, the Jains were prominent. They had close and friendly relations with members of the Muslim élite; and both communities appear to have co-operated with each other in social matters. Like the Muslim aristocrats, the Jains spent money on constructing schools where children were instructed in the traditional sciences. Once, when a school building was acquired by the government during the Sūr period (1552), the Jains approached Shaikh-ul Mashāikh Sulaimān to intercede with the Afghan governor for its restoration, which was done.[108] The land grant made by Sultan Sikandar Lodī (1488–1517) to a Jain saint, Jambūjī, earlier also tends to suggest that the Jain community had acquired much importance in western Rajasthan.[109]

We cannot here go into the details of social mobility in Gujarat. It may, however, be pointed out that rigorous social stratification was further weakened there after the establishment of the independent Sultanate. Those gifted with talent and determination appear to have escaped from their traditional caste occupations into ones bringing prestige and dignity. Fortunately, we are given interesting information about cases of this kind in the *Mirāt-i Sikandarī*. Describing the beginning of the construction of pleasure gardens

[106] *Wāqi'āt-i Mushtāqī*, ff. 76b–77a.

[107] Ibid., f. 68a.

[108] *Epigraphia Indica, Arabic and Persian Supplement*, 1955–56 as cited by W. H. Siddiqui, 'Religious Tolerance as Gleaned from Medieval Inscriptions', *Proceedings of the Seminar on Medieval Inscriptions*, Aligarh, 1970, p. 56.

[109] *Jambū Sāgar*, Shlok no. 29, pp. 319–20. For this reference, I am indebted to Munshi Sohan Lal who has cited the Jambu Sagar in his Urdu work, *Tārīkh-i Bīkāner*.

with fountains, artificial waterfalls, and channels of running water during the reign of Sultan Maḥmūd Begara, Sikandar bin Manjhū informs us that once an immigrant from Khurāsān said to the Sultan: 'I have got sufficient experience of designing the plans and supervising the construction of gardens and buildings.' He then built for the Sultan a beautiful garden with a cistern in its centre, fountains, artificial waterfalls, and channels of running water all around. During its construction the foreign architect allowed only illiterate workers to enter the enclosure so that his art could not be learnt by the Gujarati architects. One of the local workers, a carpenter named Bailū, however, observed every technique employed in constructing the garden and then applied for royal permission to build another garden like the one designed by the Khurasani. Being permitted to do so, Bailū succeeded in constructing a yet more magnificent garden. Highly impressed by Bailū's intelligence and achievement, the Sultan showered favours upon him, presented him with the *khil'at-i khāṣ* (special robe of honour) and raised him to the status of a grandee.[110]

Like skilled artists and craftsmen, capable slaves are also reported to have been appointed to important positions at the royal court. The career of Malik Sha'bān, the *wazīr* of Sultan Maḥmūd Begara, is a case in point. He was purchased as a boy by Sultan Muḥammad Shāh II (son of Sultan Aḥmad Shāh), and was trained for state service along with other slave boys, after which he made rapid progress in the official hierarchy. Ultimately he rose to be *wazīr* during the reign of Sultan Maḥmūd Begara.[111] In most cases, the slaves, being local people, would help their relations and caste people in obtaining state favours and gaining social advancement.

There were also those, belonging to low caste families, who entered the royal army as soldiers or petty officials and rose in the official hierarchy by dint of merit and hard work. Such officers offer an important illustration of social mobility.

We should note, in passing, that references to Muslim *birādarīs* in our sources suggest that by the fifteenth century, the Indo-Muslim community had been divided into numerous *birādarīs* (brotherhoods), a term of sociological significance. If anywhere it is in the formation of a *birādarī* that the influence of the Hindu caste

[110] *Mirāt-i Sikandarī*, pp. 109–10. [111] Ibid., p. 132.

system seems to have been quite strong. The Afghans in India were also divided into *birādarīs*.[112] A case can be made out that the *birādarīs*, like artisan guilds, came in the way of an artisan wishing to take up a profession other than his hereditary one, as Babur would have us believe.[113] Yet there is no dearth of evidence to show that people changed their professions if they knew that the change would benefit them. People in the urban centres seem to have enjoyed considerable freedom in this matter. In fact, education, talent, trade, and also the institution of slavery in certain cases, contributed to raise the social status of the low born. During the Sūr period, members of the weaver and Banya communities attained high rank in the nobility. As in the past, Sher Shāh's slaves and their sons also occupied key positions in the Empire.[114]

As regards men of low caste, the examples of Iqbāl Khān, a Muslim weaver, and Hemū *Bagal*, who belonged to the Dhūsar caste (a sub-caste of the Banyas) in Rewari, may be cited. Iqbāl Khān (formerly Karamullah) started his career under Sher Shāh as a soldier and ultimately rose to the command of 5,000 *sawārs* (horsemen) under Islām Shāh (1545–53). The latter is said to have honoured him with a high position at his court.[115] Likewise, Hemū started his career as a market inspector during Sher Shāh's reign, but rose to the rank of the premier noble under Sultan 'Ādil Shāh Sur (1553–57).[116]

During the period of his ascendancy, members of Hemū's caste rose in society: Rizqullāh Mushtāqī, a contemporary of Hemū, states that he destroyed the *chaudhrīs* and *muqaddams* in the territory of Rewari (probably for their recalcitrance) and replaced

[112] *Wāqi'āt-i Mushtāqī*, f. 12b, where the term *birādarī* occurs for the first time; also Shaikh 'Abdul Ḥaq Muḥaddis Dehlevi, *Zadul Muttaqīn wa Salūk-i Ṭarīqal-yaqīn*, MS personal collection of author, ff. 149b, 150a, for the division of Muslims into *birādarīs* in Gujarat.

[113] *Bāburnāma*, Eng. tr. Beveridge, Vol. II, p. 518.

[114] *Masnad-i 'ālī* Khawwāṣ Khān, the premier noble under Sher Shah, was the son of Malik Sukha, a slave of Sher Shāh. Ḥājī Khān was also Sher Shah's slave and continued to serve as the governor of Bayana, Mewat and Eastern Rajputana till the fall of the Sur Empire in 1555. Cf. Iqtidar Husain Siddiqui, *History of Sher Shah Sur*, Aligarh, 1971, pp. 66, 68, 149 (footnote 3).

[115] *Wāqi'āt-i Mushtāqī*, f. 72b; Abdul Qadir Badaoni, *Muntakhab-ut Tawārīkh*, Calcutta, 1868, I, 411.

[116] *History of Sher Shah Sur*, pp. 149–58.

them with Banyas (*baqqāls*).[117] Mushtāqī's testimony suggests that the Dhusar *zamīndārs* mentioned by Abu'l Fazl in the *sarkār* of Rewari during Akbar's reign were the creation of Hemū.[118] Hemū's relations, such as Taharpāl, Rājya and Bhagwān Das were also entrusted with important positions in the army and administration of the Empire.[119]

The revival of trade and commerce in the Sultanate of Delhi during the Afghan period seems to have contributed towards greater social mobility. Trade attracted enterprising people from the higher as well as lower strata: some members of aristocratic families preferred trade to state service, whereas petty officials enriched themselves by engaging in commerce. Two examples may be cited: the brothers of Malik Adhū Kansī (the latter being an important noble of Sultan Sikandar Lodī), who belonged to the town of Shikārpur in Panjab, travelled to Iran and Central Asia with a merchant caravan taking Indian products abroad and returned loaded with foreign merchandise.[120] Unlike the brothers of Malik Adhu Kansī, Miān Walīd, a non-Afghan army man in the contingent of Khān A'ẓam Lād Khān Lodī Sārang Khānī, the Muqta' (governor) of Jaunpur under Sultan Ibrāhīm Lodī, amassed wealth by dealing in perfumes and glassware. Himself a master craftsman, he trained his servants and slaves in manufacturing glassware and extracting perfumes of fine quality. He also purchased quality goods, stored them and then supplied them to the market when they fetched high prices. With this additional income, he was able to live like an aristocrat, holding banquets for friends and giving money to his relations.[121]

Finally, it may be stressed that demographic mobility in India during medieval times was closely linked with the process of urbanization. The expansion of old towns and construction of new

[117] In medieval times the Dhusar caste (grocers) was considered to be the lowest Banya caste, because most of its members dealt in foodgrains and other commodities on a small scale. *Baqqāl* is a word normally used in Indian Persian for Banya. See Abu'l Faẓl, *Akbarnāma*, Calcutta, 1886, I, p. 337, Eng. tr. Mrs. Beveridge, Calcutta, 1939, pp. 616–17; also I. H. Siddiqui, *History of Sher Shah Sur*, pp. 149–50.

[118] *Wāqi'āt-i Mushtāqī*, f. 74a; also Iqtidar Husain Siddiqui, *History of Sher Shah Sur*, p. 157.

[119] There are references to the Dhusar *zamīndārs* in the Persian text of the *Ā'īn-i Akbarī* but Jarrett has translated *zamīndārs* as castes which is incorrect.

[120] *Wāqi'āt-i Mushtāqī*, f. 105a.

[121] Ibid., ff. 98a–b.

metropolitan centres first in the Delhi Sultanate and then in the newly-founded regional kingdoms in the fifteenth century, led artisans, artists, craftsmen and merchants to move there in the hope of better prospects. In his account of the foundation of Ahmadabad in 1410, the author of the *Tārīkh-i Salāṭīn-i Gujarāt* mentions the arrival of masons, craftsmen and *baqqāl*s (Banyas) in large numbers, who took permanent abode in the new capital. The bazars and quarters of Ahmadabad are reported to have hummed with commercial activity, on account of the many foreign traders attracted to the mart. [122]

In 1506, when Sultan Sikandar Lodī made Agra the capital of his empire, the royal *kārkhāna*s attracted skilled workers from different parts of India. There are references to ironsmiths from Rāprī[123] and stone-cutters from Nagaur[124] who are said to have settled down in Agra and other places in the Lodi empire. The *sarrāf*s (bankers and money-changers), artisans such as skilled darners and cloth-merchants, were attracted by trade and settled in the new capital.[125]

To conclude, it may be stated that the institutions (both political and social) of the Sultanate, the process of urbanization, and the enlightened policies followed by certain Sultans were important factors making for social change in the Sultanate. In addition, the royal *kārkhāna*s, *madrasa*s, the *khānqāh*s of ṣūfī saints, and the institution of royal slave-households helped the emergence of important new social groups in the urban centres during pre-Mughal times.

[122] Maḥmūd Bukhārī, *Tārīkh-i Salāṭīn-i Gujarāt*, ed. A. A. Tirmizi, *Medieval India Quarterly*, Aligarh, Vol. 5, 1963.

[123] *Wāqi'āt-i Mushtāqī*, f. 69b.

[124] *Epigraphia Indica, Arabic and Persian Supplement*, Calcutta, 1953–54, pp. 3–4.

[125] *Wāqi'āt-i Mushtāqī*, ff. 15a, 18b, 25b, 33b, 57a, 69b, etc.

3

Irrigating Haryana: The Pre-Modern History of the Western Yamuna Canal

ABHA SINGH

It is well recognized that the Western Yamuna canal was originally cut by Fīrūz Shāh (1351–88), but the detailed history of the canal has not yet been reconstructed by assembling all the available material; nor have changes in its course and alignment down the centuries been established by collating the statements of earlier historians and documents with modern surveys and maps. I shall attempt to fill this lacuna here.

Essentially, Fīrūz Shāh's canal was designed to force water from the Yamuna (Jamuna) into the Chitang river. The Chitang, once a tributary of the Ghaggar and so ultimately of the dead river Hakra, is mentioned as the 'river of Hānsī' in the *Chachnāma* (written in Arabic in the eighth century and now surviving in an early thirteenth-century Persian translation).[1] Apparently before Fīrūz Shāh the Chitang was largely a seasonal river flowing down to Hansi.

Fīrūz Shāh's Canal

In his *Tā'rīkh-i Fīrūz-Shāhī*, Shams Sirāj 'Afīf gives us a detailed account of the canals built by Fīrūz Shāh.[2] According to him, Fīrūz Shāh had dug two canals to bring a continuous supply of water to his newly-built town of Hissar Firuza. One canal was brought from the Yamuna, and the other from the Sutlej. From the Yamuna were

[1] *Chachnāma*, ed. Daudpota, Hyderabad (Dn), 1939, p. 51.

[2] Shams Sirāj 'Afīf, *Tā'rīkh-i Fīrūz-Shāhī*, ed. Wilayat Husain, Calcutta, 1891, pp. 127–9.

taken out two canals, the Rajabwah and the Ulughkhānī.[3] The two are said to have had their head-waters near Karnal, whence, running for about eighty or ninety *kurohs*, they reached the town of Hissar. Both canals received other rivers and flowed past Safedon, Dhatrat, Jind and Hansi.

The *Tarikh-i Mubārakshāhī* of Yaḥyā Sirhindī also has some important statements to make about the canal.[4] It says that in AH 750/AD 1355 Sultan Fīrūz had made a canal which he called the canal of Firuzabad. This ran from the vicinity of the Sirmur and Mandauti Hills,[5] receiving waters from seven other different rivers, and, reaching Hansi, passed on to Arasan, where Fīrūz Shāh had founded the fort of Hissar Firuza. Here the canal helped to fill a reservoir. After referring to another canal dug from the Ghaggar river, the same work goes on to describe yet another canal drawn from the Budhi Yamuna (an old channel of the Yamuna), which too ran into the reservoir of the fort of Hissar Firuza, from which it continued for some distance. Yaḥyā's two canals running to Hissar Firuza apparently correspond to the Rajabwah and Ulughkhānī of 'Afif.

Subsequent writers do not add materially to this information. But Akbar's *sanad* of AH 978/AD 1570–1 states that Fīrūz Shāh had used for his canal the Chitang, which brought water from the *nalas* and drains in the vicinity of Sadhaura, at the foot of the hills to Hansi and Hissar.[6] The importance of Akbar's *sanad* lies in the fact that it clearly states the connection of Fīrūz Shāh's canal with the Chitang though, perhaps by oversight, there is no reference to the Yamuna as providing water to the canal. Abū'l Faẓl in the *Ā'īn*

[3] The 'Rajabwah' was named after Fīrūz's father Rajab; *wah* means canal. 'Ulughkhānī', possibly 'Ulughkhān-nī (*nī* meaning channel, river) was similarly named after his cousin and predecessor, Muḥammad Tughluq, whose pre-royal title was Ulugh Khan.

[4] Yaḥyā bin Aḥmad Sirhindī, *Tārīkh-i Mubārakshāhī*, ed. Hidayat Husain, Calcutta, 1931, pp. 125–6.

[5] The Mandauti Hills cannot be identified. Perhaps they were situated near the Sirmur Hills.

[6] Lieut. Yule, 'A Canal Act of the Emperor Akbar with some notes and remarks on the History of the Western Jumna Canal', *Journal of the Asiatic Society of Bengal (JASB)*, Calcutta, Vol. XV (1846), pp. 213–23. A translation of the *sanad* is given but not the text, which seems to have remained unpublished. The original copy of the *sanad* was obtained by S. A. Abbot, in charge of Kaithal, from Abdul Samad and Abdul Mustakim, Pirzadas, at Dhatrat. The copy ran on four leaves (pages) having been abstracted from a book of 'considerable antiquity'.

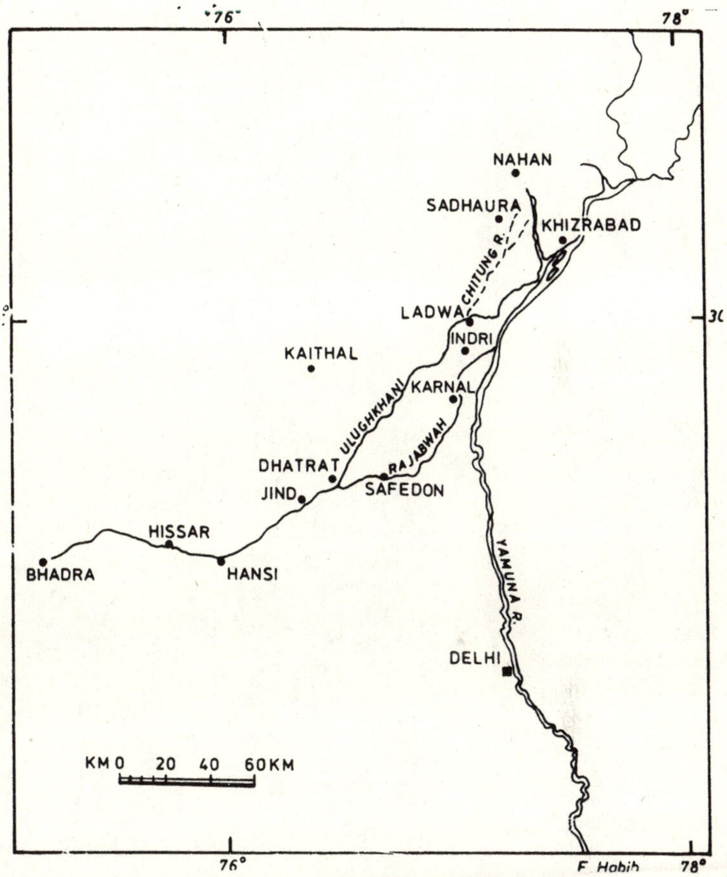

1 Fīrūz Shāh's canal

supplies this omission, saying that Fīrūz Shāh's canal was cut from the Yamuna and that it ultimately terminated in a reservoir at Bhadra,[7] thus confirming the *Tārīkh-i Mubārakshāhī* which too says it ran for a stretch beyond Hissar.

The historians of Shāhjahān's reign, Wāriṣ and Ṣāliḥ, further tell us that the canal's headwaters lay in the *pargana* of Khizrabad, and, flowing for about 30 *kuroh*s by the Mughal imperial measure (equal to about seventy-five miles) ran past Safedon, the royal hunting ground of Sultan Fīrūz.[8]

By assembling information from all these sources the course of Fīrūz Shāh's canal can be traced fairly precisely. It had two major feeder-canals. The first had its head in the Yamuna near Khizrabad, very near the point where the Yamuna debouches from the hills (the Sirmur Hills of the *Tārīkh-i Mubārakshāhī*) into the plains. In other words, it ran in the channel which is *now* known as the Budhi Yamuna ('Boodhee Jamuna' in the *Indian Atlas* (*IA*) Sheet 48), and so must have collected streams that fall into that channel. The headwaters of the second feeder lay in the 'Buddhī Jamuna' of the *Tārīkh-i Mubārakshāhī*, which could not have been the upper part of the channel now known as Buddhi Yamuna, but a lower one, such as the old channel of the Yamuna which leaves the river at about the same latitude as Indri and rejoins the river in the latitude of Karnal (*IA* Sheet 48). It approaches at one point quite close to Shāhjahān's West Yamuna Canal. It may be recalled that 'Afīf places the source of Fīrūz Shāh's canal near Karnal and this again suits the lower headwaters for the second feeder canal.

If these were the two headwaters, then the probability is that the lower one fed the 'Rajabwah', since the *IA* Sheet 48 shows 'Rajabuka canal' running from Karnal towards Safedon. In that case the upper headwaters should be those of 'Afīf's Ulughkhānī, which should then also be Yahyā's Fīrūzābād Canal. From the channels shown in *IA* Sheet 48 one can conjecture that the Ulughkhānī ran into the Chitang near Ladwah. The lower feeder canal then must have joined the northern feeder running in the Chitang near Dhatrat, precisely where the 'Hansi Canal' on *IA* Sheet 48 meets the Chitang.

[7] Abū-l Fazl, *Ā'īn-i Akbarī*, Bibliotheca Indica, ed. Blochmann, Calcutta, 1872, I, pp. 514–15.

[8] Muḥammad Wāriṣ, *Bādshāhnāma*, transcript, Department of History, Aligarh, p. 39; Muḥammad Ṣāliḥ, *'Amal-i Ṣāliḥ*, Calcutta, 1939, III, p. 29.

The two canals brought enough water to Hansi to impress contemporaries. Baranī says that the canals were so deep that one needed to be ferried over by boat. People also used to journey by boat on the canals.[9] 'Afīf mentions that during the rains the canals used to be in flood.[10]

Fīrūz Shāh's canal was excavated chiefly for irrigation purposes. The water reaching the desert tracts is said to have helped greatly in extending cultivation;[11] whereas earlier only the harvesting of the kharif crop was possible, now both the kharif and the rabi were harvested.[12] People even started harvesting high-grade crops such as wheat and sugarcane.[13] The canal raised the ground water level as well: 'Afīf writes that it could now be found at a depth of four *gaz* from ground level.[14]

Akbar's Canal, the Shekhū-Nī

By the sixteenth century Fīrūz Shāh's canal seems to have silted up. Akbar's *sanad* already quoted states that while previously the canal used to carry water for at least four or five months in the year, now it had become 'so choked that for the last hundred years the waters have not flowed past the boundary of Kythal and thence to Hissar.' Clearly, the reference is to the upper canal of Fīrūz Shāh, the Ulughkhānī, which, as we have suggested, ran into the Chitang near Ladwah. As a memorandum of 1635 shows, the Chitang actually ran through *pargana* Kaithal, and entered the *chakla* of Hissar after passing through the boundary of Kaithal.

The first repairs on the canal in Akbar's time seem to have been carried out by Shihābuddīn Khān, who was Governor of Delhi about the year 1560.[15] Since the canal is said to have run from the

[9] Ziya Baranī, *Tārīkh-i Fīrūz Shāhī*, Calcutta, 1862, p. 567.

[10] 'Afīf, p. 130.

[11] Major Colvin raises doubts as to whether Fīrūz Shāh's canal actually served the purpose of irrigation on any large scale since there are no traces of subsidiary irrigation channels along its banks ('On the Restoration of the Ancient Canals in the Delhi Territory, *JASB*, II, no. 15 (March 1833), p. 109). Water could, however, have been lifted from the canal or its main branches through water-wheels.

[12] 'Afīf, p. 128.

[13] Baranī, pp. 567–70; 'Afīf, p. 128.

[14] 'Afīf, p. 128.

[15] Abū-l Fazl, *Akbarnāma*, Calcutta, 1879, II, p. 94; 'Abdu-l Qādir Badā'ūnī, *Muntakhab-ut Tawārīkh*, Calcutta, 1864–9, II, p. 36.

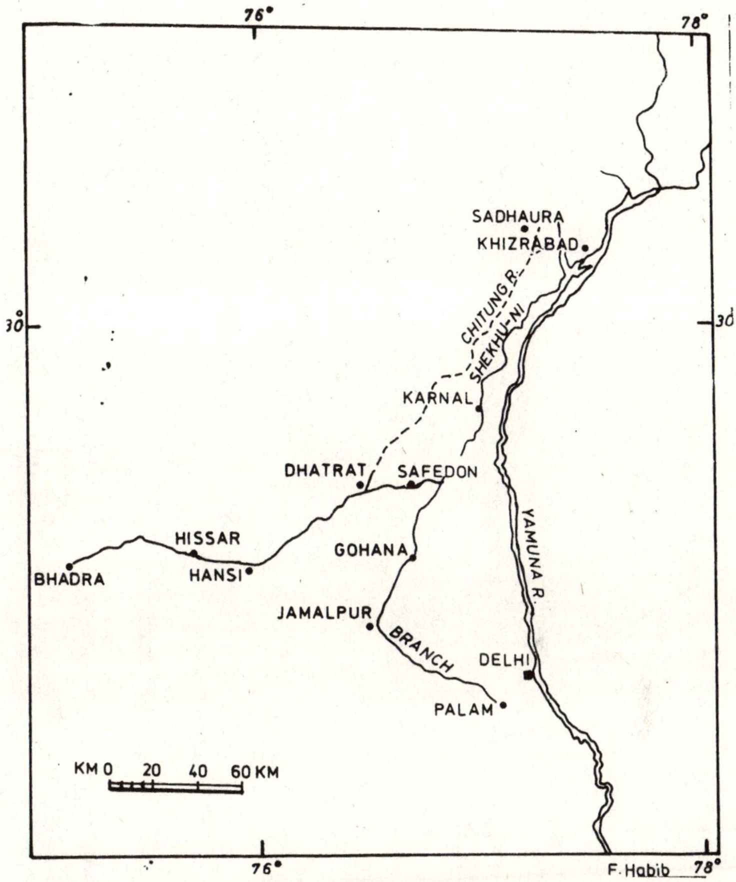

2 Akbar's canal, the Shekhū-nī

Yamuna to Safedon, it must have been the Rajabwah, and not the Ulughkhānī, that was re-excavated. The renovated canal was named by him 'Shihābnahr', after himself.[16]

Later on Akbar himself ordered the renewal of the canal in the year AH 978/AD 1570–1. A *farmān* (*sanad*) of Akbar dated AH 978/AD 1570–1 and issued from Firuzpur, is concerned with the opening of the canal, which was to be called 'Shaikhū-nī' ('Shaikhnai' in translation).[17] The name, also used by Badā'ūnī,[18] was given after Jahāngīr, whom Akbar always called Shaikhū Bābā, and who was born in 1569.[19] The *sanad* does not refer to the 'Shihābnahr', which can only be explained by assuming that the present order had in mind the Ulughkhānī rather than the Rajabwah. The *sanad* confirms this by referring to the fact that Fīrūz Shāh's canal had ceased to flow beyond 'the limits of Kaithal'. Akbar ordered the renewal of the canal right from the foot-hills near Khizrabad. The water was collected in the river Sonb from different streams and *nala*s which used to flow into the Yamuna, thus suggesting that the source of the canal was close to that of the Ulughkhānī. But the canal ran into the bed of the Rajabwah, instead of joining the Chitang directly. This is shown by Abū-l Fazl's reference to the 'Shekhū-nī' passing by Karnal.[20] Bada'ūnī also tells us that the canal ran past Karnal to Safedon.[21] Moreover, the *sanad* says that the canal flowed into the Chitang at a distance of about a hundred *kuroh*s from Khizrabad, indicating that the junction was the one near Dhatrat, where Fīrūz Shah's Rajabwah used to join the Chitang (*IA* Sheet 48), rather than the one of the Ulughkhānī with the Chitang near Ladwah. Akbar's *sanad* contains no reference to the canal's head being in the Yamuna. Apparently the canal simply took water from the streams falling into the Yamuna from the west. But the Shihāb Nahr (restored Rajabwah) which it joined above Karnal might still have been carrying water from the Yamuna. This may be the reason for Badā'ūnī's statement that the Shaikhū-nī was excavated from the Yamuna.

Akbar ordered that the canal be deepened and widened so that it might supply water all through the year upto Hansi and Hissar.

[16] Wāriṣ, p. 39; *'Amal-i Ṣāliḥ*, III, p. 29.

[17] *Sanad* of Akbar, trans. Yule, *JASB*, XV, 1864, p. 215.

[18] Badā'ūnī, III, p. 198.

[19] Jahāngīr, *Tuzuk-i Jahāngīrī*, ed. Sayid Ahmad, Aligarh, 1864, p. 1.

[20] *Ā'īn*, I, p. 520.

[21] Badā'ūnī, III, p. 198.

Wherever necessary bunds were to be built, and the *shiqdārs*, *chaudhrīs*, *muqaddams* and the *ra'iyat* (peasants) of all the *parganas* were required to give the necessary assistance, including labour. Arrangements were to be made to distribute water from the canal 'at the season of cultivation'. Bridges were to be built along with bunds. Nūruddīn Muḥammad Tarkhān, described by Bada'ūnī as the builder of the canal, is designated the *Mīr-i Āb* (Canal Superintendent) in the *sanad*. It was also ordered that the canal was to be made navigable by having a large channel, so that boats could ply on it.

As for the use of water for irrigation purposes, Akbar directed that people in each *pargana* should be made 'satisfied with the number of cuts' equally distributed among different *parganas*, and no one should take more than his due share.

Badā'ūnī confirms the statements in the *sanad* and tells us that the canal was dug by Mullā Nūruddīn Muḥammad Tarkhān, who held the *pargana* of Safedon in *jāgīr*. He named it 'Shekhū-nī' after Prince Salīm. The canal was excavated from the Yamuna, fifty *kurohs* (about 125 miles) in length, and ran past Karnal and beyond that town.[22] Badā'ūnī adds that it resulted in a considerable extension of cultivation and a great increase in the prosperity of people.[23]

Akbar's *sanad* regarding the construction of the Shaikhū-nī is dated Shawwāl AH 978; but it refers to an earlier *farman* issued in AH 977 ordering the construction of the canal. The *sanad* also contains verses apparently added to copies of the *sanad*; these contain a chronogram which yields AH 978 (AD 1570–1).[24] Badā'ūnī gives another chronogram 'Shaikhū-nī' yielding AH 977/AD 1569–70, which conforms to the year of Akbar's *farman* ordering its construction.[25] We may then say that the excavation of the canal began in AD 1569–70 and that it was completed the next year.

The Shaikhū-nī might well have been a perennial canal, to judge from the two masonry bridges over it, one at Karnal, the other at Safedon.[26] The Karnal bridge was mentioned by Monserrate in

[22] Ibid. [23] Ibid.

[24] *Sanad* of Akbar, tr. Yule, p. 216. The chronogram reads *Ābād Shaikhnī* (= AH 978/AD 1570–1)

[25] Badā'ūnī, III, p. 198.

[26] Sanderson, *A Guide to the Buildings and Gardens* [*of the Fort at Delhi*], Calcutta, 1929, p. 40 *n*.

Akbar's time,[27] and the Safedon bridge must also belong to that period, since Shāhjahān's Nahr-i Bihisht did not run past Safedon.

It seems that a branch of the Shaikhū-nī was taken beyond Safedon down to Palam to the west of the Delhi ridge. Lāhorī in his *Badshāhnāma* mentions a visit by Shāhjahān in his 11th Regnal Year to a garden irrigated from a dam built by Aṣālat Khān near Palam on 'the Karnal stream', which can, of course, only mean a branch of the Shaikhū-nī, which used to run by Karnal.[28] On *IA* Sheet 49, a channel can indeed be traced running towards Palam from the 'Rajbuka' ('Rajabwah') channel, which, as we have seen above, the Shaikhū-nī had utilized.

A Project for the Chitang, 1635

We are fortunate in possessing an anonymous memorandum on the Chitang which, though undated, belongs to the reign of Shāhjahān, since it uses the characteristic designation of that emperor—Ā'lā Ḥaẓarat.[29] The document can be more precisely dated, since it states that the *faujdārī* of *chakla* Sihrind (Sirhind) had been placed under the jurisdiction of Sayyid Bāqir Khān. The only 'Bāqir Khān' in the lists of *manṣab*-holders in Lāhorī and the *'Amāl-i Ṣāliḥ* is Bāqir Khān Najm-i Ṣānī, usually simply called Bāqir Khān. This noble served in Orissa early in Shāhjahān's reign, but was briefly appointed Governor of Delhi in the 8th Regnal Year (AD 1635), [30] being replaced by Aṣālat Khān during the same year.[31] Since *chakla* Sirhind belonged to *ṣūba* Delhi, it must have been during his brief viceroyalty of Delhi that the *faujdārī* of *chalka* Sirhind was given to him. He died in the 10th Regnal Year while holding charge of the *ṣūba* of Allahabad.[32] The word *chakla* in connexion with Sirhind

[27] F. Monserrate, *The Commentary of Father Monserrate, S.J. on his journey to the court of Akbar*, tr. J.S. Hoyland and annotated S.N. Banerjee, Cuttack, 1922, p. 98.

[28] Lāhorī, *Bādshāhnāma*, Bib. Ind., Calcutta, 1867, II, p. 112. Aṣālat Khān was appointed governor of Delhi in the 8th R.Y. of Shāhjahān's reign and retained his office till the 12th R.Y. (Lāhorī, I (ii), pp. 87, 280.)

[29] Included in the volume of letters of Bālkrishan Brahman and other papers, British Mus. Add. 16,859, ff. 107a–9b.

[30] Lāhorī, I (ii), pp. 72, 76. The 8th R.Y. happens to correspond almost wholly with the Christian year 1635.

[31] Ibid., p. 87. See M. Athar Ali, *Apparatus of Empire*, Delhi, 1985, p. 128 (entries S 1040–1).

[32] Lāhorī, I (ii), p. 274.

occurs as early as the 5th Regnal Year,[33] so that its use in our document does not itself suggest a much later date as was presumed by Irfan Habib.[34]

The year 1635 is important, because this would explain why there is no reference to Shāhjahān's construction of the West Yamuna canal in its detailed account of the water supply in the Chitang.

The memorandum begins by referring to the complaint of peasants of *chakla* Hissar, 'who are greatly distressed from the intensity of drought and lack of water and help from seasons.' They had petitioned that the channel (*nahr*) of the Chitang be opened. Accordingly, the Emperor had ordered the anonymous writer of the memorandum to proceed with a skilled *mai'mār* (architect, mason) and give a report on the expenditure and time required for bringing water into the channel, and the number of *pargana*s which would benefit from the projected work.

The writer accordingly reported that the Chitang originated in the mountains of Sadhaura, eighty *kuroh*s (over 200 miles) from Hissar. The Chitang, he said, runs through the *pargana*s of Sadhaura, Buria, Mustafabad, Indri, Karnal, Thanesar, Pundri, Fatehpur and Kaithal, all belonging to the *chakla* of Sirhind. Leaving the 'boundary of Kaithal',[35] it ran through the *pargana*s of Khanda, Dhatrat, Jind, and Hansi, before reaching Hissar. These latter *mahal*s belonged to the *chakla* of Hissar. This is precisely the course of the Chitang as shown in modern survey maps.

The Memorandum said that the peasants of the *maḥal*s of *chakla* Hissar had given an undertaking to let 'the water pass through their limits till it reaches Hissar.' But for *chakla* Sirhind, Sayyid Bāqir K͟hān, who held its *faujdārī* jurisdiction, had to be approached. For this purpose, it was recommended that a *Mīr-i Āb* (Canal Superintendent) and a *mai'mār* from the Imperial establishment be appointed and a *farman* issued to the *faujdār* of *chakla* Sirhind to furnish the *Mīr-i Āb* with the necessary information. He should also oblige the *zamindar*s and peasants of *chakla* Sirhind to give the necessary undertakings: they should join in the work, let the water

[33] Ibid., I (i), p. 409. The '*chakla*' of Hissar is also mentioned under Regnal Year 5 in Lāhorī, Vol. I (i), p. 432.

[34] *Agrarian System of Mughal India*, Bombay, 1963, p. 33 *n*.

[35] One is reminded here of Akbar's *sanad* which said that the channel ran dry before it reached the 'boundary of Kaithal'.

flow from its source, build strong dykes (*bands*) at two or three places, which could be raised by the *Mīr-i Āb* with the help of the *mai'mār* and the *zamīndār*s.

The writer recommended that funds be sanctioned for the works from the Imperial Treasury, and the amount recovered from the people of the two *chakla*s in instalments, presumably through special cesses.

The writer of the Memorandum had not himself surveyed the existing channel but reported that it was said that in earlier times it had carried water in a stream that was '4 *dir'a*s (yards) broad and one *dir'a* deep, as can be seen from the traces of its channel in this tract.' If the connexion with the mountain springs was restored, it would again be a perennial flow, but if it was fed by rain it would only carry water during the rainy season. Either way it would give much benefit. Obviously, the writer had no knowledge of any link with the Yamuna achieved through earlier canals.

The Memorandum is particularly important in that it visualizes irrigation through distributaries from the revived channel:

> Whenever the water begins to flow in this tract, most of the *zamindar*s and peasants will betake themselves, cut branches and lay out sub-channels (*kārīz-hā*) to carry the water to their fields and villages.

The Memorandum is also of some interest in showing that at this time Hissar received no water from the Shaiku-nī. It is possible that already the branch running to Palam, which we have encountered in the 11th Regnal Year of Shāhjahān, had diverted the waters of that canal in a contrary direction.

It is not known whether any action was taken on the Memorandum. It is not very likely that it was, since even clearing the channel of the Chitang would not by itself have brought much water to Hissar. It would merely have deprived the upper areas of irrigation water in the interest of the lower areas.

In any case, in Shāhjahān's West Yamuna Canal, the terminal point was firmly shifted from Hissar to Delhi, and so no water could now be taken to Hissar by any canal.

Shāhjahān's Nahr-i Bihisht

Shāhjahān decided to use the alignment of the Shaikhū-nī for a large section of his great canal, the *Nahr-i Bihisht*, also called *Nahr-i Faiz* and *Shāh-nahr.*[36] The construction of this canal was wrongly ascribed to 'Alī Mardān Khān in later accounts.[37] The official chronicler Wāriṣ, as well as Muḥammad Ṣāliḥ, mentions that it was excavated under the supervision of Ghairat Khān.[38]

Construction was started on 20 September 1638.[39] Ghairat Khān worked for about four months, after which he was transferred as Governor of Thatta. The task was now entrusted to Ilāhwardī Khān, then Governor of Delhi, who supervised the work for over two years, it being finally completed by Mukarmat Khān in 1647–8.[40] This refers to the main canal. Channels and aqueducts distributing its water in the fort of Shāhjahānābād (Delhi) are said to have been completed four years later, in 1650, at the cost of two lakhs of rupees.[41]

According to Wāriṣ and Ṣāliḥ, the canal took off from the Yamuna near Khizrabad. It used the old canal channel down to Safedon (stated to be about thirty *kurohs*, or seventy-five miles). From here a new channel (also thirty *kurohs* in length) was excavated to bring the canal to the new city of Delhi or Shāhjahānābād.[42]

[36] See Wāriṣ, p. 39, and *'Amal-i Ṣāliḥ*, III, p. 29. Also see Shaikh Muḥammad Baqā 'Baqā', *Mir'āt-al 'Alam*, Aligarh MS, 'Abdus Salām Collection 314/84, f. 253a; Sujān Rāi Bhandārī, *Khulāṣat-ut Tawārīkh*, Delhi, 1918, p. 36; Rā'i Chaturman Saksena, *Chahār-Gulshan*, Aligarh MS, 'Abdus Salām Collection 292/62 f. 47a; *Ḥālāt-i Manāzilaz-Shāhjahānābād tā-Kābul*, Aligarh MS Univ. Collection, *Fārsīa Akhbār*, 237, f. 2a.

[37] *Chahār-Gulshan*, f. 47a; *Ḥālāt-i Manāzilaz-Shāhjahānābād tā-Kābul*, f. 2a; Colvin, 'Ancient Canals', p. 107; W. Francklin, *History of the Reign of Shah Aulum*, London, 1798, p. 208.

[38] Wāriṣ, p. 39; *'Amal-i Ṣāliḥ*, III, p. 29.

[39] Ibid., Ṣāliḥ gives the date of excavation as 15 Jumādī al-Awwal AH 1049/AD 13 September 1639.

[40] Wāriṣ, pp. 39–40; *'Amal-i Ṣāliḥ*, III, 29. Ṣāliḥ says that the construction was completed by Ghairat Khān during his tenure as Governor.

[41] *'Amal-i Ṣāliḥ*, III, 116.

[42] Wāriṣ, p. 39; *'Amal-i Ṣāliḥ*, III, p. 29. The distances given by the chroniclers may be compared with map distances (as the crow flies):

	Wāriṣ	From modern maps (approximate)
Khizrabad to Safedon	30 *kurohs* (75 miles)	70 miles
Safedon to Delhi	30 *kurohs* (75) miles)	65 miles

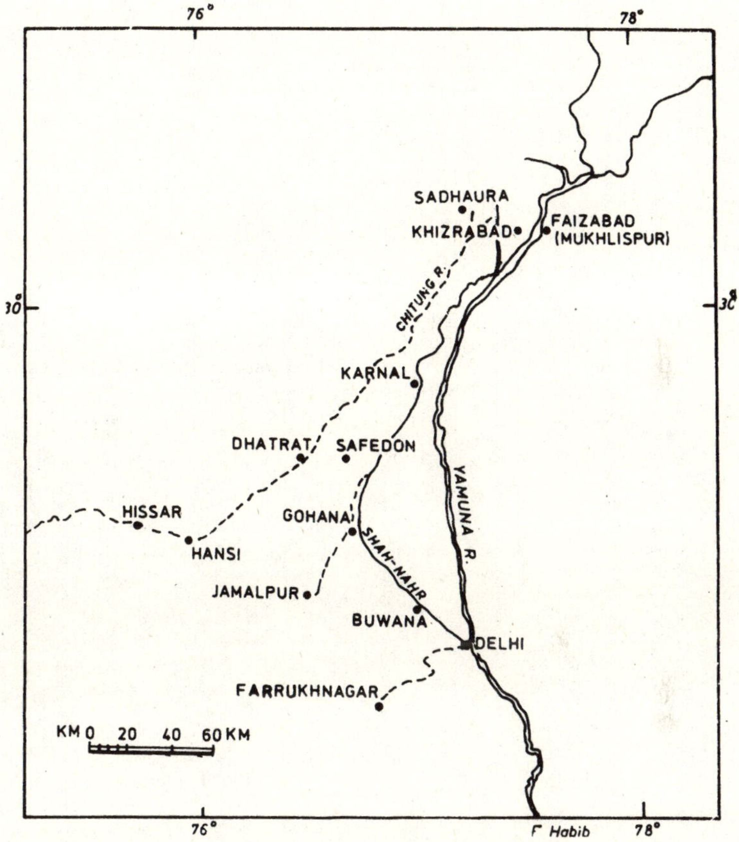

3 Shāhjahān's *Nahr-i Bihisht*

Later writers give the position of the canal headwaters more precisely as Mukhlispur on the Yamuna,[43] a spot much favoured by Shāhjahān,[44] and it is not surprising that the cut was made there. It is thus described by Sanderson: 'The river supply coming down the right bank of the Jumna was bunded up annually at Fatehgarh near Dadupur, about 14 miles below Tajawala.'[45] Thus the supply into the canal had to be maintained by annual works. The present West Yamuna canal has its headwaters at Tajewala.[46]

From its headwaters the canal ran by Karnal, as did the Shaikhūnī. This precise information comes from the route map in the *Chahār-Gulshan*.[47] From here, as Wāriṣ and Ṣāliḥ say, it ran towards Safedon.

The course of the new channel excavated by Shāhjahān from near Safedon is described by Colvin in his report of 1833.[48] The point where the canal took a southerly direction (as against south-westerly) was Madloda, some miles before Safedon. It ran south to Korana, originally with the idea of connecting it with drainage from the Farkhnagar Jhil, fifteen miles south-west of Delhi. But instead of turning, the canal waters ran on to Gohana and farther as far as Jamalpur because of a natural decline.[49] A catastrophe is said to have taken place on the first trials of the works, for the water accumulated in the deep hollow at Gohana, and resulted in the inundation of Lalpur town. Its ruins are said to exist still in a low hollow in the present Rohtak district.

The accident forced a new course to be designed for the canal. It now passed close to the natural ridge of the country, where the land falls off on each side. From Jatola the circumventing channel joined the course as first laid out.

Colvin thinks that an insurmountable difficulty would have been faced by the canal builders while making 'another detour near

[43] Sujān Rāi, pp. 29, 36–9; *Chahār Gulshan*, f. 47a; *Ḥālāt-i Manāzilaz-Shāhjahānābād tā-Kābul*, f. 2a. Sujān Rāi writes that the cut was made at the base of the hills of Sirmur, while the *Ḥālāt-i Manāzilaz-Shāhjahānābād tā-Kābul* puts it below the foothills of Nahan. The location is the same.

[44] *'Amal-i Ṣāliḥ*, III, pp. 240–1.

[45] Sanderson, p. 40 *n*.

[46] Ibid.; also see *Punjab District Gazetteers, Ambala District*, 1892–3, p. 11.

[47] *Chahār Gulshan*, f. 143a; *Ḥālāt-i Manāzilaz-Shāhjahānābād tā-Kābul*, f. 3a. It also refers to the masonry bridge near Karnal over the canal.

[48] Colvin, 'Ancient Canals', pp. 109–10.

[49] Ibid., p. 109. This is also evident from the *IA* Sheet 49.

Bhowana' where it entered the low ground around Bhowana. It appears that the builders saved the canal by providing an outlet 'at the upper end of the dangerous spot, sufficient to reduce the level of canal.'[50] From this spot 'the canal instead of being sunk in the ground is carried along an elevated mound', the bottom of which at many places rises higher than the surrounding country. 'The lowest portion of this hollow was crossed on an aqueduct of masonry', under which the surplus water of the Farrukhnagar Jhil escaped into the Yamuna. The canal then enters and strikes the base of the range of hills west of Delhi, the drain from which crosses over the canal by 'ancient aqueducts'.

The 'Poolchaddar aqueduct' near Delhi took the canal over the Najafgarh Jhil drain and acted at the same time as a 'waste weir'. The measurements of the aqueduct as given by Sanderson are: 'total length, 80 ft; thickness of the canal floor, 3½ feet; waterway, 16 feet at bed and 19 feet at the top of the parapets, which were 5 feet 9 inches high. The aqueduct was carried on massive 8 feet thick piers with cut waters and arches of 8 feet span over the drainage.'[51]

Around here was the masonry bridge built over the canal by Ba<u>kh</u>tāwar <u>Kh</u>ān, a high official of Aurangzeb. The *Mir'ātu-l 'Ālam* tells us that when the canal used to be in flood it became difficult for one to cross it; so Ba<u>kh</u>tāwar <u>Kh</u>ān had a strong bridge built over it.[52]

In order to reach Delhi, the canal had to pierce the Ridge. Colvin says that the channel is here cut out in the rock to a depth of about 60 feet from the crest.[53] According to Francklin (1798) the cut at 'Mogul Parah' was nearly 3 miles in length, 25 feet in breadth and 25 feet again in depth.[54]

Colvin's report describes how passing through this cut the canal 'enters the city [of Delhi]; and passing through it by an open channel it traverses another extensive aqueduct into the palace [the Fort].' Inside the Fort it 'ramifies in opened or covered water-courses having outlets to the Jamuna, thus permitting the passage of constant streams of fresh water.'[55]

[50] This is shown in the *IA* Sheet as the 'Buwana escape'.

[51] See Sanderson, p. 40 *n.*, where Baker's report of 1849 is cited.

[52] *Mir'āt-ul 'Ālam*, Aligarh: 'Abdus Salām, 314/84, f. 253a.

[53] Colvin, 'Ancient Canals', p. 110.

[54] Francklin, *Shah Aulum*, p. 208.

[55] Colvin, 'Ancient Canals', p. 110.

Susan Gole has now published a Persian map (apparently prepared in the eighteenth century) showing in several panels the alignment of Shāhjahān's canal.[56] It generally confirms the alignment established from our sources.

Undoubtedly, Shāhjahān's Western Yamuna Canal was a considerable feat of engineering, for which its builders have yet to receive due credit. More, the canal and its fourteenth- and sixteenth-century precursors give testimony of a concern for public welfare among the rulers, for which they too should receive some recognition.

[56] Susan Gole, *Indian Maps and Plans*, New Delhi, 1989, pp. 104–9 (reproductions with commentary). The original is stated to be in the Andhra Pradesh State Archives, Hyderabad.

4

The Mughal Assignment System During Akbar's Early Years, 1556–1575

IQTIDAR ALAM KHAN

In the Delhi Sultanate as also in the regional states which succeeded it during the fifteenth century, but most prominently during the Mughal period, the appropriation of the agricultural surplus and its orderly distribution amongst the different segments of the ruling class was conducted mainly by an elaborate system of revenue assignments introduced in India originally by the Ghorians. The central feature of this system consisted of an arrangement whereby the management and appropriation of revenues of different territorial units vested in the members of the ruling group under the supervision of the central authority. The individuals holding assignments were not allowed to acquire hereditary rights over the regions falling under their jurisdiction. Such assignments were designated *iqṭā*'s in the Delhi Sultanate and *jāgīr*s or *tuyūl*s in the Mughal empire. With the passage of time, the system tended to change in a variety of ways, often affecting or defining the degree of political centralization.

As Irfan Habib has pointed out, Fīrūz Tughlaq's 'policy of letting son succeed father to official posts' amounted 'to a complete capitulation to the sentiment in favour of permanent and semi-hereditary rights in the assignments.' Under the Lodis, this process went a step further when 'the nobility consisted of Afghan tribal leaders, whose control over the revenues of their territorial charges tended to be hereditary and derived only partly from the king's favour.'[1] But with the establishment of the Mughal empire

[1] 'The Social Distribution of Landed Property in pre-British India', in *Indian Society: Historical Probings*, ed. R.S. Sharma and V. Jha, 1977, New Delhi, p. 294.

this trend was reversed. In the Mughal system of assignments, identified with *jāgīr*s or *tuyūl*s, a noble's income from his assignment approximated to his salary fixed according to his rank in the hierarchy and the expected or actual strength of his armed contingent. It was closer to a pure revenue assignment than to an administrative-cum-fiscal charge like the *iqṭā'* of the Sultanate period. 'It was never a fixed territorial unit, and had no connection except for convenience in assignment, with the administrative units, *sarkar*s and *pargana*s.' The practice of frequently transferring assignments also reasserted itself under the Mughal rulers. Ordinarily, the *jāgīr* of a Mughal noble was transferred from one place to another after every three or four years.[2]

It is important to understand how and when this reversal of the earlier trend occurred under the Mughals. Was the emergence of the assignment system of the Mughals, with its pronounced centralizing features dictated, as Rushbrook Williams suggests, by the theory of kingship that Bābur brought with him?[3] Or was it an entirely novel arrangement conceived and enforced by Akbar along with his other far-reaching measures of 1574–5 (19 R.Y.) devised consciously for tightening control over the nobles? Or, again, would it be more correct to assume that it was an arrangement meeting the special requirements of the Mughal polity in India which evolved under the strains and stresses of the period 1526–75 when the Mughals were struggling desperately for survival in the face of persisting local hostility? Before we attempt to answer these questions on the basis of fresh research, let us briefly notice the treatment that the subject has received from Moreland and Irfan Habib, both of whom have paid little more than passing attention to the evolution of the Mughal assignment system during the first twenty years of Akbar's reign.

The distinctive features of the Mughal assignment system towards the close of the sixteenth century are mainly discernible in

[2] Ibid., p. 303.

[3] *An Empire Builder of the Sixteenth Century*, reprint, S. Chand, n.d., Delhi, p. 161. Rushbrook Williams's view may be summarised thus: Bābur, being the 'very embodiment of absolute kingship' and 'divine right', was determined to be 'no Sultan hampered by all the limitations which had beset the Lodi dynasty'. But lacking an aptitude for administration, Babur 'found it necessary to carry on the administrative plan of the Lodis'. An entirely new arrangement 'bridging the gulf between the central and local authorities' could materialize only under Akbar.

the abundant source material that becomes available for the period 1595 onwards. But, unfortunately, this material does not throw much light on the working of the system prior to 1574–5. It tends, moreover, to create the impression that the Mughal assignment system, with the features that we associate with its working during the seventeenth century, came into existence only with the introduction of *manṣab*s in 1575. Such an impression is implicit in Moreland's as well as Irfan Habib's treatment of the subject. Both seem to proceed on the assumption that prior to 1575 the assignments in the Mughal empire were not substantially different from the permanent administrative-cum-revenue charges of the Lodi period. According to Moreland, for instance, there is no important reference in the sources of Akbar's reign indicating that the assignee was permitted to realize only his sanctioned income and was 'required to account to the central treasury for any sums which he might collect in excess.' He goes on to suggest that this practice might have been 'developed gradually as an alternative to frequent revision of valuation' during the last twenty years of Akbar's reign.[4] Irfan Habib, on the other hand, implicitly suggests that as late as the 13th regnal year of Akbar, i.e. 1568–9, the practice of frequent transfers was not decisively established.[5]

These suggestions are very useful in so far as they enable one to locate the problems that need to be examined in order to appreciate the working of the Mughal assignment system prior to Akbar's measures of 1575. At the same time, it is obvious that these two authorities have drawn purely tentative inferences from a limited survey of the extant evidence. Moreland himself has alluded in passing to references in the chronicles to assignments (with various designations) given to or held by the nobles at different points of time—references that represent a store of information which, if arranged and sifted properly, could illuminate many aspects of the working of the Mughal assignment system during the early years of Akbar's reign.[6]

The insights provided by this evidence go to highlight the following problems as deserving of particular attention from

[4] *The Agrarian System of Moslem India*, reprint, Delhi, 1968, p. 98.

[5] *The Agrarian System of Mughal India*, Bombay, 1963, p. 260.

[6] Cf. *The Agrarian System of Moslem India*, p. 94, where Moreland refers to chronicles showing 'the frequency of appointments and promotions'.

researchers: (1) What were the different terms used in the sources to describe assignments as well as assignees, and to what extent do these reveal changing nuances in the system? (2) Were the assignments of individual nobles as also of nobles belonging to the same clans composed of compact territorial units or were they parcelled out in small fragments scattered over different territories? (3) Were the assignments in the nature of revenue-cum-administrative charges or did they imply the separation of administrative and fiscal jurisdiction that was so patently established in the subsequent period? (4) What was the frequency of transfers of assignment and in what way was this related to other developments like the separation of administrative and revenue charges, or the fragmentation of *jāgīr*s?

To find answers to these questions, as well as to address the wider issue of the reversal of the trend from the semi-hereditary or permanent control of nobles over their assignments, it is necessary to examine contemporary references pertaining to the receiving and holding of assignments by nobles. About 400 cases of such assignments made under Akbar down to AD 1581 have been gathered from the *Tārīkh-i Akbarī* by 'Ārif Qandahārī, the *Tazkira-i Humāyūn-wa-Akbar* by Bāyazīd Bayāt, the *Akbarnāma* by Abū'l Fazl, the *Tabaqāt-i Akbarī* by Nizamuddīn Aḥmad and the *Muntakhab-ut-Tawārīkh* by 'Abdu'l Qādir Badāunī, and a list of assignments made which covers the first twenty-four years of Akbar's reign.[7] Individual cases of assignments are arranged in chronological order and information classified under the following five heads: 'Date', 'Nomenclature', 'Locale', 'Name of assignee', and 'References'.[8]

Let us first take the nomenclature. Such an exercise is aimed at gaining insights into the dynamics and orientation of the changes that the Mughal assignment system underwent during the first five decades of Mughal rule in Hindustan. It would largely be based on a table showing the frequency with which different terms denoting assignments or assignees are used in my list of assignments.[9]

Next, I shall focus on the actual working of the Mughal assignment system down to 1567, drawing upon other more

[7] See Appendix I.

[8] For the nature of information furnished under these heads, see introductory note to Appendix I.

[9] Appendix II.

general evidence gleaned from the sources. To illustrate the frequency of *jāgīr*-transfers during this period, information furnished by the list of assignments is presented in a separate appendix, where it is arranged under two heads: 'List of Assignments held by Thirteen Leading Nobles'; and 'List of Nobles holding *sarkārs* Multan, Etawa, Narnaul, Kalpi and Sambhal as Assignments'.[10]

II

The term *jāgīr* commonly used in seventeenth-century official papers to describe the revenue assignment, does not occur in any work compiled before Akbar. Its occurrence seems to have synchronised with the transition from the semi-permanent territorial assignments of the Lodi period to the revenue assignments of the Mughal empire.

The term *jāgīr*, which by the end of the sixteenth century came to be accepted as the standard term for a revenue assignment, is actually a shortened form of the Persian *jāygīr* meaning 'possessing, occupying a place, fixing a habitation, making a settlement'.[11] It possibly originated in the popular administrative jargon of petty officials during the early years of Akbar, and came to be used in official papers only gradually. A tendency on the part of both Abū'l Faẓl and Badāūnī to spell the term as *jāygīr* and Abū'l Faẓl's deliberate attempt in the third volume of *Akbarnāma* to substitute for it the archaic expression *iqṭā'*, indicate the reluctance of these writers to use this term of vulgar origin.

Accounts of the period 1556–60 contain the term *jāgīr* much less frequently than those of the period 1561–75.[12] From the table in Appendix II it can be seen that of the total 68 references for the period 1556–60, only 22, i.e. 32.3 per cent mention the term *jāgīr*, while in the remaining 67.7 per cent cases the terms used for the assignments or the position of assignees are *ḥukūmat/ḥākim* or some other vague expression like *ḥirāsat*, *sardārī*, *dāwarī*, or *iyālat*. On the other hand, the corresponding respective percentages for 1561–75 come to 60.57 per cent and 39.43 per cent. As a matter of

[10] Appendix III.

[11] Muhammad Ghiyāṣuddīn, *Ghiyāṣ ul-Lughāt* (compiled AH 1242 AD 1825–6), Nawal Kishore, Kanpur, 1878, p. 115. Cf. Steingass, *Persian-English Dictionary*, Indian edition, 1973, s.v. *Jāygīr*.

[12] Appendix II.

fact the frequency of use of the term *jāgīr* by chroniclers seems to increase dramatically from 1561 onwards, and persists down to 1575. But then, significantly enough, it declines in narratives of the period 1575–80. As we know this was the period when in a major part of the empire revenue assignments were kept in abeyance. In the narratives of these years the term *jāgīr/jāygīr* occurs only in 9.9 per cent of cases.

It may be assumed that the varying frequency of the term *jāgīr* was caused by the changing nomenclature for different kinds of assignments in the original documents consulted by the chroniclers. This is forcefully suggested by the sudden drop in the frequency of the term *jāgīr* during the period 1575–80. The sudden and startling shift from the extensive use made of the term *jāgīr* during the preceding period was presumably caused by its absence from the royal orders conferring charges on the nobles during this period.

Proceeding on the assumption that the varying technical terms used by chroniclers reflect the changing administrative jargon of official papers, one might interpret the table given in Appendix II as suggesting that the original documents available to chroniclers for the first four years of Akbar did not always use the term *jāgīr* as a standard technical term for assignment. This in turn goes to confirm the inference drawn by Irfan Habib from his reading of two of Akbar's *farmān*s (dated AH Jumada I 971/December 1563–January 1564 and AH 24 Sha'ban 979/9 January 1572) that during the early years of Akbar's reign 'the term [*jāgīrdār*] was meant to designate the lesser assignees of revenue, and not the great nobles or commanders holding large charges.'[13]

There is another significant aspect of the nomenclature used in the chronicles of Akbar's reign for assignments. It almost entirely excludes the expressions *wajah-wa-'alufa*, *istiqāmat-wa-wajah*, *wajah-wa-istiqāmat*,[14] terms used by Bābur to describe different

[13] 'Aspects of Agrarian Relations and Economy in a Region of Uttar Pradesh during the Sixteenth Century', *The Indian Economic and Social History Review*, Vol. IV, No. 3, September 1967, p. 209.

[14] Cf. A. R. Khan, 'Babur's Settlement of his Conquests in Hindustan', *Proceedings of Indian History Congress*, 1967, p. 218. The expression *wajah-wa-istiqāmat* being misread as *wajah-i-istiqāmat*, can lead to a serious error in the study of Mughal nomenclature. For a correct reading of the formula see A. S. Beveridge, *The Bābur-Nāma, The Haiderabad Codex*, Luzac and Co., London, 1905, reprint 1971, ff. 304b, 326b etc., as well as *Tuzak-i Bāburī*, MS. BM Or. 3714, ff. 501, 531, etc. For Tatar Khan's

kinds of assignments made by him. Interestingly enough, in his Persian translation of the Turkish text of the *Bāburnāma* prepared during the 1580s, Abdur Rahim scrupulously avoids use of the newly-coined term *jāgīr*, taking care to retain the original expressions.[15] One might well suppose that in doing so he was guided by an awareness that the *wajah*s of Bābur in many respects represented a very different kind of assignment system from the one identified, in the 1580s, with the *jāgīr*s. And perhaps, it was again for the same reason that in the official papers of the first four years of Akbar's reign (when the term was yet to be fully accepted in the standard administrative parlance), instead of employing the term *wajah*, vague expressions like *ḥukūmat*, *sardārī*, *dāwarī*, *iyālat*, *ḥirāsat*, etc., were preferred.[16] It follows that the basic change in the nature of the assignment system, necessitating the coining of a new term to describe it, perhaps came about some time after Babur but before Akbar's accession. One might also consider whether this change did not occur under the Surs. It could have been the outcome of Sher Shah's policy of appointing *sarkār*-level military commanders, which was apparently a decisive step in the direction of separating the revenue assignments from administrative charges of the nobles.[17] This process is known to have been carried further by Islam Shah who attempted to put all the 'soldiery' serving under him on cash salaries.[18]

III

At the time of Humayun's death (January 1556), the Mughal empire appeared to be divided into seven or eight military zones,

assignment in Bayawa (that is Payanwan, cf. Beveridge, tr. *Bāburnāma*, p. 540 n. and Irfan Habib, *An Atlas of the Mughal Empire*, Delhi, 1982, p. 28) and Khusrau Kokaltāsh's assignment in Alwar, as in most other cases, the formula used reads *wajah-wa-istiqāmat*, not *wajah-i-istiqāmat*.

[15] See *Tuzak-i Bāburī*, MS BM Or. 3714.

[16] See Appendices I and II.

[17] A rather obscure passage in the *Tārīkh-i Sher Shāhī* (India Office, Ethe, 219, f. 114a), where Shujā'at Khān's appointment as the *ḥākim* of Malwa is mentioned, indicates that the salaries of troopers serving under a noble were paid through assignments made by the central authority within the territory under his administrative charge.

[18] Cf. 'Abdul Qādir Badāunī, *Muntakhab-ut Tawārīkh*, I, Calcutta, 1864–9, p. 384.

commanded by leading nobles from their headquarters at Kabul, Qandahar, Lahore, Multan, Delhi, Agra, Etawa, Kalpi, Kol and Sambhal. These nobles were entrusted with the responsibility of establishing regular administration after suppressing Afghan and other local resistance in the territories put under their control. Within these military zones, there existed smaller charges held by nobles placed in a subordinate position to the commanders (*ḥākim*s) of larger territories. Side by side with military commands and charges there also existed revenue assignments (sometimes termed *jāgīr*s) of the individual nobles. The *jāgīr* (revenue assignment as distinct from military–administrative charge) of a high noble covering a number of contiguous *pargana*s, sometimes even *sarkār*s, would mostly be located within the territory controlled by him. But it would not always be concomitant with his military–administrative charge. Speaking in terms of the territory covered by the two kinds of assignment, one might say that the military–administrative charge of a high noble would always extend much beyond that of his revenue assignment. On the other hand, in the case of an ordinary noble holding charge of a *sarkār* or *pargana* in a subordinate position to a high noble, the meagre evidence we have suggests that the confines of his *jāgīr* often conformed to the territory of his charge.

The system of commands and *jāgīr*s obtaining at the time of Humayun's death may be inferred from the incidental evidence shedding light on arrangements obtaining in the military zones administered from Delhi, Kabul and Qandahar. For instance, it suggests that the territory controlled from Delhi extended over a number of surrounding *sarkār*s. To the south-east of Delhi the territory is known to have covered the *sarkār*s of Mewat and Narnaul. Tardi Beg administered this entire territory from Delhi, but his own *jāgīr* was located in Mewat.[19] The *sarkār* of Narnaul apparently comprised the military charge as well as revenue assignment of one of Tardi Beg's subordinates, Majnūn Khān Qāqshāl.[20] A similar arrangement seems to have existed in Kabul.

[19] See *Akbarnāma*, II, Calcutta, 1873–87, p. 14, for Abū'l Faẓl's cryptic remark: 'servants of Tardī Beg maintained order in Mewat.'

[20] Ibid., p. 20. After Majnūn Khān Qāqshāl, who is described as the *jāgīrdār* of Narnaul, was expelled from there by the Sūr noble, Hājī Khān, Tardī Beg came there to re-establish Mughal authority. This suggests that at this time the protection of *sarkār* Narnaul was his responsibility.

While the over-all military–administrative charge of *sarkār* Kabul rested with Mun'im Khān, and he also exercised the powers to appoint or dismiss commanders of different places within that *sarkār*,[21] not all the revenues of Kabul were under his control.[22] His personal *jāgīr* or revenue assignment comprised only a part of the total estimated revenues of *sarkār* Kabul. Several places located within the Kabul *sarkār* are known to have been held as *jāgīr*s by nobles serving as Mun'im Khān's subordinates. In this connection mention may be made of Mīr Hāshim's *jāgīr* comprising Kahmard, Ghorband and Zuhak,[23] or of Khwāja Jalāluddīn Maḥmūd holding the *ḥukūmat* of Ghaznin.[24] The evidence on arrangements existing in *sarkār* Qandahar is still more revealing. The *sarkār* of Qandahar is described by Abū'l Faẓl as Bairam Khān's *jāgīr* administered by his deputy, Shāh Muḥammad Qalātī.[25] But he also seems to suggest that Zamindawar, described in the *Ā'īn-i Akbarī* as one of the '*vilāyat*s' constituting 'Gharbī-i Qandahār[26] was held by Bahādur Khān Uzbek as his military and revenue assignment.[27] From this one might infer that the revenue assignment of Bairam Khān was actually confined to only a part of *sarkār* Qandahar. This inference finds support in Nizamuddin's more cautious statement that Bairam Khān's *jāgīr* consisted of 'the town (*balda*) of Qandahar and its environs (*muzāfāt*)'.[28]

The available evidence on the working of this arrangement during the first four or five years of Akbar's reign indicates also a growing tension between the commandants (*hākim*s) of the different regions and the central authority over the question as to what kind of jurisdiction was to be allowed to them within the territories under them. One specific point of dispute appeared to be whether the commandant of a larger territory should control the

[21] For Mun'im Khān's position as the *ḥākim* of Kabul, see Iqtidar Alam Khān, *The Political Biography of a Mughal Noble*, New Delhi, 1973, pp. 35–51.

[22] From an incidental statement in Bāyazīd Bayāt's memoir (*Taẕkīra-i Humāyūn-wa-Akbar*, ed. Hidāyat Ḥosain, Calcutta, 1941, p. 221) that in 1557 Mun'im had gone to Nangnahar and Mandrawar to collect revenue, one might suppose that his *jāgīr* was located in the region around *Jū-i Shāhī* (later Jalalabad).

[23] *Akbarnāma*, II, p. 17.

[24] Ibid., p. 53.

[25] Ibid., p. 14.

[26] *Ā'īn-i Akbarī*, Bib., Ind., I, p. 589.

[27] *Akbarnāma*, II, p. 52. Abū'l Faẓl uses the term *dāwarī* to describe Bahādur Khān's position at Zamindawar. Beveridge has by a slip rendered the word *dāwarī* as *dīwānī* (Eng. trans., II, p. 53).

[28] Nizamuddīn Aḥmad, *Ṭabaqāt-i Akbarī*, ed. B. De, Calcutta, 1931, II, p. 128.

entire revenues of the area or his fiscal authority should remain confined to his personal *jāgīr*, so that all the *maḥal*s and *sarkār*s of his charge not within his own *jāgīr* and also not reserved for the *khālisa* might be given as *jāgīr*s to other nobles by the central *dīwān*. Conflicting orientations of the central authority and regional commandants on this issue can be seen at work in the Court's relations with 'Alī Qulī Khān, the commandant of Lucknow and the adjoining *sarkār*s, during 1558–60. Some time in 1558, *pargana* Sandila was assigned by 'Alī Qulī Khān to one of his relatives, Ismā'īl Khān. But this assignment was superseded by the central *dīwān*, which assigned it in *jāgīr* to Ḥusain Khān Jalāir. Although Ismā'īl Khān tried to resist Ḥusain Khān Jalāir's taking over charge of the *pargana*, he was not successful. 'Alī Qulī Khān, who initially encouraged Ismā'īl Khān in his resistance, subsequently, appears to have accepted the *fait accompli*.[29]

There is yet another incident which throws light on this tension from a slightly different angle. In 1557, Mun'im Khān, the commandant of Kabul, arbitrarily removed Khwāja Jalāluddīn Maḥmūd from his charge of Ghaznin and, then, out of anxiety to prevent the aggrieved noble from reporting the matter to the Court, had him imprisoned. From Mun'im Khān's behaviour on this occasion it becomes apparent that he was not very sure if he really had the authority to remove an assignee and for this reason feared that he might be accused of acting beyond his competence.[30]

Contrary pulls operating within the Mughal assignment system during the early years of Akbar's reign seem to have given rise to a number of the features assumed by the system as it operated down to 1575. One of these features appears to be the growing demarcation between the revenue assignments and the jurisdiction of the commandants over the territories controlled by them. The revenue assignment or *jāgīr* of a noble was increasingly conceived in terms of a fixed income assigned against specific *maḥal*s rather than a portion of the revenue collected from the territory administered by a noble. Also the locale and the nominal value of the *jāgīr*s of all the nobles, including the *jāgīr*s of those serving in different regions in subordinate positions to the superior *ḥākim*s, would be decided by the central *dīwān*. This is illustrated by an interesting passage in

[29] *Akbarnāma*, II, pp. 68–9.

[30] Ibid., p. 71. See *Political Biography of a Mughal Noble*, p. 52.

Bāyazīd Bayāt, who tells us that in 1560, 'Alī Qulī Khān, then *ḥākim* of Jaunpur and adjoining *sarkārs*, assigned *sarkār* Banāras to his younger brother, Bahādur Khān, in a manner that bordered on defiance of the royal wishes. But he took care to make this assignment formally on behalf of the king (*az qibl-i pādshāhī*) which was apparently the reason why the Court was eventually persuaded not to make an issue out of this episode.[31] This was an exceptional case, however, in so far as the actual decision on assignment was taken by the commandant of a region without prior authorization. The standard procedure of the distribution of *jāgīrs* within a region appears to be that at the time of the appointment of a high noble as the *ḥākim* of a certain region, an official of the central *dīwān* would be deputed for supervising the distribution of *jāgīrs* among the nobles stationed there. Abū'l Faẓl reports this procedure in connexion with the assignment of *jāgīrs* in Malwa in the year 1562.[32] One might also suppose that the locale and value of the *jāgīrs* of even the highest nobles was expected to be properly defined through *sanads* issued by the central *dīwān*, and refusal by the commandants of the regions to fully abide by this procedure was not condoned. It seems that one of the causes of the breach between the Uzbek nobles and the Court in 1565 was the refusal of 'Alī Qulī Khān and other Uzbek nobles to accept such control.[33] But at the same time one does come across occasional instances of the King virtually delegating his authority of assigning *jāgīrs* in different regions to local commanders.[34]

[31] *Taẓkira-i Humāyūn-wa-Akbar*, p. 244.

[32] At the time of 'Abdullāh Khān Uzbek's appointment to Malwa in the 7th R.Y./1562–3, Mu'īnuddīn Khān Farankhudī, then a *wazīr* in the *dīwān-i-buyūtāt*, was deputed to supervise the distribution of *jāgīrs* there. He was under instructions to return to Agra after performing this task (*Akbarnāma*, II, pp. 168–9).

[33] It is noteworthy that while agreeing to stop military operations against 'Alī Qulī Khān in 1565 without insisting on his surrender, Akbar still insisted that he would only be allowed to reoccupy his *jāgīr* after obtaining a formal *sanad* from the central *Dīwān*. Again, during the brief peace of 1566, 'Alī Qulī Khān was persuaded to send his agent to Agra to obtain formal papers of his *jāgīr* from the court. Cf. *Akbarnāma*, II, pp. 260, 285; *Ṭabaqāt-i Akbarī*, II, p. 181; *Muntakhab-ut Tawārīkh*, II, p. 82. See also *Taẓkira-i Humāyūn-wa-Akbar*, pp. 339–40.

[34] One such case pertains to 1574 when Mun'im Khān was authorised by Akbar to recommend the assignment of *jāgīrs* in the eastern *sarkārs*. Akbar is reported to have told Mun'im Khān: 'I recognize your handwriting. [A noble] will be assigned a *jāgīr* [only] after receiving a recommendation in your handwriting.' It may be assumed that this practice had existed earlier as well.

Down to 1560 or 1561, apparently, the revenue assignments covered a compact territory of contiguous *pargana*s or *sarkār*s. This is suggested by references in the sources to the assignment of *jāgīr*s and appointments of *ḥākim*s. Before October 1560 one does not come across any case where one part of the salary of a noble was assigned against a fraction of the revenues of one *pargana* and the other part against a fraction of the revenues of some other *pargana*s. It would appear that till 1560 the salaries of the nobles were arbitrarily settled in terms of the *jama*ʻ of the *pargana*s against which it was assigned.[35] Under this practice, a noble could hold as his *jāgīr* part of a *pargana*, one whole *pargana*, or several contiguous *pargana*s and a fraction of another adjacent *pargana*, but it was never assigned in parts against the partial *jama*ʻ of two or more *pargana*s. When around December 1560, an attempt was made by the officials of the central *dīwān* to fragment the *jāgīr* of a senior noble by assigning it against the partial *jama*ʻ of two different *pargana*s, it provoked the noble to accuse the officials of vindictiveness.[36] There is also other evidence which suggests that earlier the *pargana*s assigned to a noble were always contiguous ones. Bāyazīd Bayāt tells us that in December 1560 ʻAlī Qulī K͟hān was assigned (*jāgīr kardand*) *sarkār*s Jaunpur, Banaras, Ghazipur and some of the *pargana*s of *sarkār*s Manikpur and Awadh.[37] Apparently, part of ʻAlī Qulī K͟hān's salary that exceeded the total *jama*ʻ of *sarkār*s Jaunpur, Banaras and Ghazipur, was assigned against some of the *pargana*s of the two neighbouring *sarkār*s. It is significant that both the *sarkār*s bordered upon *sarkār* Jaunpur. This would strongly suggest that these *pargana*s were contiguous to the rest of the

[35] This was apparently a practice dating from Bābur's time. Bābur's use of the term *pargana* for *wajah* is an indication that he perceived assignments basically in terms of fiscal units. For a reference of this kind, see for instance, *Tuzūk-i Bāburī*, f. 411b, where resumption of the nobles' assignments is described as resumption of their *pargana*s.

[36] *Akbarnāma*, II, p. 120. In Shamsuddīn Muḥammad Atka's letter to Akbar, written around December 1560, he complains bitterly that of one crore copper *tanka*s sanctioned as his '*juldū*', the authorities had assigned 40 *lakh*s (80 lakh *dām*s) against Firuzpur. We know that at the time of the compilation of the *Āʻin-i Akbarī* (Bib. Ind., I, p. 554) the *jama*ʻ of Firuzpur amounted to 1,14,79,404 *dām*s. This indicates that the rest of the revenues of the *pargana* were either assigned to some other noble or were reserved for the *k͟hālisa*. The remaining 60 *lakh* copper *tanka*s (120 *lakh dām*s) of Shamsuddīn Muḥammad Atka's assignment were to be given to him elsewhere. This was, apparently, viewed by him as a deviation from established practice.

[37] *Taẕkira-i Humāyūn-wa-Akbar*, p. 239.

territory of 'Alī Qulī Khān's *jāgīr*, of which *sarkār* Jaunpur was a part. Thus one would be quite justified in interpreting this evidence as indicating the current emphasis on compact *jāgīr*s.

During Akbar's early years the *maḥal*s of the *khāliṣa* were not clearly demarcated. The Centre's share in the revenues of the different regions was no doubt fixed, but its collection and transmission to the central treasury was made the responsibility of the *ḥākim*s. This situation is suggested by two statements furnished by Bāyazīd Bayāt. First, he vaguely alludes to the existence of an arrangement, down to the beginning of 1561, where the responsibility for collecting central revenues rested with the senior nobles acting as *ḥākim*s.[38] Secondly, he makes a cryptic reference to '*sarkār* Banāras' being 'in excess of his ['Alī Qulī Khān's] *jāgīr*' in 1560. This *sarkār* was assigned by 'Alī Qulī Khān to his brother Bahādur Khān 'on behalf of the king'.[39] From this statement it may be construed that before *sarkār* Banaras came to be assigned to Bahādur Khān at the beginning of 1561, its revenues were at par with those of the *khāliṣa* but these were actually managed by the *ḥākim* of the Jaunpur region, of which Banaras was a part. Thus there emerges a general picture of high nobles managing the *khālisa* revenues of the regions administered by them, which they could always be tempted to misappropriate. Such a tendency was bound to be aggravated by the inflated *jama*' on the basis of which the value of the assignment was calculated. It was, perhaps, because of the general tendency of the regional *ḥākim*s to withhold central revenues that towards the beginning of 1561 the central treasury was completely exhausted.

One noteworthy consequence of the working of the *jāgīr* system during the first four years of Akbar's reign was the concentration in particular regions of *jāgīr*s of nobles belonging to the same clans. This emerges from evidence relating to the Turānī nobles during 1563–7. Already by 1565, the following concentrations seem to have existed: Uzbeks in the Jaunpur region; Qāqshāls in Kara-Manikpur; Jalāirs in Lucknow and Awadh; Mirzās in Sambhal; and

[38] Ibid., p. 244. While commenting on the depletion of the central treasury around December 1560, Bāyazīd observes: 'After His Majesty started paying attention to the affairs of his *sarkār* (*sarkār-i khwud*), the people have seen how much treasure has accumulated in each one of the towns, *pargana*s and villages of Hindustan.'

[39] *Tārīkh-i Humāyūn-wa-Akbar*, p. 244.

the Atka clan in the Panjab. A number of factors seem to have contributed to this situation. Firstly, it could have been created by the Court's policy, down to 1560, generally to assign *jāgīrs* to members of a clan in a region administered by their leader. One comes across several such instances. In 1559, for instance, the entire Jalāir clan was assigned *jāgīrs* in and around *sarkār* Lucknow. In August–September 1560, Akbar decided to confer the 'whole of Punjab on him [Shamsuddīn Muḥammad Atka] and his brothers'.[40] Again, the concentration of clans in particular regions was also facilitated by an overt tendency on the part of high nobles to procure *jāgīrs* for their own clansmen within the territory of their charge. Sometimes this was sought to be achieved even by violating or twisting the rules.[41]

From the central authority's point of view, one negative result of this development was the marked slowing down of the process of transfers of *jāgīrs*. The list of assignments prepared by me shows that transfers were more frequent during the first four years of Akbar's reign than during 1560–7. This result is derived from Appendix III. It comes out clearly from the list of assignments held by Muḥammad Qāsim Barlās, Bahādur K͟hān, 'Alī Qulī K͟hān, Qayā K͟hān Gung and Iskandar K͟hān. The same trend is also suggested by the list of nobles holding assignments in *sarkārs* Multan, Etawa, Narnaul, Kalpi and Sambhal. The concentration of different clans in particular regions by 1560 was responsible, at least partly, for this slower rotation of *jāgīrs* during the ensuing six years.

IV

In the evolution of the *jāgīr* system under Akbar, 1561 appears as a crucial turning point. It is around this time that certain far-reaching changes in the working of the *jāgīr* system become discernible. These changes may be regarded as the precursors of Akbar's measures of 1574–5. In this section, I propose briefly to notice some of these changes, and, to the extent that the available evidence permits, I also propose to investigate the question as to

[40] *Akbarnāma*, II, pp. 82, 116.

[41] As in the case already mentioned, 'Alī Qulī K͟hān's assigning Banaras as *jāgīr* to his brother on the presumption that he was doing it on behalf of the king (*az qibl-i pādshāhī*). Cf. *Tazkīra-i Humāyūn-wa-Akbar*, p. 244.

how the changes of 1561 were related to the better-known developments of 1566–7 and 1574–5.

A significant change introduced around 1561 pertained to the manner in which the *jāgīrs* were assigned. From the second half of 1560 onwards, the *jāgīrs* of great nobles came to be assigned in fragments scattered over a number of *parganas* located at considerable distances from each other. It seems that this was done as a matter of conscious policy. This change in the assignment policy seems to have synchronised with the rise of a new concept of assignment, which, in the post-1561 period, was increasingly perceived as pre-sanctioned income determined in accordance with the status and obligations of the assignee.

The basic evidence suggesting this change is vague, even problematic in nature. The earliest indication of it is furnished by Shamsuddīn Muḥammad Atka's letter of December 1560 to Akbar already referred to in the preceding section, in which he accuses the officials of the central *dīwān* of being slow in assigning to him and his son the *jāgīrs* which had already been sanctioned by the King. He also complains that the officials were being vindictive towards him. In this context he makes two specific points: that the full assignment of *jāgīrs* sanctioned by the king in October 1560 was being delayed indefinitely; and that an attempt was being made to fragment his *jāgīr* by assigning it in pieces in different *parganas*. The second point is not made directly, but is clearly implied in the statement, 'out of the entire amount [of one crore copper *tankas*] the authorities have assigned [only] forty lakhs (i.e., 80 lakh *dams*) on Firuzpur.'[42] The implication of this statement becomes clear in the light of the *Ā'in-i Akbarī*'s figure for the *jama'* of *pargana* Firuzpur, which in 1595 stood at 1,14,79,404 *dāms*[43] which means it outstripped the *jama'* of Shamsuddīn Muḥammad Atka's assignment against the same *pargana* by 34,79,404 *dāms*. The corresponding *jama'* figure for 1560 would have been still higher, owing to the fact stated by Abū'l Fazl himself that the earlier *jama' raqami* figures were inflated. It can thus be seen that in assigning only 40 lakh copper *tankas* (i.e. 80 lakh *dams*) out of Shamsuddīn Muḥammad Atka's sanctioned income of one crore *tankas* or two crore *dāms* against a *pargana* whose *jama'* exceeded

[42] *Akbarnāma*, II, p. 120.

[43] *Ā'in-i Akbarī*, Bib. Ind., I, p. 554.

one crore, fourteen lakhs, the officials of the central *dīwān* were seen to be deviating from the norm followed till then.

It may, however, be pointed out that Shamsuddīn Muḥammad Atka's grouse was not fully justified. Official deviations from the hitherto adhered norm were not confined to his case. Some time between 1561 and 1563 Mun'im Khān's compact *jāgīr* at Hisar Firuza was also reduced by almost half and for this he was compensated by being assigned *jāgīrs* in the widely-scattered *sarkārs* of Etawa and Khairabad and the *parganas* of Shahpur (in *sarkār* Bari Doab), Jalandhar (in *sarkār* Bet Jalandhar Doab) and Indri (in *sarkār* Saharanpur).[44]

Till April 1561, *sarkār* Hisar Firuza was administered by a certain Khwāja Kalān, described by Bayazid as a servant of Mun'im Khān. In April 1561, the same *sarkār* was placed under a *ḥākim* appointed from the central *dīwān*. The person entrusted with this charge was Bāyazīd Bayāt, who till this time had been a personal servant of Mun'im Khān; his appointment as *ḥākim* of Hisar Firuza was considered a promotion to the position of an officer of the king. His new status was underlined by the conferment of the title *sulṭānī*.[45] It is very likely that the curtailment of Mun'im Khān's administrative jurisdiction in *sarkār* Hisar Firuza suggested by the above change not only accompanied but actually resulted from the decision of the authorities to reduce his assignment in that *sarkār*.

Here it would not be out of place to note that the identical cash rates given in the schedule of *Ā'in-i dahsāla* for the widely dispersed *dastūr*-circles comprising Kishni and Ibrahimabad in

[44] *Tazkira-ī Humāyūn-wa-Akbar*, pp. 240, 248, 299: In October 1560, '*sarkār* Hisar Firuza' was given to Mun'im Khān as his *jāgīr*. Presumably, the entire revenues of Hisar Firuza were assigned to him. He appears to have held this *jāgīr* without any change till 1561, when an order was issued for the transfer of *sarkār* Hisar Firuza to the *khālisa*, but on Mun'im Khān's agreeing to its being governed by a *ḥākim* appointed by the central *dīwān* he was allowed to hold a *jāgīr* there. (See also *Akbarnāma*, II, p. 189.)

The extent to which Mun'im Khān's *jāgīr* in *sarkār* Hisar Firuza was reduced can be gauged by comparing the figure for its income in 1567 furnished by Bāyazīd Bayāt, i.e. 3 crore (*dāms*?), with the *jama'* of the *sarkār* given in the *Bāburnāma* (1,30,75,174 copper *tankas*, equal to 2,61,50,346 *dāms*) and *Ā'in-i Akbarī* (5,23,54,905 *dāms*). Bāyazīd has not specified the currency in which he has stated the *ḥal-i ḥāsil* of Mun'im Khān's *jāgīr* at Hisar Firuza. But it could not be a figure in copper *tankas*. If Bāyazīd's figure for the actual collection in 1567 is treated as being stated in copper *tankas* then it would exceed the *jama'* of the *sarkār* both for 1526 as well as 1595.

[45] *Tazkira-i Humāyūn-wa-Akbar*, pp. 249–50.

Awadh are quite different from the rates sanctioned for Awadh, but are similar to those of Manikpur and Rae Bareli. Regarding these *dastūr*-circles, Shireen Moosvi's guess that these were 'included in the *jāgīrs* of some big nobles who held the other circles within their *jāgīrs* and wished to have identical *dastūrs* in the various parts of their *jāgīrs*', seems very plausible. Thus the pattern of cash rates shown for different *dastūr*-circles in *Ā'in-i dahsāla* may also be interpreted as testifying to the fragmentation of the *jāgīrs* of some of the high nobles during 1575–80 when these rates were actually worked out.[46]

Shamsuddīn Muḥammad Atka's letter is perhaps the earliest document where the value of the *jāgīr* of a noble is stated in terms of sanctioned income rather than the yield of the *parganas*/*sarkārs* against which it was assigned. This evidence seems to point to a quite different conception of the system from the one where a revenue-assignment was conceived basically as the allocation of the revenues of a territory to a person entrusted with its administration. It is in this sense that Atka K͟hān's reference to the presanctioned value of his *jāgīr* represents an entirely different situation from what is suggested by the statements in *Bāburnāma* specifying the amounts assigned to individual nobles against different *parganas*/*sarkārs*. Moreover, it is integral to the conception of a *jāgīr* representing the presanctioned income of a noble that its value would be fixed, keeping in view the status of the noble and the actual strength of his contingent. In this context, Shireen Moosvi's interpretation of the passage in *Akbarnāma* on the fixing of the strength of the nobles' contingents in 1566 seems to be especially relevant.[47] It is very likely that the money rates per horseman mentioned there were used for specifying the strength of the contingent against the expected income of *jāgīrs* under the newly-established *jama'*. But it is also possible that these criteria were formulated on the basis of previous practice, having been worked out by taking into account the ratio to be maintained between the strength of a noble's contingent and his actual income. This is partly borne out by the figures furnished by Bāyazīd Bayāt for the *ḥāl-i ḥāṣil* of Mun'im K͟hān's *jāgīr* in *sarkār* Hisar Firuza, and the strength of the contingent that he maintained on that income. In

[46] Shireen Moosvi, 'Formulation of Land Revenue Rates under Akbar', *Indian Historical Review*, January 1978, IV, No. 2, pp. 324–5.

[47] Shireen Moosvi, 'The Evolution of the *Manṣabdāri* System under Akbar until 1596–7', *Journal of the Royal Asiatic Society*, London, No. 2, 1980, p. 175.

1565, from 700 to 800 horsemen were maintained on the income of Mun'im K͟hān's *jāgīr* in *sarkār* Hisar Firuza;[48] and the actual collection (*ḥāl-i ḥāṣil*) of the same *jāgīr* in 1567 came to three crore *dāms*.[49] From these figures the rate of per horseman payment works out to 42,857 *dāms* if the strength of the contingent is taken as 700, and 37,500 *dāms* if it is accepted as 800. The rates per horseman fall within the range of the second category (32,000) and third category (48,000) of horsemen given by Abū'-l Faẓl. One might even conjecture that the new conception of the *jāgīr* suggested by Shamsuddīn Muḥammad Atka's reference to the pre-sanctioned value of his assignment tended to make the income of a noble's *jāgīr* and the number of troops commanded by him contingent on each other.

The process of the fragmentation of *jāgīrs* and the consequent separation of *jāgīr* from administrative jurisdiction inevitably impeded the regional concentration of *jāgīrs* of the nobles. But there also arose a definite policy of not allowing the clans to remain concentrated in particular regions. During 1564–7, even the groups siding firmly with the King in his conflict with the recalcitrant Turani nobles were not exempted from the operation of this policy. Soon after the suppression of the Uzbek nobles in 1567, members of the Atka K͟hail were transferred from the Punjab. Subsequently, their *jāgīrs* were scattered all over the empire. Akbar regarded Atka K͟hail's dispersal a greater achievement than the suppression of defiant sections of the nobility.[49a]

In conclusion, it would be useful to specifically enumerate some of the important points that emerge from this discussion.

An analysis of the nomenclature used for the Mughal assignments strengthens the impression that the system identified with the *jāgīrs* of Akbar's reign was a different kind of arrangement from the one represented by the military-cum-revenue assignments of Bābur. In so far as this suggests that the origin of the Mughal assignment system lay in the administrative policies of the Sūr rulers, it points to a line of inquiry which has yet to be pursued with vigour. It also goes to underline M. Athar Ali's emphasis on

[48] *Taẕkira-i Humāyūn-wa-Akbar*, p. 285.

[49] As already argued, this figure could not have been in copper *tankas*. It is obvious that Bāyazīd has converted the original figure of copper *tankas* into *dāms*.

[49a] *Taẕkira-i Humāyūn-wa-Akbar*, p. 253.

the contribution made by the Sūr regime to the structure of the Mughal polity.[50]

The division of the Mughal empire at the time of Humāyūn's death into a number of military zones administered by senior nobles seems to resemble the administrative plan that, according to Abū'l Faẓl, was contemplated by Humāyūn in 1555, a scheme characterized by S. Nurul Hasan as aimed at the decentralization of authority.[51] But from references to assignments during the first four years of Akbar's reign it appears that the organization of military command inherited by him from Humāyūn, was actually superimposed on a system of revenue assignments closely regulated by the central authority. This in turn points to a similarity with the structure of commands and assignments established by Sher Shāh. From its very inception, then, this arrangement appeared to carry an inbuilt tendency towards the separation of the revenue assignments from the assignees' military and administrative jurisdictions.

The working of this system during the last two years of Bairam K͟hān's regency, when he was forced to act in important matters in consultation with the leading nobles,[52] seems to have given rise to certain features which thwarted its intrinsic centralizing propensity. But this imperfection of the Mughal assignment system in the early years of Akbar's reign was speedily remedied after he had succeeded in establishing his personal authority in the central government around 1561. One might even suggest that the changes discernible in the Mughal assignment system between 1561 and 1567, such as the linking of a noble's income with his status and military obligation, fragmentation of *jāgīrs*, a clear demarcation of the *jāgīr* jurisdiction from routine administration, went much beyond the structural possibilities of the system handed down by Humāyūn. In many respects, it now tended to resemble the *jāgīr* system of the post-1575 period, which, it goes without saying, was increasingly conditioned by the operation of a new mode of revenue assessment and collection and also by the gradual introduction of an elaborate system of military hierarchy and obligations.

[50] 'Towards An Interpretation of the Mughal Empire', *Journal of the Royal Asiatic Society*, London, No. 1, 1978, p. 39.

[51] S. Nurul Hasan, 'New Light on the Relations of Early Mughal Rulers with their Nobility', *Proceedings of the Indian History Congress*, 1944, pp. 389–97.

[52] For the curtailment of Bairam K͟hān's powers around April 1558 see Iqtidar Alam Khan, 'The Mughal Court Politics during Bairam Khan's Regency', *Medieval India—A Miscellany*, Vol. I, 1969, p. 33.

APPENDIX I

This Appendix seeks to assemble information pertaining to the assignments conferred upon, or held by, individual nobles at different points of time during the first twenty-four years of Akbar's reign (1556 to 1580). The references listed have been taken from the four major histories of Akbar's reign, namely, *Tārīkh-i Akbarī* by 'Arif Qandahārī, *Tazkīra-i Humāyūn-wa-Akbar* by Bāyazīd Bayāt, *Akbarnāma* by Abū'l Fazl, *Ṭabaqāt-i Akbarī* by Niẓāmuddīn Aḥmad, and *Muntakhab-ut Tawārīkh* by 'Abdul Qādir Badāunī.

The available information is presented under five heads:

Date This is either established with the help of specific dates furnished by the chronicles or is suggested by the sequence of reporting in Abū-l Fazl's chapters arranged by regnal years.

Nomenclature If, in a particular reference the fact of a noble holding an assignment is alluded to only by implication without using any specific expression to denote the nature of his jurisdiction, the entry in this column simply reads: '(assignment)'.

Locale Where the place assigned is identified with the *pargana*-headquarters or a small town (*qaṣba*) located within a *sarkār*, its name is entered under *Pargana/Qaṣba*. For the purpose of this list, the *tumān*s of *sarkār*s Kabul and Qandahar are also identified as *pargana*s. The name of the *sarkār* within which the *pargana/qaṣba* under reference was included is entered under the column *sarkār* within parentheses. (In the case of *qaṣba* Kahmard situated in Balkh this rule could not be adhered to as it was not included in any one of the *sarkār*s listed in *Ā'īn-i Akbarī*.) To indicate whether a particular place-name in this column refers to a *pargana* or *qaṣba*, the letter 'Q' is written within parentheses against the names of the *qaṣba*s (e.g., 'Mama Khatun (Q)'). The location of places other than *pargana* or *sarkār*-headquarters have been determined with the help of Irfan Habib's *Atlas of the Mughal Empire* (Oxford University Press, 1982). In a few cases, where the information is vague and alludes only to the assignment of unspecified *pargana*s in a particular *sarkār* it is entered as '*Parganas*' in the column '*Pargana/Qaṣba*' with the name of the *sarkār* within parentheses under '*Sarkār*'.

If the place is identified with the name of a *sarkār*-headquarters or the territory of a *sarkār* (e.g., *sarkār* Punjab) it is placed under *Sarkār*; this applies to cases where the same place happened to be the *ṣūba*-headquarters as well, in view of the fact that during our period, i.e. down to AD 1580, regular *ṣūba*s did not exist.

In all cases where the place assigned is identified by the sources with a territory that later came to comprise a *ṣūba* (e.g., Malwa, Punjab, etc.) or appears to have corresponded to a territorial unit that was larger than a *sarkār* but was not constituted into a *ṣūba* in 1580, it is placed under

'*Vilāyat/Ṣūba*' but against the latter type of territory, 'V' is added in parentheses (e.g.,) 'Badakhshan (V)'.

The spellings of place names given by Irfan Habib in his *Atlas* are generally used.

References: The following abbreviations are used: 'Arif ('Arif Qandahārī, *Tārīkh-i Akbarī*, Rampur, 1962); Bāyazīd (Bāyazīd Bayāt, *Tazkīra-i Humāyūn-wa-Akbar*, Calcutta, 1941); *AN* (Abū'l Fazl, *Akbarnāma*, Calcutta, 1873–87); *TA* (Niẓāmuddīn Aḥmad, *Ṭabaqāt-i Akbarī*, Calcutta, 1931); Badāunī ('Abdul Qādir Badāunī, *Muntakhab-ut Tawārīkh*, Calcutta, 1864–69). Where the sources cited for the same reference have varying versions of technical terms or of names, etc., the earlier version is preferred.

List of Assignments: AD 556–80

Date	Nomenclature	Locale: Pargana/ Qaṣba	Sarkār	Ṣūba/ Vilāyat	Name	Reference
1556 March	*ba-arāmash w asāish-i mulk*			Badakhshan [V]	Mīrzā Sulaimān	*AN*, II, p. 14
„	*intiẕām dāsht*		Kabul-wa-Ghazni		Mun'im Khān	Ibid.
„	*jāgīr*		Qandahar		Bairam Khān	„ *TA*, II, p. 128
„	*Niẕām-i Sarkār*		Sambhal		'Alī Qulī Khān	*AN*, II, p. 14
„	*ḥukūmat*		Agra		Sīkandar Khān Uzbek	„
„	*ba-sardārī*		Kalpi		'Abdullāh Khan Uzbek	„
„	*amnīyat bakhsh*			Mewat (V)	*mulāzmān-i* Tardī Beg	„
„	*lawāzim-i khidmat*		Kol-wa Jalali		Qayā Khān Gung	„
„	*ijrā'-i aḥkām-i pādshāhī namūd*	Bayana	(Agra)		Ḥaidar Muḥammad Khān	„
„	*jāgīr*	Ghorband Kahmard (Q) Zuhak	(Kabul) (Kabul)		Mīr Hāshim	Ibid., p. 17

Date	Nomenclature	Locale: *Pargana/ Qaṣba*	Locale: *Sarkār*	Locale: *Ṣūba/Vilāyat*	Name	Reference
1556						
March	*jāgīr*		Narnaul		Majnūn Khān Qāqshāl	Ibid., p. 20
„	*ṣawāb-i intimā*		Delhi		Tardī Beg Khān	„
September–October	*ḥākim*		Agra		Sikandar Khān Uzbek	Ibid., p. 129
„	(assignment)		Etawa		Qayā Khān Gung	Badāunī, II, p. 13
„	(assignment)		Kalpi		'Abdullāh Khān Uzbek	„
„	(assignment)	Bayana	(Agra)		Ḥaidar Muḥammad Khān	„
November	(assignment)		Sambhal *ba-sair-i pargana-hā-i miān-i doāb*		'Alī Qulī Khān (titled Khān-i Zamān)	'Arif, p. 52; *AN*, II, p. 45
„	*ikhtiṣāṣ*		Kalpi		'Abdullāh Khān Uzbek (titled Shujā'at Khān)	*AN*, II, p. 45
„	*bakhshīdand*					
„	*ba intizām nāmzad shud*		*dār-ul mulk Agra-wa an hudūd*		Qayā Khān	„
November	*ba ḥirāsat*		*Shahar-i* Lahore		Ḥājī Muḥammad Sistānī	Ibid., p. 47
„	*ba ḥirāsat*		Delhi		Mahdī Qāsim Khān	Ibid., p. 48
„	*ḥukūmat*		Ghazni		Khwāja Jalaluddīn Bujūk	Ibid., p. 55
December	*jāygīr*	Sialkot	(Rachnao Doab)		Sikandar Khān	Ibid., p. 47

Date	Nomenclature	Locale			Name	Reference
		Pargana/ Qaṣba	*Sarkār*	*Ṣūba/Vilāyat*		
1557 March	(assignment)		Multan		Muḥammad Qulī Khān Barlās	Ibid., p. 53
„	*jāgīr*		Multan		Bahādur Khān Uzbek	„
„	*jāgīrdār*		Nagaur *wa an-ḥudud*		Muḥammad Qulī Barlās	„
23 July	*jāgīr*		Kharid, Bihar *wa an ḥudud*		Sikandar Sūr	Ibid., p. 59
„	*ḥirāsat*		Qila'-i Mankot		Abū'l Qaṣīm	„
December	*ḥukūmat*		Lahore		Husain Khān	Ibid., p. 46
1558 March	*mutakafil-i intizām*		Ajmer		Muḥammad Qāṣim Khān Nishāpūrī	Ibid., p. 66
March–October	*jāygīr*	Surharpur	(Jaunpur)		'Abdul Raḥmān Beg	Ibid., p. 83; *TA*, II, p.137; Badāunī, II, p. 23
1558	*jāygīr*	Sandila	(Lucknow)		Sulṭān Ḥusain Khān Jalāir	*AN*, II, p. 69
„	*jāgīr*	Fatḥpur Haswa, etc.	(Kara-Manikpur)		Kamāl Khān Ghakkar	Ibid., p. 78, 192; *TA*, II, p. 161
„	*jāgīr*	Hatkant	(Etawa)		Adham Khān	*AN*, II, p. 78

Date	Nomenclature	Locale: Pargana/ Qaṣba	Locale: Sarkār	Locale: Ṣūba/Vilāyat	Name	Reference
1558	*wajah-i jāygīr*	Bayana	(Agra)		Ḥabib ʻAlī Khān	Badāunī, II, p. 31
„	*muqarrar shud*	Bhasawar Toda Bhim	(Agra)		Chaghtāī Khān	Ibid.
1559 March–September	*jāygīr*		Dipalpur		Bahādur Khān Uzbek	*AN*, II, p. 102; Badāunī, II, p. 11
1559	(assignment)		Lucknow		ʻAlī Qulī Khān	*AN*, II, p. 82; *TA*, II, p. 141
„	*ba taskhīr*		Jaunpur		ʻAlī Qulī Khān	Ibid.
„	*supurda*		Lucknow		Jalāirs	*AN*, II, p. 82
„	*ḥākim*		Hisar Firuza		Beg Mīrak	Bāyazīd, p. 279
1560 March	(assignment)	Indri	(Saharanpur)		Ḥusain Khān	Badāunī, II, p. 35
„	*ḥākim*		Delhi		Shahābuddīn Aḥmad Khān	*AN*, II, p.94; *TA*, II, p. 143
„	(assignment)	Sikandra Rao	(Kol)		Muḥammad Bāqi Baqlānī	*AN*, II, p. 94
„	(assignment)	Bhera	(Chinhat Doab)		Shamsuddīn Muḥammad Khān Atka	Ibid., p. 95
„	(assignment)		Lahore		Qāsim Mahdi Khān	„

Date	Nomenclature	Locale			Name	Reference
		Pargana/ Qaṣba	*Sarkār*	*Ṣūba/Vilāyat*		
1560						
March	(assignment)		Lahore		Mīr Muḥammad, Khān-i Kalān	„
„	(assignment)		Alwar		Bairam Khān	Ibid., p. 98
March–April	*ḥākim*		Dipalpur		Durwesh Uzbek	'Arif, p. 61; Bāyazīd, p. 226
„	*jāgīr*	Bhatnair	(Hisar Firuza)		Sher Muḥammad Dīwāna	'Arif, p. 61; Bāyazīd, p. 225; *AN*, II, p. 109; *TA*, II, p. 147; Badāunī, II, p. 40
May	*ḥukūmat*		Kabul		Ḥaidar Muḥammad Khān Akhta Begī	*TA*, II, p. 162
April–May	(assignment)		Bahraich		Qayā Khān	*AN*, II, p. 100
„	*muqarrar shud*		Nagaur		Mīrzā Sharfuddīn Ḥusain	Ibid., p. 104
„	*jāgīrdār*	Pathaura/ Thara	(Bari Doab)		Mīrzā 'Abdullāh Mughal	Bāyazīd, p. 225; *AN*, II, p. 110
August–September	(assignment)		Multan		Muḥammad Qulī Khān Barlās	*AN*, II, pp. 114–15
„	*jāygīr*		Multan		Muḥammad Qāsim Nishāpūrī and others	Ibid.
„	*jāygīr*	Etawa	(Etawa)		Bahādur Khān	Ibid., p. 115
July–August	*ḥukūmat*		Delhi		Khwāja 'Abdul Mājid	Ibid., p. 111

Date	Nomenclature	Locale: *Pargana/ Qaṣba*	Locale: *Sarkār*	Locale: *Ṣūba/Vilāyat*	Name	Reference
1560						
August–September	*ḥukūmat*			Punjab	Shamsuddīn Muḥammad Atka and brothers	Ibid., p. 116
October	*juldū*	Firozpur	(Dipalpur)		Shamsuddīn Muḥammad Atka	Ibid., p. 121
"	*jāygīr*		Nagaur		Mīrzā Sharfuddīn Ḥusain	Ibid., p. 128
October–December	*jāgīr*	Patiali			Ḥusain Khān	Badāunī, II, p. 43
December	*jāgīr*	*Parganas*	Jaunpur Baranas Ghazipur (Awadh & Manikpur)		'Alī Qulī Khān-i Zamān	Bāyazīd, p. 239
"	*dīwān*		Hisar Firuza		Khwāja Muzaffar 'Alī	Ibid., p. 240
"	*jāgīr*		Hisar Firuza		Mun'im Khān	"
1560	*ḥukūmat*		Kalpi		'Abdullāh Khān Uzbek	Badāunī, III, p. 6
1561						
January–March	(assignment)		Etawa		Bahādur Khān Uzbek	Bāyazīd, p. 244
"	*jāgīr*		Banaras		Bahādur Khān Uzbek	"
March	*sardārī-i ṣūrī*			Malwa	Adham Khān	*AN*, II, p. 138
"	*ikhtiṣaṣ yāft*		*Sarangpur*		*Adham Khān*	"
"	*sardār-i m'anavī*			Malwa	Pīr Muḥammad Khān	"

Date	Nomenclature	Locale: Pargana/ *Qaṣba*	Locale: *Sarkār*	Locale: *Ṣūba/Vilāyat*	Name	Reference
1561						
March	*muqarrar shud*		Mandu		Pīr Muḥammad Khān	„
			Ujjain			„
	mufauwaz gasht		Handia		Qayā Khān Gung	„
„	*nāmzad kardand*		Mandasor *wa ān ḥudūd*		Ṣādiq Khān	„
„	*jāygīr*		Kalpi		‘Abdullāh Khān	„
April	*jāgīr*		Hisar Firuza		Mun‘im Khān	Bāyazīd, p. 249
24 May	*jāgīrdārs*	[*Parganas*]	*ān ḥudūd* (Jaunpur and the eastern *sarkārs* in general)		Ibrāhīm Khān Uzbek Majnūn Khān Qāqshāl Shāham Khān Jalāir Kamāl Khān Ghakkar	*TA*, II, p. 154
August	*ḥākim*		Jaunpur		‘Alī Qulī Khān	‘Arif, p. 68
„	*jāgīr*		Banaras		Bahādur Khān	*TA*, II, p. 154
„	*ḥākim*		Kalpi		‘Abdullāh Khān	Bādaunī, II, p. 49
„	*ḥukūmat*		*Sarkār* Punjab		Shamsuddīn Muḥammad Khān Atka (entitled Khān-i A‘ẓam)	Bāyazīd, p. 245; *TA*, II, p. 155
October–November	*ḥirāsat*		Chunar (Q)		Ḥasan ‘Alī Khān Turkmān	*AN*, II, p. 150
1562						
January	*jāygīr*			Mewat (V)	Mīrzā Sharfuddīn Ḥusain	Ibid., p. 155
January	*ḥukūmat*			Malwa	Pīr Muḥammad Khān	‘Arif, p. 68; *AN*, II, p. 152; *TA*, II, p. 156

Date	Nomenclature	Locale			Name	Reference
		Pargana/ Qaṣba	*Sarkār*	*Sūba/Vilāyat*		
1562						
January–February	*jāygīr*		Ajmer		Mīrzā Sharfuddīn Ḥusain	Badāunī, II, p. 50
„	*jāygīr*		Ajmer		Tarsūn Muḥammad Khān Shāh Budagh Khān 'Abdul Muṭṭalib Khurram Khān Muḥammad Ḥusain Shaikh	*AN*, II, p. 157
March–April	*jāygīr*	Sakit	(Kannauj)		Ibrāhīm Badakhshī	Ibid., p. 163
March–May	*jāygīr*	Birka	(Bet Jalandhar Doab)		Jān Muḥammad Bihsūdī	Ibid., p. 169
July–August	*jāygīr*	Sarut	(Saharanpur)		Mīr Muḥammad Munshī	Ibid., p. 180
„	*shiqdār*	Sarut	(Saharanpur)		Qāsim 'Alī Sīstānī	Ibid., *TA*, p. 159; Bādāunī, II, p. 54
August	*ḥākim*		Mandu		'Abdullāh Khān Uzbek	'Arif, p. 68; Bāyazīd, p. 243; *AN*, II, p. 168; *TA*, II, p. 157
„	*jāygīr*	(*Parganas*)		Malwa	Qayā Khān Gung Shāh Muḥammad Qalātī Ḥabib Khān	*AN*, II, p.168

Date	Nomenclature	Locale			Name	Reference
		Pargana/ Qaṣba	*Sarkār*	*Ṣūba/Vilāyat*		
1563						
January	*jāygīr*	Mama Khatun (Q)	(Kabul)		Tūlak Khān	Ibid., p.184
"	(assignment)	Ghaznin	(Kabul)		Mīrzā Khizr Khān Hazāra	Ibid., p. 186
March	*jāygīr*		Kara		Khwāja 'Abdul Mājid (Aṣaf Khān)	Ibid., p. 182
"	(assignment)	Peshawar	(Kabul)		Ḥamza 'Arab	Bāyazīd, p. 255
"	*ḥākim*		Multan		Muḥammad Qulī Khān Barlās	*AN*, II, p. 187
"	*jāygīrs*	(*Parganas*)	Hisar Firuza		Mun'im Khān	Ibid., p. 189
		"	Etawah			
		"	Khairabad			
		Shahpur	(Karli/Bari Doab)			
		Kalanaur	(Karli/Bari Doab)			
		Jallandhar	(Bet Jallandhar Doab)			
		Indri	(Saharanpur)			
"	(assignment)		Kabul		Ghanī Khān	*TA*, II, p. 162
April–May	*hirāsat*		Chunar		Ḥasan Khān Turkmān	Badāunī, II, p. 63
August	*shiqdār*		Narnaul		Gesū Khān	'Arif, p. 73; *TA*, II, p. 165; Badāunī, II, p. 60

Date	Nomenclature	Locale: Pargana/ Qaṣba	Locale: Sarkār	Locale: Ṣūba/Vilāyat	Name	Reference
1563						
August	*jāgīr*	*Pargana*	(Narnaul)		Khānzāda	*TA*, II, p. 166
,,	*jāygīrs*			Punjab	Mīr Muḥammad Khān Quṭbuddīn Khān Mahdī Qāsim Khān Sharīf Khān Jān Muḥammad Bahsūdī Rājā Kabūr Deo Rāja Ram Chand	*AN*, II, p. 193, Bāyazīd, p. 270
September	*dārāī*	*Pargans*	(Punjab)		Kamāl Khān Ghakkar	Arif, p. 72; *TA*, II, p. 161
,,	*jāgīr*		Ajmer Nagaur		Ḥusain Qulī Beg	*AN*, II, pp. 195–6
,,	(assignment)	Qil'a Merta	(Nagaur)		Jag Mal	*AN*, II, p. 196
,,	*muqarrar shud*		Narnaul		Shujā'at Khān	Ibid., p. 199
,,	(assignment)	Hajipur	(Jodhpur)		Ḥusain Qulī Khān	Badāunī, II, p. 59
,,	*jāgīr*	Ponian	(Hisar Firuza)		Shāh Qurbān	Bāyazīd, p. 278
1563	*ḥākim-i vilāyat*	Danduana	(Nagaur)		Ḥusain Qulī Khān	'Arif, p. 73
,,	*jāgīrdār*	Sahaswan	(Badaun)		Qulīch Chaugān Begī	Badāunī, III, p. 121
1564						
January	*ḥākim*		Delhi		Tātār Khān	Bāyazīd, p. 284

Date	Nomenclature	Locale: *Pargana/ Qaṣba*	Locale: *Sarkār*	Locale: *Ṣūba/Vilāyat*	Name	Reference
1564						
January	*jāgīrdār*	Safadaon	(Delhi)		Nūruddīn Muḥammad Tarkhān	„
March–June	*jāygīrdār*		Kara Bhatta Garah-Katanga		'Abdul Mājid Aṣaf Khān	*AN*, II, p. 209; *TA*, II, p. 170
June–July	*ḥukūmat*		Sarangpur		Muḥammad Qāsim Nishāpurī	*AN*, II, p. 224; *TA*, II, p. 172
July–August	*ḥukūmat*			*Vilayat-i Malwa wa Mandu*	'Abdullāh Khān Uzbek	'Arif, pp. 79–80; *TA*, II, p. 172
„	*guzāshta būd*		Handia		Khān Qulī	*AN*, II, p. 230; *TA*, II, p. 174
„	*jāygīr*		Handia		Muqarrab Khān	„
„	*ḥukūmat*		Mandu		Qara Bahādur	*AN*, II, p. 232; *TA*, II, p. 174
Sept. 1564–March 1565	*ḥukūmat*			Punjab	Mīr Muḥammad Khān (titled Khān-i Kalān)	*AN*, II, p. 239
„	*ḥākim*		Multan		Muḥammad Qulī Khān Barlās	„
„	(assignment)			Punjab	Quṭbuddīn Khān Mahdī Qāsim Khān Ḥasan Ṣūfī Sultān Jān Muḥammad Bihsūdī	„

Date	Nomenclature	Locale: Pargana/ Qaṣba	Locale: Sarkār	Locale: Ṣūba/Vilāyat	Name	Reference
Sept. 1564– March 1565					Kamāl Khān Ghakkar Fāẓil Muḥammad Khān Muḥammad Qulī Khān	
1565 March	*jāgīr*		Jaunpur		'Alī Qulī Khān-i Zamān	*TA*, II, p. 180; Badāunī, II, p. 75
„	*jāygīr*		Awadh		Sikandar Khān Uzbek	'Arif, p. 85; *AN*, II, p. 249; *TA*, II, p. 180; Badāunī, II, p. 75
„	*jāygīr*	Surhurpur	(Jaunpur)		Ibrāhīm Khān Uzbek	*AN*, II, p. 249; *TA*, II, p. 180; Badāunī, II, p. 75
March–June	*ḥukūmat*		Garah-Katanga		'Abdul Mājid Aṣaf Khān	*TA*, II, p. 181
„	*jāgīr*		Kara		'Abdul Mājid Aṣaf Khān	„
June	*jāygīrdār*		Maṇikpur		Majnūn Khān Qāqshāl	*AN*, II, p. 249
„	*jāgīrdārān*			Awadh	Shāham Khān Jalāir Shāh Budagh Khān Amîr Khān Muḥammad Amīn Dīwāna	*AN*, II p. 250

Date	Nomenclature	Locale			Name	Reference
		Pargana/ Qaṣba	*Sarkār*	*Ṣūba/Vilāyat*		
1565 June					Sulṭān Qulī Khāldār Chalma Tawāchī Shāh Ṭāhir Badakhshī Khalilullāh Gadā ʻAlī Tōlkchī Khān Qulī Sārbān Yūsuf Taghāī etc	
„	*jāgīrdār*	Nimkhar	(Khairabad)		Amīr Khān-i Jamīl	Bāyazīd, p. 286
„	(assignment)	Nimkhar	(Khairabad)		Shāh Budāgh Khān	ʻArif, p. 84
September	*jāgīr*		Kara		Khwāja ʻAbdul Mājid Aṣaf Khān	Bāyazīd, p. 287
1566 January	(assignment)		Jaunpur Banaras Ghazipur		Mun'im Khān	Bāyazīd, pp. 294–5
„	(assignment)		Banaras		Bāyazīd Bayāt	„
„	(assignment)	Zamania (Q)	(Ghazipur)		As'adullāh Khān Tabrizī	Bāyazīd, p. 296
January–March	*faujdār*	Samana (Q)	(Sirhind)		Muḥammad Tarkhān	*AN*, II, p. 263
„	*mahāmm-i vilāyat*			Malwa	Shahābuddīn Aḥmad Khān	Ibid., p. 271
March–July	*nāẓim-i ashtāt*		Garaha		Mahdī Qāsim Khān	Ibid., pp. 272, 273

Date	Nomenclature	Locale			Name	Reference
		Pargana/ Qaṣba	*Sarkār*	*Ṣūba/ Vilāyat*		
1566						
March–July	*ta'yin namuda*		Garaha		Shāh Qulī Khān Nāranjī Kākar 'Alī Khān	Ibid., p. 273; Badāunī, II, p. 85
„	*jāygīr*	Azampur	(Sambhal)		Ibrāhīm Ḥusain Mīrzā	Badāunī, II, p. 85
November–December	*shiqdār*		Balda-i Sirhind		Ḥāfiẓ Rakhna	*TA*, II, p. 202
„	*Sarkārdārī*		Sirhind		Ḥāfiẓ Rakhna	„
„	*muntazim mahāmmāt*		Kabul		Mīrzā Farīdūn	*AN*, II, p. 275
1567						
January–March	*ba-kharch-i ma'īshat*	Azampur	(Sambhal)		Muḥammad Sulṭān Mīrzā	Ibid., p. 279
„	*jāygīr*		Sambhal		Ibrāhīm Ḥusain Mīrzā	Ibid., pp. 279–80
„	*jāygīr*	Nihtaur	(Sambhal)		Ulugh Mīrzā Shāh Mīrzā	Badāunī, II, p. 91
„	*jāygīr*	Nimkhar.	(Khairabad)		Yār Shāhī	*AN*, II, p. 280
„	*muqarrar shuda*			Malwa	Muḥammad Qulī Khān Barlās	„
„	*istaḥkām dād*		Ujjain		Khwāja Hādī	„
„	(assignment)		Handia		Qadam Khān	„
„	(assignment)	Satwas (Q)	(Handia)		Muqarrab Khān	„

Date	Nomenclature	Locale			Name	Reference
		Pargana/ Qaṣba	*Sarkār*	*Ṣūba/Vilāyat*		
1567						
Jan.–March	*jāygīr*	Patyali Shamsabad	(Kannauj)		Ḥusain Khān	Bādāunī, II, p. 86
22–3 March	*ḥukūmat w dārāī*			*Vilāyat-i* Punjab	Mīr Muḥammad Khān	'Arif, p. 94; *AN*, II, p. 286; *TA*, II, p. 207
"	*taqsīm namudand*	(*Parganas*)		Punjab	Mīr Muḥammad Khān Quṭbuddīn Khān and their relations	*AN*, II, p. 286
"	*muḥafzat*		Kara Manikpur		'Abdul Mājid Aṣaf Khān Majnūn Khān Qāqshāl	Ibid., p. 283; *TA*, II, p. 207
"	*jāygīr*	Hindaun	(Agra)		Junaid Karārānī	*AN*, II, p. 284
"	*ḥukūmat*		Delhi		Tātār Khan	Ibid., p. 288; *TA*, II, p. 208
"	*jāygīrdār*	Bhojpur (Q)	Delhi		Shahābuddīn Khān Turkmān	Ibid.
March	*jāygīr*	Surhurpur	(Jaunpur)		Ibrāhīm Khān Uzbek	*AN*, II, p. 289
"	*ḥākim*		Kannauj		Mīrzā Yūsuf Khān	'Arif, p. 97; *AN*, II, p. 289; Badāunī, II, p. 94
April–May	*jāygīrdār*		Manikpur		Muḥibb 'Alī Khān	*AN*, II, p. 291
"	*dar qala'*		Manikpur		Majnūn Khān Qāqshāl	'Arif, p. 100
"	*ḥākim*		*Qala-'i* Chunār	Ḥasan Khān	Ibid., p. 106	

Date	Nomenclature	Locale: Pargana/ Qaṣba	Locale: Sarkār	Locale: Ṣūba/Vilāyat	Name	Reference
1567 June	*jāygīr*		Jaunpur Banaras Ghazipur Chunar		Mun'im Khān	'Arif, p. 107; Bāyazīd, p. 299 *AN*, II, 298; *TA*, II, p. 213; Badāunī, II p. 101
"	*jāygīr*		*Qaṣba* Kora		Farḥat Khān	*AN*, II, p. 298
"	*gumashta-i Khān-i Khānān Mun'im Khān*	Zamania	(Ghazipur)		Qāsim Mushkī	Bāyazīd, p. 300; *AN*, II, p. 325
"	*supurdand*	Sultanpur & a few other *parganas* of Ḥasan Khān Bachgoti	(Awadh)		Asadullāh	Bāyazīd, p. 300
July–August	(assignment)		*Qaṣba-i* Etawah		Shujā'at Khān	*AN*, II, p. 298
September	*jāgīr*	Bayana	(Agra)		Ḥājī Muḥammad Khān Sīstānī	*TA*, II p. 215
"	*jāgīr*	Bayana Bhasawar Wazirpur Mandalgarh	(Agra) (Agra) (Agra) (Mewar)		Aṣaf Khān	Ibid.; Badāunī, II, p. 102
"	*jāygīr*		Awadh		Muḥammad Qulī Khān Barlās	*AN*, II, p. 300; *TA*, II, p. 214

		Locale				
Date	Nomenclature	*Pargana/ Qaṣba*	*Sarkār*	*Ṣūba/Vilāyat*	Name	Reference
1567						
September–October	*ḥukūmat wa ḥirāsat*	Qila'-i Siwi Super	(Ranthambhor)		Naẓar Bahādur	*AN*, II, p. 303; *TA*, II, p. 215; Badāunī, II, p. 102
"	*ḥukūmat*	Kota	(Hadauti)		Shāh Muḥammad Khān Qalātī	*AN*, II, p. 303; *TA*, II, p. 215; Badāunī, II, p. 102
September–October	*jāygīrs*			*Vilāyat-i* Malwa	Shahābuddīn Aḥmad Khān Shāh Budagh Khān Murād Khān Ḥājī Muḥammad Khān Sīstānī	*AN*, II, p. 313; *TA*, II, p. 215; Badāunī, II, p. 102
"	*jāygīr*		Gagraun		Aṣaf Khān Wazīr Khān	*AN*, II, p. 313
1568						
January	(assignment)		Rohtas		Muḥibb 'Alī Khān	Bāyazīd, 302
February	*jāgīr*	Daryabad	(Awadh)		L'al Khān Badakhshī	Ibid.
February–March	*makarmat farmud*		Chittor		Khwāja 'Abdul Mājid Aṣaf Khān	*AN*, p. 324; *TA*, II, p. 219

Date	Nomenclature	Locale			Name	Reference
		Pargana/ Qaṣba	*Sarkār*	*Ṣūba/Vilāyat*		
1568						
Feb.–March	*jāygīrdār*		Ujjain		Murād Khān	*AN*, II, p. 330
„	(assignment)	(*Parganas*)	Ujjain		Mīrzā 'Azīz Mashhadī	*TA*, II, p. 222; Badāunī, II, p. 106
„	*ḥākim*	Sironj	(Chanderi)		Shahābuddīn Aḥmad Khān	„
„	*ḥākim*		Sarangpur		Shāh Budāgh Khān	„
August–September	*ḥukūmat*			*Vilāyat-i* Punjab	Ḥusain Qulī Khān Ismā'īl Qulī Khān	*TA*, II, p. 223; Badāunī, II, p. 106
„	*jāygīr*		Sambhal		Mīr Muḥammad Khān-i Kalān	*AN*, II, pp. 332–3; Badāunī, II, p. 106
„	*mukaramat shud*			*Sarkār* Malwa	Quṭbuddīn Muḥammad Khān	*AN*, II, p. 333
„	*makhṣūṣ gasht*		Kannauj		Sharīf Khān	„
June–December	*jāygīr*		Lucknow		Ḥusain Khān	Badāunī, III, p. 18
„	*jāygīr*		Lucknow		Mahdī Qāsim Khān	Ibid., II, p. 125; *AN*, II, p. 336
„	*wajah-i jāygīr*	Kant Gola	(Badaun)		Ḥusain Khān	Badāunī, II, p. 126

Date	Nomenclature	Locale			Name	Reference
		Pargana/ Qaṣba	*Sarkār*	*Ṣūba/Vilāyat*		
1569						
February–March	*jāygīr*	Saronj	(Chanderi)		Shahābuddīn Aḥmad K͟hān	*AN*, II, p. 331
„	*ḥukūmat*		Sarangpur		Shāh Budag͟h K͟hān	Ibid.
21 March	*ḥukūmat w ḥirāsat-i qila'*		Ranthambhor		Mahtar K͟hān	Ibid., p. 338; *TA*, II, p. 224
June–August	*jāgīr*	(*Parganas*)	Kalinjar		Majnūn K͟hān Qāqshāl	*TA*, II, p. 226
„	*muḥāfiẓat w ḥirāsat-i qala'*		Kalinjar		Majnūn K͟hān Qāqshāl	„
„	*jāygīr*	Arail	(Allahabad)		Rāja Rām Chand of Bhatta	Badāunī, II, p. 120
1570						
September	*jāygīrdār*	Pakpattan	(Bet Jalandhar Doab)		Mīrzā 'Azīz Koka, titled K͟hān-i 'Aẓam	Ibid., p. 133
„	(assignment)		Lahore		Ḥusain Qulī K͟hān	Ibid., p. 134
October–November	*ḥukūmat*		Nagaur Ajmer Jodhpur & the frontier of Gujarat		Mīr Muḥammad K͟hān titled K͟hān-i Kalān	'Arif, p. 131; *AN*, II, p. 357

Date	Nomenclature	Locale			Name	Reference
		Pargana/ Qaṣba	*Sarkār*	*Ṣūba/Vilāyat*		
1571						
March–April	*jāygīr*	Dipalpur	(Punjab)		Mīrzā 'Azīz Koka titled Kh̲ān-i A'ẕam	'Arif, p. 132; *AN*, II, p. 363; *TA*, II, p. 232
„	*ḥākim*		Punjab		Ḥusain Qulī Kh̲ān	'Arif, p. 133; *AN*, II, p. 364; *TA*, II, p. 232
„	*ḥākim*		Multan		Sa'īd Kh̲ān Mug̲h̲al	*TA*, II, p. 233; Badāunī, II, p. 134
„	*jāygīr*		Multan		Muḥibb 'Alī Kh̲ān	*TA*, II, p. 233; Badāunī, II, p. 134
1572						
June–July	*jāgīr*		Kh̲iṯṯa-i Lucknow		Sikandar Kh̲ān Uzbek	'Arif, p. 155; *AN*, II, p. 368; Bāyazīd, p. 307; *TA*, II, p. 235
June	*jāgīr*	Saraon	(Manikpur)		Qulīj Kh̲ān	Bāyazīd, p. 307
„	*jāgīr*	Saraon	(Manikpur)		Mun'im Kh̲ān	„

Date	Nomenclature	Locale			Name	Reference
		Pargana/ Qaṣba	*Sarkār*	*Ṣūba/Vilāyat*		
1572						
July–August	*ḥukūmat wa dārāi*		Nagaur Ajmer Jodhpur upto Gujarat frontier		Mīr Muḥammad Khān	'Arif, p. 157
18 September	*jāgīr*		Lucknow		Sikandar Khān Uzbek	'Arif, p. 155; Badāunī, II p. 135
7 November	*maraḥmat farmud*		Patan		'Abdur Raḥīm, titled Mīrzā Khān	*AN*, III, p. 6
„	*shiqdārī*		Patan		Saiyed Aḥmad Khān Bārah	'Arif, p. 159; *AN*, III, p. 6; *TA*, II, p. 238; Badāunī, II, p. 140
December	*ḥukūmat*		Ahmadabad		Mīrzā 'Azīz Koka titled Khān-i A'ẓam	'Arif, p. 162; *AN*, III, p. 8–9; *TA*, II, p. 241; Badāunī, II, p. 164
„	*ḥukūmat*	Bandar Khambayat	(Ahmadabad)		Ḥasan Khān Khazānchī	*AN*, III, p. 11
„	(assignment)			Malwa	Quṭbuddīn Muḥammad Khān	Ibid., p. 18

Date	Nomenclature	Locale			Name	Reference
		Pargana/ Qaṣba	*Sarkār*	*Ṣūba/ Vilāyat*		
1572						
December	*jāygīr*		Kalpi		Shāham K̲h̲ān	Ibid., p. 19
1573						
January	(assignment)	Zamania	(Ghazipur)		Qāsim Muhrdār (same as Qāsim Mushkī)	Ibid., p. 22
"	*ḥirāsat-i qala'*		Patan		Saiyed Aḥmad K̲h̲ān Bārah	Ibid., p. 23; *TA*, II, p. 252
"	(assignment)		Nagaur		Farruk̲h̲ K̲h̲ān	Badāunī, II, p. 150
"	*jāgīrdārs*		Malwa		Quṭbuddīn Muḥammad K̲h̲ān Shāh Budag̲h̲ K̲h̲ān Muṭṭalib K̲h̲ān	*AN*, III, pp. 23–4; Badāunī, II, p. 147
"	(assignment)	Dholqa	(Ahmadabad)		Shaik̲h̲ Muḥammad Buk̲h̲ārī	*AN*, III, p. 24
January–February	*jāgīrdār*		Gorakhpur		Pāyanda Muḥammad Sulṭān Sag-kush	Bāyazīd, p. 314
"	*jāgīrdār*		Ghazipur		Ṭālib Sulṭān	"
"	*jāgīrdār*	Bhadohi	(Allahabad)		Mīrzā Qulī Sulṭān	"
"	*jāgīrdār*	Dostpur	(Jaunpur)		Nadīm Sulṭān	"
February	(assignment)		Gorakhpur		Pāyanda Muḥammad Sulṭān Sag-kush	Ibid., p. 317
February	*jāgīrdār*	Qila'-i Zamania	(Ghazipur)		Qāsim Mushkī	Ibid., p. 318

Date	Nomenclature	Locale: *Pargana/ Qaṣba*	Locale: *Sarkār*	Locale: *Ṣūba/Vilāyat*	Name	Reference
1573						
February	*jāgīr*	Qila'-i Zamania	(Ghazipur)		Muḥammad Kh̲ān	„
February–March	*jāgīr*	Bhojpur Bahia-Jit Ballia	(Rohtas) (Rohtas) (Gorakhpur)		Rāja Gajpatī	Ibid., p. 319
„	*jāgīrdār*	Rae Bareli	(Manikpur)		Nauram Sulṭān Uzbek	Ibid., p. 322
„	(assignment)		Qala'-i Surat		Shuja'at Kh̲ān	„
March–April	*tafwīẓ farmūd*		Ahmadabad		'Azīz Koka	'Arif, p. 173; *AN*, III, p. 33; *TA*, II, p. 253
„	*'anāyat namūd*		Patan		Mīr Muḥammad Kh̲ān-i Kalān	*AN*, III, p. 33; Bāyazīd, p. 334
„	*'anāyat namūd*	 Sultanpur	Baroach Baroda Nandurbar (Nandurbar)		Quṭbuddīn Kh̲ān	*AN*, III, p. 33; Bāyazīd, p. 334
„	*ayālat*		Sargnpur Ujjain	*Vilāyat-i* Malwa	Muẓaffar Kh̲ān	'Arif, p. 173; *AN*, III, p. 33; *TA*, II, p. 253; Badāunī, II, p. 149

Date	Nomenclature	Locale			Name	Reference
		Pargana/ Qaṣba	*Sarkār*	*Ṣūba/Vilāyat*		
1573						
March–April	*jāgīr*		Qala'-i Surat		Qulīj Khān	'Arif, p. 172; Bāyazīd, p. 333; *AN*, III, p. 31; *TA*, II, p. 249
„	*ḥirāsat*		Nagaur		Farrukh Khān	*AN*, III, p. 34
„	*jāygīr*	Sujat	(Jodhpur)		Rāi Rām	„
„	*ḥākim*	Merta	(Nagaur)		Farrukh Khān	*TA*, II, p. 253
„	*jāygīr*	Kant Gola	(Badaun)		Ḥusain Khān	Badāunī, II, p. 151
„	*jāgīrdār*		Sambhal		Mu'īnuddīn Khān Farankhudī	Ibid., p. 153
„	*ṣāhib-i ṣūba w jāygīrdār*			Delhi	Mu'īnuddīn Aḥmad Khān	Ibid., p.154
„	*wajah-i jāygīr*	Nagarkot	(Bari Doab)		Rāja Bīr Bar	*AN*, III, p. 37; *TA*, II, 256
„	*jāygīrdār*	Patiali	(Kannauj)		Ḥusain Khān	*AN*, III, p. 36
„	*ḥākim*			Multan	Sa'īd Khān Chaghta	Ibid., p. 38
June	*ḥākim*			Punjab/ Lahore	Ḥusain Qulī Khān titled Khān-i Jahān	'Arif, p. 163; *AN*, III, p. 40; *TA*, II, p. 254

Date	Nomenclature	Locale: Pargana/ Qaṣba	Locale: Sarkār	Locale: Ṣūba/Vilāyat	Name	Reference
1573						
June	(assignment)		Multan		Sa'īd Khān Chaghta	'Arif, p. 163; Badāunī, II, p. 165
June–August	*ḥākim*		*Qala'-i* Chunar		Ḥasan 'Alī Khān	Bāyazīd, p. 310
„	*jāgīr*	Sanjauli	(Jaunpur)		Sa'adat Yār	Ibid., p. 312
July	*jāygīr*	Idar	(Ahmadabad)		Mīrzā Muqeem	*AN*, III, p. 41
„	*qila'dārī*		Surat		Qulīj Khān	Ibid., p. 42
„	(assignment)		Broach		Quṭbuddīn Aḥmad Khān	Ibid.; *TA*, II, p. 262; Badāunī, II, p. 165
„	*shiqdār*	Khambayat	(Ahmadabad)		Ḥasan Khān Karkarāq	*AN*, III, p. 42; *TA*, II, p. 261
September–October	(assignment)	Dholka Dandhuka	(Ahmadabad) (Ahmadabad)		Wazīr Khān	*TA*, II, p. 273; Badāunī, II, p. 170
„	*ḥukūmat*		Lahore		Ḥusain Qulī Khān titled Khān-i Jahān	*AN*, III, p. 43; *TA*, II, p. 264
„	(assignment)			Punjab	Sa'īd Khān Chaghta	*AN*, III, p. 43
October–November	*jāgīr*	(*Parganas*)		Punjab	Mīrzā Yūsuf Khān Makhṣus Khān	„

		Locale				
Date	Nomenclature	*Pargana/ Qaṣba*	*Sarkār*	*Ṣūba/Vilāyat*	Name	Reference
1573						
August	*jāgīr*	Kachiwara	(?)		Kunwar Mān Singh	"
October–November	*ḥukūmat*		Patan		Mīr Muḥammad Khān-i Kalān	Ibid., p. 64; *TA*, II, p. 273; Badāunī, II, p. 170
"	*wajah-i jāgīr*	Dholka Dandhuka	(Ahmadabad) (Ahmadabad)		Wazīr Khān	*AN*, III, p. 64
"	*ḥukūmat*	Deesa	(Patan)		Shāh 'Alī Langāh	Ibid.; *TA*, II, p. 266
"	*dar an sar zamīn guzāshtand*		Sirohi		Ṣādiq Khān	*AN*, III, p. 65
"	*jāgīr*	Harba (Q)	Ajmer		Rām Dās Kachwāha	*TA*, II, p. 274
November	*ḥukūmat*		Sarangpur		Muẓaffar Khān	Ibid., p. 276; Badāunī, II, p. 171
1573	*ḥākim*		Dehli		Ṭayab Khān	*TA*, II, p. 266
1574						
March	*jāygīr*		Saran		Ḥasan Khān Batanī	*AN*, III, pp. 82–3
May–June	*ḥirāsat*		Agra		Shahābuddīn Aḥmad Khān	Badāunī, II, p. 175
"	*jāgīrdār*	Chekur (Q)	(Manikpur)		Bābā Khān Qāqshāl	*TA*, II, p. 285

Date	Nomenclature	Locale: Pargana/ Qaṣba	Locale: Sarkār	Locale: Ṣūba/Vilāyat	Name	Reference
1574						
July–August	*jāgīr*	Kant Gola	(Badaun)		Ḥusain Khān	Badāunī, II, p. 179
„	*ḥākim*	Bayana	(Agra)		Saiyed ‘Abdullāh Khān Chaugān Begī	Ibid., p. 180
21 August	*jāygīr*			Jaunpur (V)	Mun‘im Khān	*AN*, III, p. 103
„	*wazārat*		Jaunpur Banaras Chunar etc.		Mīrzā Mīrak Riẓvī Ibrāhīm Sikrīwāl	‘Arif, p. 194; *AN*, III, p. 103; *TA*, II, p. 296; Badāunī, II, p. 182
July–October	*jāgīr*	Jhusi Payag	(Allahabad)		Niyābat Khān	Ibid., p. 289
„	(assignment)		Patna Bihar		Mun‘im Khān	‘Arif, p. 193
„	*jāgīr*		Khiṭṭa-i Hajipur		Muḥammad Qulī Khān Barlās	Ibid.; Bāyazīd, p. 341
July–October	(assignment)		Rohtas		Farḥat Khān	‘Arif, p. 194; Badāunī, II, p. 182
August	*ḥākim*		Patna		Muḥsin Khān	Bāyazīd, p. 347
„	(assignment)		Ghoraghat		Majnūn Khān Qāqshāl Bābā Khān Qāqshāl	Ibid., p. 341
„	*dādand*		Tirhut		Khān-i A‘lam	„
„	*‘ināyat kardand*	Khalgaon	(Monghyr)		Wazīr Khān-i Jamīl	„

Date	Nomenclature	Locale: Pargana/ Qaṣba	Locale: Sarkār	Locale: Ṣūba/ Vilāyat	Name	Reference
1574						
August	(assignment)		Sonargaon		Saiyed Khān Tōghpāī	„
„	(assignment)	Burdwan	(Sharifabad)		Qayā Khān	„
„	*'ināyat kardand*		Satgaon		Tukhta Alabam	„
October	*muḥāfiẓat*		*Qala'-i* Bhakkar		Mīr Gesū	'Arif, p. 200; *TA*, II, p. 301
October–November	*jāygīr*	Kant Gola	(Badaun)		Ḥusain Khān	*AN*, III, p. 110
1575						
January	(assignment)		Lucknow		Khwāja Amīna titled Khwāja Jahān	Badāunī, II, p. 186
January–March	*jāgīr*	*Parganas*		(Bengal)	Mun'im Khān	Bāyazīd, p. 342; *AN*, III, p. 116
„	*ba ṭarīq-i dar bast-i wajah-i julduī*		Chunar		Mun'im Khān	Ibid., pp. 312, 341–2
„	*jāgīr*	(*Parganas*)	Chunar		Bāyazīd Bayāt	Ibid., p. 250
„	(assignment)		Ghoraghat		Majnūn Khān Qāqshāl	'Arif, p. 204; *TA*, II, p. 303
„	*ḥukūmat*		Ahmadabad		Mīrzā 'Azīz Koka	'Arif, p. 204
April–May	*tuyūl*			Orissa	Dāud Karārānī	*AN*, III, p. 131
June	(assignments)		Patna Bihar		Mun'im Khān	Ibid., p. 133

Date	Nomenclature	Locale			Name	Reference
		Pargana/ Qaṣba	*Sarkār*	*Ṣūba/Vilāyat*		
1575						
June	*jāgīr*	Sasaram	(Rohtas)		Muẕaffar K͟hān	Bāyazīd, p. 348
"	*jāgīrdār*		Ghazipur		Ṭālib Sulṭān	Ibid., p. 347
"	*jāgīr*		Bihar		Tangar Qulī Sulṭān	"
16 July	*jāygīr*	Merta	(Ajmer)		Kala s/o Ram Rai	*AN*, III, p. 159
August–September	*ḥākim*			Punjab	K͟hān-i Jahān	*TA*, II, p. 316
June–October	*iyālat*	Thanesar	(Sirhind)		Malik Ashraf	*AN*, III, p. 142
September–October	*ḥākim*		Lahore		B͟hagwān Dās	*TA*, II, p. 315; Badāunī, II, p. 214
October	*jāgīr*	Tajpur	(Tirhut)		K͟hwāja Muḥammad Zakariyā	Bāyazīd, p. 351
8 October	(assignment)		Ahmadabad		'Azīz Koka titled K͟hān-i A'ẓam	*TA*, II, p. 315
October–November	*tuyūl*		Hajipur		Muḥammad Qulī K͟hān	*AN*, III, p. 136
"	*ḥukūmat*		Hajipur		Muẕaffar K͟hān	'Arif, p. 210; *AN*, III, p. 136
"	(assignment)		Hajipur		Mīr Muḥammad Shaūkatī	"
"	*ḥākim*			Punjab	K͟hān-i Jahān	Badāunī, II, p. 216

Date	Nomenclature	Locale			Name	Reference
		Pargana/ Qaṣba	*Sarkār*	*Ṣūba/Vilāyat*		
1575						
Oct.–Nov.	*mutaṣaraf shud*		*Qila'-i* Chunar		Bāyazīd Bayāt	Bāyazīd, 352
„	*karorī*		Jaunpur		Mīrzā Mirak	„
„	*ḥukūmat*			Bangala	K̲h̲ān-i Jahān	*TA*, II, p. 319; Badāunī, II, p. 218
„	*iyālat*		Bhakkar		Mīr Saiyed Muḥammad *Mīr-i 'adl*	*AN*, III, p. 158
4 November	*jāygīr*		Garaha		Rāī Surjan	„
„	*jāygīr*		Garaha		Ṣādiq K̲h̲ān	„
„	*jāygīr*		Chunar		Rāī Surjan	„
November–December	*ḥākim*		Patan		Mīr Muḥammad K̲h̲ān-i Kalān	'Arif, p. 206
1576						
March	*ḥukūmat*		Surat		Qulīj K̲h̲ān	*TA*, II, p. 319
March–April	*ḥākim*		Patna		Muẓaffar K̲h̲ān	Badāunī, II, p. 230
May–June	*ḥākim*	Sambhar	(Ajmer)		Rājā Lon Karaṇ	Ibid., p. 231
„	*jāygīrdār*	Arrah	(Rohtas)		Farḥat K̲h̲ān	*AN*, III, p. 169
„	(assignment)		Ghazipur		K̲h̲ān-i Jahān	Ibid., p. 170
August–September	(assignment)	Arrah	(Rohtas)		Farḥat K̲h̲ān	Badāunī, II, p. 237

Date	Nomenclature	Locale			Name	Reference
		Pargana/ Qaṣbā	*Sarkār*	*Ṣūba/Vilāyat*		
1576						
September–October	*iyālat*		Patan		Tarsūn Khān	*AN*, III, p. 190
December	(assignment)		Ujjain		Bāyazīd Bayāt	Bāyazīd, p. 353
December–January 1577	(assignment)		Rohtas		Shahbāz Khān	‘Arif, p. 221
„	(assignment)		Rohtas		Muḥibb ‘Alī Khān	Ibid., p. 222
„	*jāygīrdār*	Ishhar	Rohtas		Muḥammad M‘aṣūm Kābulī	Ibid., pp. 222, 223
„	(assignment)	Islampur Mohi	(Chittor)		Ghāzī Khān	Badāunī, II, p. 242
„	(assignment)	Madaria	(Chittor)		‘Abdur Raḥmān Beg	Ibid.
1577						
February–March	*ḥukūmat*		Bhakkar		Mīr Saiyed Muḥammad, *Mīr-i ‘Adl*	Ibid., p. 245
„	(assignment)	Siwi	(Bhakkar)		Mīr Saiyed Abū’l Faẓl	„
„	(assignment)	–		Malwa	Shahābuddīn Aḥmad Khān	Ibid., pp. 241–2
March–April	(assignment)		Sarangpur		Shahābuddīn Aḥmad Khān	Ibid., p. 353
„	(assignment)		Ahmadabad		Shahābuddīn Aḥmad Khān	„
„	(assignment)		Sarangpur		Bāyazīd Bayāt	Bāyazīd, p. 353
„	*jāgīr*		Sarangpur		Shujā‘at Khān	„

Date	Nomenclature	Locale: Pargana/ Qaṣba	Locale: Sarkār	Locale: Ṣūba/ Vilāyat	Name	Reference
1577						
April–May	*jāygīr*		Baroach Baroda		Quṭbuddīn Muḥammad Khān	Badāunī, II, p. 250
„	*faūjdārī*	Bareilly	(Badaun)		Deep Chand Manjhula	„
„	*ḥākim*			Gujarat (V)	Wazīr Khān	Ibid., p. 249
June–July	*iyālat*			*Ṣūba-i* Ajmer	Dastām Khān	*AN*, III, p. 210
„	*tuyūl*		Ranthambhor		Dastām Khān	„
August–September	*iyālat*			Multan	Saiyed Ḥāmid	*AN*, III, p. 213
September	*ṭhānedārī*	Islampur Mohi	(Chittor)		Mujāhid Beg	Ibid., p. 216
October–November	*iyālat*			Malwa	Shahābuddīn Aḥmad Khān	Ibid., pp. 217–18
„	*iyālat*			Gujarat (V)	Shahābuddīn Aḥmad Khān	Ibid., p. 218
„	(assignment)	Idar	(Ahmadabad)		Wazīr Khān	„
„	(assignments)			Malwa	Qāsim Khān Ṭāhir Khān Naqīb Khān Qamar Khān Fīrūz Shaikh M'uazzam Shaikh Junaid	„

Date	Nomenclature	Locale: Pargana/ Qaṣba	Locale: Sarkār	Locale: Ṣūba/ Vilāyat	Name	Reference
1577						
13 November	*muqarrar gasht*		Bihar		Shujā'at Khān Mīr Mu'izzul Mulk	Ibid., p. 227
November–December	*shafqat kardand*		Sarangpur		Shujā'at Khān	'Arif, p. 233
"	*ḥukūmat*			Gujarat (V)	Quṭbuddīn Muḥammad Khān Shihāb Khān	"
"	*shafqat kardand*		Ujjain Mandu		Shāh Fakhruddīn Khān Shāh Budāgh Khān	"
1578						
5 January	(assignment)		Hisar Firuza		Mehr 'Alī Khān Silduz	Ibid., p. 232
January	(assignment)	Thara/ Pathaura	(Bari Doab)		Chaman Qulī the *Qush-begī*	Ibid., p. 235
March–April	*ḥukūmat*			Punjab	Sa'īd Khān	Badāunī, II, p. 254
2 May	*ḥukūmat*		Dehli		Muḥibb 'Alī Khān	*AN*, III, p. 248; Badāunī, II, p. 276
May	*ḥākim*			Gujarat	Wazīr Khān	*TA*, II, p. 322
"	(assignment)		Nandurbar		Bāz Bahādur s/o Sharīf Khān	"
1 December	(assignment)			Punjab	Rājā Bhagwant Dās Jagannāth Rājā Gopāl Jag Mal Panwār	*AN*, III, p. 262

Date	Nomenclature	Locale: Pargana/ Qaṣba	Locale: Sarkār	Locale: Ṣūba/Vilāyat	Name	Reference
1579						
February–March	*ḥukūmat*			Bangala	Muzaffar Khān	‘Arif, p. 246
June–December	(assignment)		Sarangpur		Shujā‘at Khān	Badāunī, II, p. 284
September	(assignment)			Ajmer	Dastam Khān	*AN*, III, p. 326
September–October	*ḥākim*		Patan		Tarsūn Muḥammad Khān	Badāunī, II, p. 274
„	*ḥukūmat*		Jaunpur		M‘aṣūm Khān Farankhūdī	Ibid., pp. 276, 282
„	*ḥākim*		Kalpi		Qāsim ‘Alī Khān Baqqāl	Ibid., p. 282
„	*ḥākim*		Rohtas		Muḥibb ‘Alī Khān	„
„	(assignment)		*Qila‘-i* Patna		Bahār Khān Khāṣa Khail	Ibid., p. 283
„	(assignment)			Malwa	Sharīf Khān Atka	Ibid., p. 285
„	*tuyūldārī*		Jalesar		Khāldīn Khān	*AN*, III, p. 292
„	(assignment)		Jalesar		Mīr Jamāluddīn Ḥusain Anjū	„
November–December	*tuyūl*		Etawa		Zain Khān Kōka	Ibid., p. 278
1580						
February–March	(assignment)		Khitta-i Jaunpur		Ma‘ṣūm Khān Farankhūdī	Ibid., p. 281
„	(assignment)		Ghazipur		Ma‘ṣūm Khān Farankhūdī	„

Date	Nomenclature	Locale: Pargana/ Qaṣba	Locale: Sarkār	Locale: Ṣūba/Vilāyat	Name	Reference
1580						
Feb.–March	(assignment)		Khiṭṭa-i Jaunpur		Tarsūn Muḥammad Khān	"
"	*iqṭā'*			Orissa	M'aṣūm Kābulī	"
"	*iqṭā'*		Patna		M'aṣūm Kābulī	Ibid., p. 285
"	*jāygīrdār*	Sasaram	(Rohtas)		Sa'īd Beg Bakhshī	"
"	(assignment)	Nanor	(Rohtas)		Sa'ādat 'Alī	"
"	*tuyūl*	Dilwara	(Tajpur)		Ḥājī Kōlābī	"
"	(assignment)		Tirhut		Sa'īd Khān Bakhshī Bahādūr s/o Sa'īd Khān Durvesh 'Alī Sanjar	"
"	*jāygīrdār*		Hajipur		Shāham	"
"	*dashtand*	Arrah	(Rohtas)		Mīr Muizul Mulk Mīr Akbar 'Alī Samājī Khān	"
"	*iqṭa'dārān*	Khiṭṭa-i Baksar	(Rohtas)		Kamāluddīn Ḥusain Sīstānī Saiyed Ḥasan Dūd Rāj	Ibid., p. 287
"	*jāgīrdār*			Awadh Allahabad	Tarsūn Khān M'aṣūm Khān Farankhūdī Ghāzī Khān Badakhshī Rai Surjan & others	"
May	*ḥukūmat*			Bangala	A'ẓam Koka titled Khān-i A'ẓam	Ibid., p. 308; Badāunī, II, p. 285

Date	Nomenclature	Locale			Name	Reference
		Pargana/ Qaṣba	*Sarkār*	*Ṣūba/Vilāyat*		
1580						
January–June	(assignment)		Manikpur		As'ad Khān Turkmān	*AN*, III, p. 309
June–July	(assignment)	(*Pargana*)		Malwa	Sharīf Khān	Ibid., p. 314
August–September	*iqṭā'dārān*			Ajmer	Pāyanda Muḥammad Khān Saiyed Hāshim Saiyed Qāsim	Ibid., p. 318
"	*iqṭā'*		Patan		I'timād Khān Gujarātī	"
"	*tuyūl*		Fathabad	(Bangala)	Murād Khān	Ibid., p. 320
September–October	(assignment)	Qila'-i Kant (Q)	(Rohtas)		Sa'ādat 'Alī Pāyand Rustam Rūp Narāyan Būmī	Ibid., p. 324
October–November	*jāgīr*		Sarangpur		Shāham Khān	"
"	(assignment)		Ḥājīpūr		'Azīz Koka	Ibid., p. 325
"	(assignment)		Patna		Shāhbāz Khān	"
"	*intiẓām*			Ajmer	'Abdur Raḥīm	Ibid., p. 327
"	*iqṭā'*		Ranthambour		'Abdur Raḥīm	"
"	*bungāh*	Boni	(Ranthambour)		Achla s/o Balabdhar	Ibid., p. 326
November–December	(assignment)		Kara		Ism'aīl Qulī Khān	Ibid., p. 328; Badāunī, II, p.289

Date	Nomenclature	Locale			Name	Reference
		Pargana/ Qaṣba	*Sarkār*	*Ṣūba/Vilāyat*		
1580						
Nov.–Dec.	*ḥākim*		Kara		Iliyās	„
„	*jāygīr*	Jhusi Payag	(Allahabad) (Allahabad)		Niyābat Khān	„
„	*jāygīr*		Awadh		Ma'ṣūm Khān Farankhūdī	*AN*, III, p. 330
„	(assignment)		Jaunpur		Tarsūn Khān	Badāunī, II, p. 289
„	*iqṭā'dār*		Sind Sagar Doab		Mīrzā Yūsuf	*AN*, III, p. 336
„	(assignment)	Sialkot	(Rachna o Doab)		Mān Singh	„
November–December	(assignment)		Sind Sagar Doab		Mān Singh	„
„	(assignment)	Safadun	(Hisar Firuza)		Mullāh Nūruddīn Muḥammad Tarkhān	Badāunī, III, p. 199
„	*gumashtagān-i* Man Singh	Nilab	(Sind Sagar Doab)		Zainuddīn 'Alī and others	*AN*, III, p. 336
„	(assignment)	Bhera Rohtas	(Channat Doab) (Sind Sagar Doab		Muḥibb 'Alī Khān	Ibid., p. 324

APPENDIX II

Frequency of Different Terms used for Assignment
(based upon Appendix I)

	jāgīr	*tuyūl*	*iqṭā'*	*bungāh*	*ḥākim*	*shiqdār*	*faujdār*	*thānedār*	*dīwān*	*gumāshta*	Other terms and vague expressions	Total
1556	4	—	—	—	3	—	—	—	—	—	16	23
1557	3	—	—	—	1	—	—	—	—	—	2	6
1558	5	—	—	—	—	—	—	—	—	—	2	7
1559	1	—	—	—	1	—	—	—	—	—	4	6
1560	9	—	—	—	6	—	—	—	1	—	10	26
1561	6	—	—	—	3	—	—	—	—	—	7	16
1562	7	—	—	—	2	1	—	—	—	—	—	10
1563	8	—	—	—	2	1	—	—	—	—	8	19
1564	3	—	—	—	6	—	—	—	—	—	2	11
1565	8	—	—	—	1	—	—	—	—	—	1	10
1566	1	—	—	—	—	1	1	—	—	—	8	11
1567	15	—	—	—	6	—	—	—	—	1	10	32
1568	6	—	—	—	4	—	—	—	—	—	5	15
1569	3	—	—	—	3	—	—	—	—	—	—	6
1570	1	—	—	—	1	—	—	—	—	—	1	3

Appendix II continued

	jāgīr	*tuyūl*	*iqṭā'*	*bungāh*	*ḥākim*	*shiqdār*	*faujdār*	*thānedār*	*dīwān*	*gumāshta*	Other terms and vague expressions	TOTAL
1571	2	—	—	—	2	—	—	—	—	—	—	4
1572	5	—	—	—	3	1	—	—	—	—	2	11
1573	22	—	—	—	9	1	—	—	—	—	17	49
1574	7	—	—	—	2	—	—	—	—	—	11	20
1575	10	2	—	—	7	—	—	—	—	—	10	29
1576	2	—	—	—	3	—	—	—	—	—	8	13
1577	2	1	—	—	3	—	1	1	—	—	15	23
1578	—	—	—	—	3	—	—	—	—	—	4	7
1579	—	2	—	—	5	—	—	—	—	—	5	12
1580	6	2	6	1	2	—	—	—	—	1	18	36

APPENDIX III

Transfers of Assignments During 1556–75

I. Assignments held by thirteen leading nobles at different points of time

Date		Locale
MUN'IM <u>KH</u>ĀN		
March	1556	Kabul-wa-Ghazni
December	1560	Hisar Firuza
April	1561	Hisar Firuza
March	1563	[*Parganas*] Hisar Firuza
		„ Etawah
		„ Khairabad
		Shahpur [Karli/Bari Doab]
		Kalanaur [Karli/Bari Doab]
		Jallandhar [Bet-Jallandhar Doab]
		Indri [Saharanpur]
January	1566	Jaunpur
		Banaras
		Ghazipur
June	1567	Jaunpur
		Banaras
		Ghazipur
		Chunar
June	1572	Saraon [Manikpur]
August	1574	Jaunpur
July–October	1574	Patna
		Bihar
January–March	1575	[*Parganas*] Bengal
January–March	1575	Chunar
June	1575	Patna
		Bihar
'ALĪ QULĪ <u>KH</u>ĀN		
March	1556	Sambhal
November	1556	Sambhal
March–September	1559	Lucknow
March–September	1559	Jaunpur

Date		Locale
'ALĪ QULĪ K̲H̲ĀN *continued*		
December	1560	Jaunpur Banaras Ghazipur
August	1561	Jaunpur
March	1565	Jaunpur
SIKANDAR K̲H̲ĀN UZBEK		
March	1556	Agra
September–October	1556	Agra
December	1556	Sialkot [Rachnao Doab]
March	1565	Awadh
September	1572	Lucknow
'ABDULLĀH K̲H̲ĀN UZBEK		
March	1556	Kalpi
November	1556	Kalpi
December	1560	Kalpi
March	1561	Kalpi
August	1562	Mandu
July–August	1564	Malwa-wa-Mandu
QAYĀ K̲H̲ĀN GUNG		
March	1556	Kol-wa-Jalali
September–October	1556	Etawah
November	1556	Agra
April–May	1560	Bahraich
March	1561	Handia
August	1562	[*Parganas*] Malwa
August	1574	Burdwan (Sharifabad)
ḤAIDAR MUḤAMMAD K̲H̲ĀN		
March	1556	Bayana
September–October	1556	Bayana
May	1560	Kabul

Date		Locale
MAJNŪN KHĀN QĀQSHĀL		
March	1556	Narnaul
May	1561	[*Parganas*] Jaunpur and the eastern *sarkārs* in general
March	1567	Manikpur
April–May	1567	Manikpur
June–August	1569	Kalinjar
August	1574	Ghoraghat
January–March	1575	Ghoraghat
MAHDĪ QASIM KHĀN		
November	1556	Delhi
August	1563	[*Parganas*] Punjab
March	1565	[*Parganas*] Punjab
March–July	1566	Garaha
June–December	1568	Lucknow
MUHAMMAD QULĪ KHĀN BARLĀS		
March	1557	Multan
March	1557	Nagaur
August–September	1560	Multan
March	1563	Multan
March	1565	Multan
January–March	1567	Malwa
September	1567	Awadh
July–October	1574	Hajipur
BAHĀDUR KHĀN UZBEK		
March	1557	Multan
March–September	1559	Dipalpur
January–March	1561	Etawah
January–March	1561	Banaras

Date		Locale
SHAHĀBUDDĪN AḤMAD KHĀN		
March	1560	Delhi
January–March	1566	Malwa
February–March	1568	Saronj (Chanderi)
February–March	1569	Saronj (Chanderi)
MĪR MUḤAMMAD KALĀN		
March	1560	Lahore
August	1563	Punjab
March	1565	Punjab
March	1567	Punjab
August–September	1568	Sambhal
October–November	1570	Nagaur
		Ajmer
		Jodhpur
July–August	1572	Nagaur
		Ajmer
		Jodhpur
March–April	1573	Patan
October–November	1573	Patan
November–December	1575	Patan
ḤUSAIN QULĪ KHĀN		
September	1563	Hajipur (Jodhpur)
September	1563	Danduana (Nagaur)
August–September	1568	Punjab
September	1570	Lahore
March–April	1571	Punjab
September–October	1573	Punjab
October–November	1575	Bangala

II. Nobles holding *sarkārs* Multan, Etawah, Narnaul, Kalpi and Sambhal as assignments

Date	Nomenclature for Assignment or Assignee	Assignee	Reference
Sarkār Multan			
March 1557	*jāgīr*	Muḥammad Qulī Khān Barlās	*AN*, II, p. 53
March 1557	(assignment)	Bahādur Khān Uzbek	Ibid.
Aug.–Sept. 1560	*jāygīr*	Muḥammad Qāsim Nishāpurī	*AN*, II, pp. 114–15
March 1563	*ḥākim*	Muḥammad Qulī Khān Barlās	*AN*, II, p. 187
Sept. 1564–March 1566	*ḥākim*	Muḥammad Qulī Khān Barlās	*AN*, II, p. 239
March–April 1571	*jāygīr*	Muḥibb 'Alī Khān	*TA*, II, p. 233
March–April 1571	*ḥākim*	Sa'īd Khān Chaghta	Ibid.
March–April 1573	*ḥākim*	Sa'īd Khān Chaghta	*AN*, III p. 38
June 1573	(assignment)	Sa'īd Khān Chaghta	'Arif, p. 163
Sept.–Oct. 1573	(assignment)	Sa'īd Khān Chaghta	*AN*, III, p. 43
Sarkār Etawah			
Sept.–Oct. 1556	*ḥākim*	Qayā Khān Gung	Badāunī, II, p. 13
1558	*jāgīr* (*pargana* Hatkant)	Adham Khān	*AN*, II, p. 78
Aug.–Sept. 1560	*jāygīr*	Bahādur Khān Uzbek	*AN*, II, p. 115

Appendix III *continued*...

Date	Nomenclature for Assignment or Assignee	Assignee	Reference
Jan.–March 1561	(assignment)	Bahādur K͟hān Uzbek	Bayāzid, p. 244
March 1563	*jāgīr* (*parganas*)	Mun'im K͟hān	*AN*, II, p. 189
July–August 1567	(assignment)	Shujā'at K͟hān	*AN*, II, p. 298
Sarkār Narnaul			
March 1556	*jāgīr*	Majnūn K͟hān Qāqshāl	*AN*, II, p. 20
August 1563	*jāgīr* (*parganas*)	K͟hānzāda	*TA*, II, p. 166
August 1563	*shiqdār*	Gesū K͟hān	'Arif, p. 73
September 1563	*maqarrar shud*	Shujā'at K͟hān	*AN*, II, p. 199
Sarkār Kalpi			
March 1556	*ba-sardārī*	'Abdullāh K͟hān Uzbek	*AN*, II, p. 14
Sept.–Oct. 1556	(assignment)	'Abdullāh K͟hān Uzbek	Badāunī, II, p. 13
November 1556	*ikhtiṣāṣ bak͟hshidand*	'Abdullāh K͟hān Uzbek	*AN*, III, p. 45
1560	*ḥukūmat*	'Abdullāh K͟hān Uzbek	Badāunī, III, p. 6

Appendix III *continued...*

Date	Nomenclature for Assignment or Assignee	Assignee	Reference
Sarkār Kalpi			
March 1561	*jāygīr*	'Abdullāh Khān Uzbek	*AN*, II, p. 138
August 1561	*ḥākim*	'Abdullāh Khān Uzbek	Badāunī, II, p. 49
December 1572	*jāygīr*	Shaham Khān	*AN*, III, p. 19
Sarkār Sambhal			
March 1556	*niẓām-i sarkār*	'Ali Qulī Khān Uzbek	*AN*, II, p. 14
November 1566	(assignment)	'Alī Qulī Khān Uzbek	*Arif*, p. 52
March–July 1566	*jāygīr* (*pargana* Azampur)	Ibrāhim Ḥusain Mīrzā	Badāunī, II, p. 85
Jan.–March 1567	*bakhарch-i ma'īshat* (*pargana* Azampur)	Muḥammad Sulṭān Mīrzā	*AN*, II, p. 279
Jan.–March 1567	*jāygīr*	Ibrāhīm Ḥusain Mīrzā and brothers	*AN*, II, pp. 279–80
Jan.–March 1567	*jāygīr* (*pargana* Nihtaur)	Ulugh Mīrzā & Shāh Mīrzā	Badāunī, II, p. 91
Aug.–Sept. 1568	*jāygīr*	Mīr Muḥammad Khān-i Kalān	*AN*, III, pp. 332–3
March–April 1573	*jāgīrdār*	Moinuddīn Khān Farankhudī	Badāunī, II, p. 153

5

Political Structures of the Islamic Orient in the Sixteenth and Seventeenth Centuries[1]

M. ATHAR ALI

It is possible to place the four major empires of Asia, apart from China, during the sixteenth and seventeenth centuries into a single category according to three distinct and separate modes of classification. First of all, the Ottomans (West Asia), the Safavids (Iran), the Uzbeks (Central Asia), and the Mughals (India) can be seen as belonging to the category of Islamic states; and Islam (and the law, polity and culture historically associated with it) can be regarded as one of the distinguishing features of this class of states. Secondly, one may adopt, with François Bernier, the frankly Eurocentric view that these states shared among themselves a negative characteristic, namely, they lacked the merits of European law and polities, especially full-scale private property in land. Finally, there is the classification which flows from the question asked by Marx: Was there something common to these state-systems that inhibited their societies from growing into capitalism? So stated, these classifications appear simplistic, even banal; I propose to show, however, that studies on the lines opened by these simple questions can nevertheless give us insights, just as they also compel us to offer many qualifications and even reservations to the standard theories.

The Islamic associations of the four empires are so obvious that one need not labour the point. The crucial question is whether Islam was a substratum or only a veneer. It must be admitted that

[1] Presented at a Colloquium, Woodrow Wilson International Centre for Scholars, Washington, D.C., June 1986. Research for this was completed under a Fellowship at the Wilson Centre.

these states set out to enforce the *Sharia* (the Muslim civil and criminal law), as it was understood by the school that carried official sanction—any of the four schools of jurists among Sunnis in three of the four empires, while Ṣafavid Irān followed the *Sharia* as interpreted by the Shi'ite theologians. By and large, it gave a universal civil and criminal law (with only minor shades of differences) to all these countries. The Qazi, however corrupt and however frequently the butt of ridicule, yet represented a unique legal universality over a region extending from the Bay of Bengal to the Atlantic. Conversely, this universality meant that, however absolute, the state lacked the power to legislate. The Tudor monarchy, with its control over Parliament and its legislation, was thus surely far more absolute or despotic than any Great Mughal.

The *Sharia* not only delimited the sovereignty of the state in this crucial manner; it also tended to define more positively how this could be constituted. During the first two centuries after the death of the Prophet (AD 632), the concept of the Khilāfat (Caliphate) had taken shape, based not on the Quran,[2] but on the political history of Islam during the period. The institution of the Caliphate, as it decayed after the ninth century, became more and more the object of theological or scholarly definition (as in Māwardī): who could be a Caliph and what the Caliph could or could not do would be rigorously laid down. As the Caliph's place came to be taken increasingly by kings (Sultans), the latter could be visualized as deputies of the Caliphs, so to speak; if so, they could not have any powers which the Caliph did not enjoy. At best, Muslim rulers could begin claiming to be Caliphs themselves as was done by the Ottomans and, more indifferently, by the Mughals. Only the Safavids claimed a distinctly higher position—that of the representative of the *Imam*. But when Akbar, the Mughal Emperor, in 1579 obtained from his doctors a declaration (*maḥẓar*) that he could sit in judgement over various interpretations of Muslim law, this created much indignation among the devout and helped to bring about a revolt which almost shook his throne.

Nonetheless, it is true that political tradition within Islam too was of historical growth, and the powers and pretensions—and

[2] Except for one verse asking the faithful to 'obey God, His Prophet and those in authority among you', the Quran has almost nothing to offer on the nature and functions of sovereignty.

not only the nominal titles of the Sultans—grew with time. Other traditions like the ancient Iranian, the Turkic and Mongol were either invoked or absorbed, and it is possible to say that the Sultans after Timur took the Mongol Khāns rather than the Sāmānids for their models. This brings me to the consideration of another important strand in the political and social history of the Islamic world—the conflict between nomadism and civilization.

If one looks at the physical map of the Old World, one finds starting from China north of the Great Wall, a huge band of steppe and desert generally heading west, while tending slightly to the south. The Gobi and Takla Makan Deserts turn into the arid grasslands of central Asia and southern Russia, after the band crosses the Tienan Shan Range. Sweeping across Iran with its waterless plateau, it encompasses the Arabian desert; and, then, across the Red Sea and the Nile, the great Sahara, dividing Africa into two. In this brief description we have not been able to list the many smaller deserts and steppes identified and named by the geographers. Suffice it to say that this vast waterless band with deserts and grasslands, has been the largest known reservoir of nomadic peoples. As it cut right across the Islamic world it made it consist essentially of deserts and oases, the biggest of the latter being the Fertile Cresent (Egypt, Syria, and Iraq), followed closely by Mavraunnahar (itself divided into the three 'Oases' of Ferghana, the Zarafshan valley and Khwarizm or Khiva).

The two regions which offer exceptions to this infestation of steppe and desert are India and the Balkans, both of which were brought under the ambit of Islam in the secondary phase of its expansion (after the twelfth century); their populations also remained non-Muslim in the larger part. For the history of the core-area of the Islamic world, in general, the nomad-city syndrome seems to set the red thread; and it is the particular virtue of Ibn Khaldūn, the great historian of the fourteenth century, to have perceived this fact and to have built a theory of historical development on its basis.[3]

Historians often see the steppe element as a dynamic source of much of Islamic polity. The Arabs themselves were, after all, desert nomads. Founders of all the dynasties of the four empires we are concerned with here, the Ottomans (from Seljuqs), the Uzbeks

[3] Cf. Muhsin Mahdi, *Ibn Khaldun*'s *Philosophy of History*, Chicago, 1964, pp. 193 ff.

(from Mongols of the Golden Horde) and the Mughals (from the Chaghtāi Horde) had steppe ancestors; and Ismā'īl, the founder of the Ṣafavid dynasty, had his following initially among the Turkoman nomads, so that Turkish remained for long the language of the Ṣafavid court. It is easy, as we look closer, to drill holes in this generalization. Paul Wittek[4] has already shown that the impulse behind the rise of the Ottoman State even in its earliest phase was not of nomadic origin, but lay in a combination of the Ghāzi tradition with the conditions of government associated with Higher Islam. The Mughal Empire in India certainly displayed no feature that could be identified as direct importations from nomadism.

Going beyond this, even the widespread attribution of the origins of Islam and its success as one of great nomadic movements needs qualification. The Prophet himself was not a nomad but a merchant of the Quraish tribe, which was a settled community of the Arabian peninsula's biggest town, Mecca. The Qurān in a well-known passage doubts the Bedouin's genuineness of belief.[5] Clearly, Islam both subdued and utilized the nomad; its own urbanism[6] saved it from the fate of other nomadic traditions, that of a total absorption among the conquered civilized societies.

Yet the fact remains that the Bedouin formed the bulk of Arab soldiers who demolished the Iranian and (in part) the Byzantine empire. So also the fact that the successive nomadic conquests by the Seljuqs, the Qarā Khitai, and the Mongols, all originated from the nomadic reservoir of the Asian steppes. The infiltration of nomadic notions and institutions was thus bound continuously to modify the political tradition and 'applied' law in the Islamic world.

It is possible to see the influence of nomadism in the evolution of the concept of an implicit state property in land. As Kovalevsky noticed long ago, Islamic law has a fairly well-developed concept of private property in land (as behoves an urban tradition codified so largely in Iran).[7] The nomads on the other hand, could only have a

[4] *The Rise of the Ottoman Empire*, Royal Asiatic Society, London, 1971.

[5] Quran, *Surah* IX, 98.

[6] See F. Lokkegaard's description of Islam as 'a religion for townspeople' (*Islamic Taxation in the Classic Period*, Copenhagen, 1950, p. 32).

[7] *Communal Landholding* (in Russian), 1879, cited by Rosa Luxemburg, *The Accumulation of Capital*, tr. A. Schwarzchild, London, 1951, pp. 372–3 *n*.

concept of tribal possession of a territory; and individual possession of a particular strip of land had no meaning for the Bedouin or other nomadic peoples.[8] A conquered territory belonged to the tribe, and was not divisible among its individuals. The personal *iqṭā'* of early Islam was thus contrasted to territory belonging to the entire Islamic (or rather Arab-Islamic) community, of which the Caliph was the head. Thus the *iqṭā'* now came to mean merely a temporary assignment of the claims to surplus from the land which were thought to vest in the Caliph. The doctrine of State property could seldom be distinctly enunciated, in view of the lack of its reconcilability with Islamic law; but it came to arise in practice nevertheless.

This implicit concept was nomadic; in itself it could have little significance but for its being combined with the purely sedentary notion of land-tax. The classic Islamic concept of *kharāj* (land-tax on non-Muslims ranging from a fifth to half of the produce) and *'ushr* (tithe on Muslims), seems quite alien to the later development of the land-tax. *'Ushr* disappeared, except as a concessionary arrangement with favoured elements; and Muslim peasants too had normally to pay *kharāj*. Finally, the *kharāj* approached or exceeded half of the produce wherever this could be realized. In other words, it tended to approximate to the surplus, or potential rent. This enlargement of the state demand could take place only by a corresponding destruction of private property; and it is extremely tempting to see in this process the evolution of an idea initially germinated by tribal nomads: the tribal possession over land converted into state property. This development was crucial for what may be regarded as the common fiscal feature of all the four states we are considering, an identification, which so far as we can see, grew within the fold of Islam under repeated nomadic tribal impulses.[9]

But if the Islamic background provided such a unifying factor in the fiscal system of all these four states, we must remember that the Ottoman Empire and, still more, the Mughal Empire, had large non-Muslim populations. Even if one were to attribute the Ottoman control over the Balkans to simple military subjugation

[8] Lokkegaard, *Islamic Taxation*, p. 20.

[9] One recalls that in 1853 Marx attributed to Muslims the creation of state property in land in Asia under the principle of 'no property in land' (letter of 14 June 1853 in *Selected Correspondence*, ed. Dona Torr, Calcutta, 1945, p. 62).

through an outward expansion of Islam (though this too is questionable, since the Ottomans conquered the Balkans first, and the Islamic lands outside Anatolia only later), it is difficult to say the same about the Mughal Empire, which did not have any Islamic hinterland at all. The successful implantation in India, and possibly in the Balkans, of forms of political organization developed in the Islamic world, must then be regarded as a singular historic achievement. Once formed, the institutions of 'Islamic' polity offered immense advantages to those at the head of power. In this sense it is even possible to say that the Rajput states of north India in the fifteenth and sixteenth centuries or the contemporary Vijayanagar Empire of the south were 'Islamic' polities though they did not accept the Islamic faith, while accepting its tradition in crucial matters like taxation and state property.[10] The advantage of these Islamic institutions to a Hindu ruling class was just as great as was that of the caste system among its Hindu subjects for the Muslim ruling class, which thereby derived cheap artisan labour for its own use.

II

With such features as we have touched upon, how far were these Islamic states different from those that developed with the absolute monarchies in Europe during the sixteenth and seventeenth centuries? The question was asked and sought to be answered by François Bernier in his remarkable description of oriental states and societies on the basis of personal observations in the East during the twelve years 1656–68.[11]

Bernier came to India after visiting Constantinople, Syria and Egypt and was familiar with the conditions of the Ottoman Empire. Thereafter he spent nine years in India. He was, therefore, no bird of passage, no superficial sightseer. What gives additional weight to his interpretation of the Orient is his scientific background and his association with the new philosophical school of which Pierre Gassendi was a notable representative. Earlier European travellers of the sixteenth century, like Bernier's own

[10] I may mention in passing that I consider Burton Stein's application of the segmentary state thesis to the Vijayanagar Empire in *Cambridge Economic History of India*, ed. T. Raychaudhuri and I. Habib, 1982, rather unconvincing.

[11] *Travels in the Mughal Empire, A.D. 1656–68*, tr. A. Constable, 2nd ed. revised V. A. Smith, Oxford, 1916.

fellow-countryman Pyrard de Laval, had based their assumption of European superiority on the well-known fact that Christianity was a superior religion; otherwise, in commerce and crafts the people in India were similar to them or even more skilled.[12] In Bernier's eyes, on the other hand, European superiority lay essentially in its science, arts, technology, property laws and social system. Furthermore, not only was Europe ahead, but the Orient was receding. This major difference between the West and East, Bernier located in the nature of the state. European states recognized private property and so created all the stability, security and public welfare that private property generates. It was otherwise with Oriental states like those of the Ottomans and the Mughals. Their indifference to private property was causing a steady devastation of the economies and societies of these empires: 'I have carefully compared the condition of European States, where that right [of private property] is recognized, with the condition of those countries where it is not known, and am persuaded that the absence of it among the people is injurious to the best interest of the Sovereign himself.'[13]

Specifically speaking, the absence of private property, according to Bernier, affected the Oriental states in the following manner. The King, being the owner of the soil, distributed the right to collect taxes over particular territories to assignees or tax-farmers who had temporary tenures. These assignments were known in the Ottoman Empire as *timār*, and in the Mughal Empire as *jāgīr*. Being temporary, the attitude of the assignees to the land under their jurisdiction could be summed up as follows:

> The Timariots, Governors, and Revenue Contractors on their part reason in this manner: Why should the neglected State of this land create uneasiness in our minds? And why should we expend our own money and time to render it fruitful? We may be deprived of it in a single moment, and our exertions would benefit neither ourselves nor our children. Let us draw from the soil all the money we can, though the peasants should starve or abscond, and we should leave it, when commanded to quit, a dreary wilderness.[14]

[12] Pyrard de Laval (1607–10) says of Indians: 'They are all cunning folk, and owe nothing to the people of the West, themselves endowed with a keener intelligence than is usual with us, and hands as subtle as ours' (*The Voyages of François Pyrard de Laval to the East Indies, the Maldives, the Moluccas and Brazil*, tr. and ed. A. Grey, assisted by H.C.P. Bell, II, Part I, Hakluyt Soc., London, 1888).

[13] Bernier, *Travels*, p. 226.

[14] Ibid., p. 227.

This, said Bernier, was at the root of the visible ruin of eastern states. Bernier's theory has received much attention from historians of the Mughal Empire, notably because he gave a fairly accurate depiction of the *jāgīr* system. The Empire was indeed divided up into the *jāgīr*s or assignments held by nobles in lieu of pay under their *manṣab*s, or numerical ranks, that also defined the size and composition of the military contingents they were to maintain. In a sense the lands reserved for the king's own revenues, called *khāliṣa*, could be termed his *jāgīr*s. The *jāgīr*s, including the *khāliṣa*, were constantly transferred, each period of assignment on average barely exceeding two or three years.[15] There has, therefore, been a strongly-held view that the *jāgīr*-system brought about the collapse of the Mughal Empire as a viable economic system, just as Bernier had suggested.[16]

But to generalize this view for all the Islamic empires would overlook the fact that the other three empires of our period did not have a system of assignment-transfers working as rigorously as in the Mughal Empire. Take, for instance, the Ottoman *timār*. The *timār*, or 'military fief', was transferable only in name; a timariot was not removed so long as he brought troops; and the son usually succeeded his father. Centralization of the grant of *timār*s in the sixteenth century had the result only of creating large estates at the cost of the small ones, leading to disaffection among the timariots, which made some small timariots leaders of peasant uprisings in Anatolia.[17] There would be little here to support the Bernier thesis of devastation of peasants by 'temporary' timariots.

If we turn to the Ṣafavid Empire the picture is almost the same. The counterpart of *jāgīr* in that empire was the *tuyūl*. Bernier's contemporary, Chardin, reported that the *tuyūl*s were virtually the property of those to whom they were assigned; and wherever the holder expected to hold the land in his lifetime and transfer it to his son, the peasants were correspondingly better treated.[18] Rapid transfers of *tuyūl*s appear, in fact, to have been very rare.

[15] See Irfan Habib, *Agrarian System of Mughal India*, Bombay, 1963, Chapter VII. The only non-transferable *jāgīrs* were the *watan jāgīrs*, which did not cover a relatively significant area.

[16] Ibid., Chapter IX.

[17] Cf. Fernand Braudel, *The Mediterranean and the Mediterranean World in the Age of Philip II*, Eng. tr., Fontana ed. 1975, II, pp. 718–24.

[18] Cf. Ann K. S. Lambton, *Landlord and Peasant in Persia*, London, 1953, p. 110.

As far as the Uzbek Empire is concerned, the Mughal *jāgīr* system was so alien to its organization that when in the 1640s Naẕar Muhammad, the Kh̲ān of Bokhara, tried to imitate the Mughals and transfer his governors and commanders from their territories, he brought about a rebellion against himself, which ultimately resulted in his expulsion from the Kh̲anate.[19]

It seems, then, fairly clear that the rigorous system of temporary assignments was a characteristic feature of the Mughal Empire alone, but not of the other three empires, where transfer and resumption of fiefs was in the nature of an ultimate weapon and only occasionally exercised.

This would remove much of the universality in Bernier's explanation of the decline of Oriental empires. What he says, then, was at best true of India alone as far as the *jāgīr* system is concerned; as to its consequences even in India there remains some room for doubt.[20]

While the agrarian aspect of Bernier's theory has excited the most interest, it must be remembered that he extended the ill effects of Oriental Despotism to trade and industry as well. Merchants' wealth was subject to usurpation and confiscation; so they had to hide their wealth and hoard treasure (and so not set it to use as capital). The craftsmen were unable to apply themselves because they could always be forced to work at low wages.[21] Thus the contempt for private property led to a constriction of commerce and crafts as well.

While abuses of the kind Bernier mentions can be illustrated from individual instances of oppression and injustice, there seems to be no reason to believe that the merchants were not allowed to have private property or that the artisans were semi-servile. Halil Inalcik has shown how commerce expanded in the Ottoman Empire, and Irfan Habib has referred to the growth of merchant capital in India aided by institutions like deposit banking and insurance.[22] It can hardly be said that the Oriental despots throttled commerce by continuous confiscation of merchant property, or

[19] Abdu'l Ḥamīd Lāhorī, *Badshah Nama*, Bib. Ind., Calcutta, 1867–8, pp. 295, 401–2.

[20] See Athar Ali, 'The Passing of Empire: The Mughal Case', *Modern Asian Studies*, Cambridge, 1975, IX, Part 3, pp. 385–96.

[21] Bernier, *Travels*, pp. 225–9.

[22] See both writers' contributions in *The Journal of Economic History*, XXIX, No. 1, March 1969.

that such confiscations were a characteristic feature of the Asian Empires we are studying.

In other words, Bernier has given us brilliant answers to a cogent question; but the answers tend to become less and less convincing as we look closer into the evidence.

III

Bernier's work won a considerable readership in Europe and much of European writing on Oriental Despotism down to the nineteenth century bore marks of his influence.[23] Karl Marx read him in 1853 and was certainly impressed by the acuteness of his observations. Yet Marx's own perception of the Oriental state was intrinsically different; with all its imperfections it may be said to make a fundamental break with the earlier traditions, though Marx had little before him except for some information directly or indirectly derived from reports of British administrators in India.

The essential question asked by Marx was whether there were any social and political obstacles to growth (particularly, growth into capitalism) in Oriental societies, as a result of which their civilization seemed to have atrophied. Marx found the answer in a combination of two institutions, the Village Community and Oriental Despotism. The Village Community, a primitive 'republic', was based on a hereditary division of labour (e.g., caste), and by its stable but pliant nature enabled the surplus it produced to be extracted by the external power, the despotic ruling class. Land-tax and rent, therefore, coincided. The tax rent was usually taken in kind; it was then sold by the state, since money economy and commerce existed only outside the village communities. The 'economic' basis of the extra-economic coercion by the despot lay in the irrigation works that the state provided to the village communities.[24]

The cycle of production and re-production was here completed without any need of capitalistic intervention. More, since the

[23] Cf. Perry Anderson, *Lineages of the Absolutist State*, London, 1974, pp. 462 ff.

[24] Marx formulated his views on India initially in 1853, and articles in the *New York Daily Tribune* of that year (conveniently collected by Shlomo Avineri in *Karl Marx on Colonialism and Modernization*, Anchor Books, New York, 1969) are a particularly important source of his views. His classic statement on the village community occurs in *Capital*, I, Eng. tr., ed. Dona Torr, London, 1938, p. 35. For tax and rent coinciding, see *Capital*, III, Moscow, 1959, pp. 771–2.

villages remained autonomous and almost amoebic units, the emergence and fall of individual dynasties or empires had no significance for the system, which expanded or contracted, but never grew.

Marx's model of the Oriental state has an inner logical consistency that is most persuasive; it is accordingly open to extreme over-simplification as in the hands of Karl A. Wittfogel (*Oriental Despotism*, 1957). But there are a number of factual weaknesses in the theory. The 'Village Community' of Marx is largely an ideal reconstructed by British administrators who tended to ignore the realities of internal stratification within the village just as they tended partly to overlook the universality of individual land-holding existing within it. Furthermore the Village Community model of Marx could hardly apply to the Ottoman Empire and Iran which has no caste system to supply a hereditary, fixed division of labour.[25] In most parts of India, moreover, the peasants normally paid rent in money and only partly or occasionally in grain, so that grain-rent cannot be taken to be as universal a basis for the fiscal systems of Oriental states as Marx had thought. As for the State structures proper, Marx wrote too little about them to enable one to argue with him over this crucial aspect of Oriental polities. It may, however, be said that irrigation works were not very important sectors of state activity in the four empires that we are discussing, with the possible exception of Ṣafavid Iran. In the north Indian plains, at any rate, irrigation was largely looked after by the peasants themselves, mainly through the digging of wells, though the state too laid out canals.

If many of the perceptions that Marx obtained must now be rejected or heavily qualified, three essential features of his 'Asiatic Mode' seem still valid in relation to the four empires with which we are concerned: first, the practical identity of tax with rent; second, the identity of the rent-appropriators and the bureaucracy (this point is implicit rather than explicit in Marx's writings); and, finally, the parasitic nature of the urban economy based on the expenditure of the state's tax-income.

Are these features sufficient to set the Oriental states apart from

[25] Conversely, because of the other identities in these civilizations, this may be treated as a refutation of the thesis popularised by Louis Dumont in *Homo Hierarchicus*, Paladin ed., London, 1972, that the caste system made India into a totally different civilization from any other.

the European absolutist states of the sixteenth and seventeenth centuries? In the absolutist European states we have the rent in more or less pure form, it being appropriated by individual landowners and not by the state; hence follows a separation of state bureaucracy and the landowning aristocracy; a standing army paid directly by the state replaces landowners' retainers; and an urban economy arises marked by the growing importance of the Middle Classes. The Oriental states by their structures appear to have inhibited such developments within the societies they controlled; but whether this led to a total absence of such features is another question.[26]

I have discussed successively the three types of major analytical framework in which the western, central and south Asian states of the sixteenth and seventeenth centuries can be studied. Their unities and specificities must be set by the side of contemporary systems in other parts of the world to understand them better. In other words, there has to be an inward as well as outward comparison of the structures of their polities. What has been offered above represents merely preliminary suggestions towards developing a suitable basis for classifying (or trying to classify) premodern states, with the four empires of the Islamic Orient seen as a possible single category. No sure success can be claimed for such an enterprise; it is only claimed that an attempt to explore the possibility can yet yield a number of important new perceptions of the general or individual characteristics of the polities of these empires.

[26] Here attention may be drawn to a strong body of opinion among scholars in India which holds that the Mughal Empire did create a middle class. The first salvo was fired by W. C. Smith, 'The Mughal Empire and the Middle Classes', *Islamic Culture*, Hyderabad, 1944, pp. 349–63. See also Iqtidar Alam Khan, 'The Middle Classes in the Mughal Empire', presidential address, Medieval India section, *Indian History Congress, 36th Session* (Aligarh), 1975.

6

Hindu Shrines and Practices as Described by a Central Asian Traveller in the First Half of the 17th Century

IQBAL HUSAIN

The Institute of Central and West Asian Studies of the University of Karachi has published a tract called *Baḥ-rul Asrār* by Maḥmūd bin Amīr Walī Balkhī, who came to India in A.D. 1624–5 during Jahāngīr's reign. He travelled from Balkh in northern Afghanistan to Cape Comorin, visiting important places such as Peshawar, Lahore, Sirhind, Delhi, Mathura, Allahabad, Banaras, Patna, Rajmahal, Midnapore, Jagannath (Puri), Hyderabad and Mangalgiri. He returned home in 1631 after an eventful voyage from Sri Lanka to Orissa, where he was shipwrecked. On his return journey he travelled through Agra and Jaisalmer, Bhakkar (near Rohri in Sind) and Bust (Afghanistan). Maḥmūd Balkhī has left a detailed account of his observations and experiences. These are particularly remarkable because of his deep interest in Hindu rituals, practices and temples of which he has offered very valuable descriptions.

Unluckily Maḥmūd Balkhī's ornate style of writing, with long and confusing sentences, and extensive use of Arabic phrases and words increases his verbosity without clarifying the sense. Nevertheless, with all his Arabicisms he also uses Hindi words such as *penth*, *dominis*, *kanchanis*, *patras*, *dandwat*, *bhog*, and *jog* (yoga). Since he stayed in the country for over six years, his Hindi vocubulary must have increased considerably with time, and we note the use of a larger number of Hindi words towards the concluding parts of his account.

In this article, attention is confined to those portions of Maḥmūd Balkhī's account which relate to Hindu rituals, beliefs and places of worship. The translated extracts are in chronological order according to the route travelled by the author. Comments are restricted to establishing the historical significance of the descriptions.

Maḥmūd Balkhī left Balkh in 1624–5, when he was 29 years old. He tells us that the journey was undertaken out of curiosity alone, and accordingly he has recorded whatever he found strange. As he entered India he came into contact with the *jogis* of Gor Khattri[1] (near Peshawar) probably in 1625:

Since it was purely a desire for sight-seeing and observation of the world, I left Kabul for Peshawar without any plan. In that area of heretical practices I obtained sight of ascetics living at the Kattri's [Khattri's] Seat. There I collected a lot of details of their mysterious affairs and sayings. Kor Kattri (Gor Khattri) is a place in the above mentioned district consisting of grand buildings made of stone and brick.[2] In the middle of that complex, there is a tall building resembling mosques and *khānqāhs* (hospices). At its gateway is a deep cell, with a small open dome which has a door in it. After descending about twelve yards from the top, one sees a recess. Candles are lighted where perfume is burnt. Some 'exercise-worshippers' sitting in a circle engage themselves in the practices of jog (*yoga*), which means 'controlling of breath'. The above place is called the seat of Baba Ratan.[3]

In the building which is like a temple, a person of the sect of *jogis* sat as the

[1] Gor Khattrī was a well-known place of the time, its visitors including Akbar and Jahāngīr. Guru Nanak is also said to have visited it. Sujān Rai Bhandari says that it was destroyed during the reign of Shāh Jahān.

There are two possible theories for the name. First that it was named after Gorakhnāth, and stands for *Gorakh-hatrī*. The other that it was, *Kor-Khattri*, *Kor* standing for *Kothī*, house/shop, and Khattrī meaning Hindu in general. It is very likely that the first was the original name, and the second a popular derivation from false etymology. It seems that our author followed the popular etymology of the term, describing Gor Khattrī first as *Khattrī-nishīn*, Khattrī's Seat. See Erskine, *Memoirs of Bābur*, tr. Jarret, ed. J. Sarkar, II p. 165; *Akbarnāma*, III, ed. 'Abdu'r Raḥīm, Asiatic Society of Bengal, pp. 528. 856; *Tuzūk-i Jahāngīri*, tr. Rogers and Beveridge, I, p. 102; Moḥsin Fāni, *Dabistān-i Mazāhib*, Nawal Kishore, Kanpur, p. 179; S. M. Jaffar, *Peshawar: Past and Present*, 1945, pp. 74–88; Sujān Rai Bhandārī, *Khulāṣat-ut Tawārīkh*, Delhi, 1918, p. 86; *Baḥrū-l Asrār*, ed. Riāzul Islam, Karachi, 1978, p. 31 *n*; S. A. A. Rizvi, *A History of Sufism in India*, I, New Delhi, 1978, p. 389. There are no grounds for supposing a Buddhist origin for the place.

[2] *Miniatures of Bābur Nāma*, ed. Ḥāmid Sulaimān, Tashkent, 1970, pp. 28–9. I am indebted to Dr S. P. Verma for this reference.

[3] Identified as Shaikh Bāba Ratan. He is said to have been a resident of Tabarinda (Tabarhindi); he also visited Arabia and is said to have met the Prophet there! He died in AD 1300–1 and is buried at Tabarhind (*Ā'īn-i Akbarī*, tr. Jarrett, III, p. 401).

Preceptor. Nearly one thousand persons from amongst the Hindus such as *jogis*, *sannyasis*, *bairagis*, etc., have become his disciples. The asceticism and endeavour of all these consists in holding back their breath, and seeking the sight in [their mind's] eye, they keep sitting with legs tucked under their bodies. In the view of this wayward sect, the sign of perfection is to take just one breath from one morning to another. When this stage is reached by one of this arrogant set, they seat him in the position of Preceptor, and the previous Preceptor (*murshid*) is put alive inside one of those buildings the doors of which are sealed with stone and brick so that he dies within a few days, and going to Hell is ensnared in eternal Perdition. In this matter their belief is that since he held perfection in controlling the breath, he would, therefore, transfer his soul to a better body[4] than what he possessed before and return to this world again. [The Sultans] and the Hindus of that area have assigned pensions and lands for the maintenance of this accursed group so that they obtain their subsistence without delay or difficulty. The writer of these lines met their above-mentioned Preceptor without any sign of enmity or prejudice. I had his company for an hour. According to the saying of the Prophet: 'The Right prevails and is not prevailed upon.' With one out of the several arguments for the unity of God I put that wayward person in the position of the accused and reduced him to shamefaced embarrassment.

There I also saw an old *jogi* among them whose beard was so long that nearly half a yard of it was dragged over the ground and his moustache encircled his neck like the rope of Satan; he had thirteen knots on each side of it. His act of asceticism consisted in this that he had tied to himself a chain weighing ten maunds so that he was unable to move. At that time, a wealthy Hindu, Ram Ḍas by name, passed that way. After offering him a sum of one thousand rupees, he desired that that self-opinionated person should free himself from the [iron] chain. But his answer was that there had to be a generous person who would give twenty thousand rupees and so secure his release from that beard and moustache.[5]

Maḥmūd Balkhī's description of the buildings and *yogi* practices at Gor Khattri are remarkably corroborated by Babur's account of the place.[6] The miniature paintings of the *Bābur Nāma*[7] where Babur is shown visiting the place further supports the authenticity of Maḥmūd Balkhī's account. Abū'l Faẓl also visited the place with Akbar in his fortieth regnal year.[8]

[4] Sujān Rai writes that the *jogis* were capable of transferring their soul to another body (*Khulāṣat-ut Tawārīkh*, p. 22).

[5] *Baḥr-ul Asrār*, pp. 4–6.

[6] *Memoirs of Bābur*, tr. S. A. Beveridge, II, pp. 111–12.

[7] *Miniatures of Bābur Nāma*, pp. 28–9.

[8] *Akbar Nāma*, III, Pt. I, p. 359.

The *jogī*s (*yogi*s) of Gorakhattri, however, seemed to have lost to a considerable extent the traditional knowledge of Yoga and Hindu religion by the time of our traveller's visit. Jahāngīr himself describes the *jogi*s of the place as 'a herd without any religious knowledge'.[9]

The practices of these *jogi*s at Gorakhattri were probably those of the Gorakhnath *jogi*s. Sujān Rai Bhandari says that the *jogi*s specialize in 'holding the breath' (*ḥabs-i dam*) which is supposed to prolong their life.[10] A similar statement is made by the author of *Dabistān-i Mazāhib*, who says that Gorakhnath was the founder of this sect of *jogi*s.[11] He also refers to the practice of burying a *jogi* alive,[12] confirming Maḥmūd Balkhī's account. Sujān Rai Bhandari ascribes to the *jogi*s alchemical practices;[13] and this again is in line with Maḥmūd Balkhī's *jogi* subjecting himself to physical torture in the hope of gaining a fortune.

From Gorakhattri, Maḥmūd Balkhī came to Lahore on 23 September 1625. His observations of the celebrations of Muḥarram at that place are of great interest since he says that the first ten days of Muḥarram were divided into two parts.[14] The first five days were of festive celebration on the ground that the Imams had permitted marriages during these days. During these days 'young Khattris' wore the dress of Khattri women and leaving their homes spent the whole day 'shamelessly' in pleasure. During the next five days mourning was observed with black dresses being worn. On the 10th Muḥarram, 'all the Shias and all Hindus close the doors of their houses and shops, and conceal themselves inside like bats.' In this particular Muḥarram observance, which the author saw, a clash occurred in the market, in which many were killed: 50 Shias and 25 Hindus. Property worth Rs 1,20,000 was lost.[15] The reason for the clash occurring is not stated. It is, however, significant that Hindus participated in the observance of Muḥarram, though there is no known basis for rejoicing in the first five days of Muḥarram.

[9] *Tuzūk*, I, p. 102.

[10] *Khulāṣat-ut Tawārīkh*, p. 22.

[11] *Dabistān-i Mazāhib*, p. 183.

[12] Ibid.

[13] *Khulāṣat-ut Tawārīkh*, p. 22.

[14] *Baḥru-l Asrār*, pp. 8–10.

[15] Ibid.

Passing through Sirhind and Delhi, Maḥmūd Balkhī arrived at Mathura.[16] He describes it thus:

At last I reached the unique place of worship of the Hindus known as Matura (Mathura). Matura in fact is the name (seat?) of the tenth *avatār* (incarnation) of the Hindus, who is also called Kishan (Krishna). The temple where his idol is worshipped is situated there. That place is also known after the name of that false (god). The said *deora* (temple) is one of the wonderful things of that locality. The first is a building which is conically shaped. Its height is more than a hundred yards and the circle of its interior about forty yards (80 *arash*) constructed of stone and brick from the bottom to top. There are some other buildings on both sides of it. But they are neither so grand nor so large. An idol made of black stone has been fixed, its height around 12 *arash* (6 yards) and breadth four yards. This building is situated near the bank of Jamuna river, and was erected by Raja Man Singh, one of the nobles of Emperor Akbar. Their practice of pilgrimage and worship is that, on the coming of the morn, the Brahmins, who are the attendants and servants (of the god), toll the giant bell which would be more than five maunds in weight, and which those misled ones call *nāqūs*. The echo of the bell reaches six *kuroh*s (15 miles!), and men and women, old and young, rich and poor among the Hindus, go to the bank of river. Beaming with joy, men and women, without shame mixing together but committing no impropriety, try to outdo each other in performing their rites, *rasoī* and all their false prayers. In the meantime a few thousand pleasure-seekers assemble at the other side of the bank of the river with the object of witnessing the scene, obtain a sight thereof. Such a sense-enticing sight is obtained that one might lose the rein of Islam and become a follower of the Hindus! Verily, from the heresy of the faces, figures and features of those modest blossoming-faced (women), it is no wonder that one's faith may be shaken and the glass of shame broken by stone; all self-control disappears! In short, after the prescribed rites, they go to the temple, they perform the *puja*, prostration and *dandwat*, as is laid down in their religion. The Brahmans, Bairāgīs, Bishnen (Vaishnavas) and other men of learning and wisdom lead one another in delivering sermons. The Kalawants, and singers of Bishen-patta (probably *Bishen pads*), *badi'* and *dhrupad* (two styles of classic singing) with such music so that every one achieving ecstacy, great excitement is created. This assemblage of music and noise lasts till the full morning. After making the ritual offerings, they return to their respective homes, and engage themselves in their daily affairs.[17]

It may be noted that our author refers to Raja Man Singh's temple (Govind Dev) at Vrindaban, five miles north of Mathura.

[16] Ibid., pp. 10–13.

[17] *Baḥru-l Asrār*, pp. 13–16.

The construction of the temple was started in the thirty-fourth year of Akbar's reign.[18] Jahāngīr also visited the temple.[19]

From our author's account it transpires that it had become a great centre of worship by his time. The idol of Krishna which was the main attraction of worship is said to have been removed to Jaipur during the reign of Aurangzeb.[20] The transfer or perhaps the change in the course of the river seems to have been one of the major factors for the temple decaying in the later period. It was in great neglect when Growse completed his work.[21]

From Mathura, Maḥmūd Balkhī went to Agra where he seems to have developed some interest in Sannyasis.[22] His stay at Agra was, however, short. While travelling further east, he joined a group of Sannyasis, and gives an interesting account of his journey from Agra to Allahabad.

In the course of my journey I joined the company of some Sannyasis. I broke my (previous) resolve of ostentatious appearance. On reaching Allahabad—which may God keep populous!—they said to this novice in their sect that here there was a pleasant place; if I wished to see it, the opportunity was worth taking. That is the place where the river Jamuna joins the Ganga; and for the Hindus it is a place of great veneration and respect. No one dares to annoy any one here in respect of life and property. Accompanying them all, I reached the said place [the Sangam] and began to enjoy the scene. My colleagues, other travellers and those present at the place, tried to precede each other in getting their hair, beard and moustache shaved. Traders and rich people threw considerable sums of money, amounting to twenty thousand rupees, into that vast river. Due to this undesirable act, I lost my patience and began to speak mockingly with Narayan Das, one of the Sannyasis with whom I had developed closer intimacy than with the others. Thereupon he became exceedingly annoyed and said, 'Of what value is wealth at this sacred place. This is the place where people wish to die.' For some time he burnt with much rage, walking slowly as he went, and then he sat beneath a heavy dagger which was set hanging. He beckoned a Brahman so that he may perform his prescribed duty. Without hesitation the Brahman drew the dagger and drove its point into that arrogant one's breast, so that it pierced his body right through.[23]

There is no confirmation of such a method of sacred suicide ever

[18] Sanskrit inscription cited by Growse, *Mathura—A District Memoir*, pp. 243–4.

[19] *Tuzūk*, II, pp. 103–4; Prasad tells us that the external part of the temple remained incomplete (*Raja Man Singh of Amber*, Calcutta, 1966, p. 158).

[20] *Mathura—A District Memoir*, p. 245.

[21] Ibid.

[22] *Baḥru-l Asrār*, pp. 18–19.

[23] Ibid., pp. 19–20.

having been practised at the Sangam. But this is a matter of enquiry into local traditions.

From Allahabad, the author travelled to Banaras. During the course of his journey he underwent an unusual experience. He records:

During the course of the journey a strange and rare incident took place. What happened was that before reaching Banaras, we had to pass by a village. At a well we were struck by lightning. Three of my companions who could not stand it, died and four others became unconscious. I lost my senses for a short while. However, two Bairagis who were old and had a vast experience remained unharmed from that stroke of lightning. These two persons, who had throughout seen what had befallen me, took me and my friend—let God forgive us!—upon their shoulders and took us from that inimical place to Banaras. I regained consciousness after one night while my friend did so after two days. I began to enquire about the lightning. They said that a person in this condition is called 'Padmini'[24] among the Hindus. It is said that the thunderbolt sometimes strikes all of a sudden.

Since the signs of constraint were manifest from my manner, they hastened to extinguish the extensive fire burning in my soul. At first, taking me by the hand, they brought me to the bank of the Ganges. When I opened my eyes, I saw a concourse of beautiful women, perfectly decorated and ornamented. (Couplets follow)

One of the strange affairs of that place that I witnessed was that twenty-three Muslims fell captive to their charms. Having fallen in love, they had deserted their religion and accepted their creed. (Couplets)

For some time I held the company of them (Muslim converts') and questioned them about their mistaken way. They pointed towards the sky and put their fingers on their foreheads. By this gesture, I understood that they attributed it to Providence and fate.

Having left them in this state, I proceeded to see the temple of Lala Bir Singh.[25] This temple is situated in the heart of the city of Banaras, and is made of stone and brick. Its height is 130 *ẕirā'* (yards) and the interior circumference is one hundred *ẕirā'* (yards), consisting of wonderful aspects and high verandahs. Outside this grand and matchless building are a school, a worship house, an inn, about 80 houses in all, fully occupied and engaged. Although the worship was coming to an end the men and women were dispersing, nearly thirty thousand women and men together and close (to each other) were present on that unique place. Orators, reciters (*indrāz-goyān*) of holy books, *dominis*, and all the administrators of affairs and others were present. Everyone stayed with their respective guides. Due to the large crowd and the ecstacy due to religious songs, it was difficult to keep one's bearing there.[26]

[24] Reading in the text needs to be corrected.

[25] Riazul Islam reads it Bar Singh (*Baḥru-l Asrār*, p. 23).

[26] Ibid., pp. 20–3.

It seems that the Muslims converted to Hinduism as cited by our author were Muslim Bairagis, who were not very uncommon in the medieval period.[27] The author of the *Dabistān-i Mazāhib* states that Mirzā Ṣāliḥ and Mirzā Ḥaidar, belonging to respectable Muslim families, had become Sannyasis.[28]

The details of temples in Banaras given in modern works do not help us to identify the temple described by our author. The descriptions given by Sherring and Fuhrer, however, suggest that several temples existed in medieval times which later fell to ruins.[29] The builder of the temple might well have been Raja Bir Singh, the famous Bundela noble of Jahāngīr, who had built a famous temple at Mathura.

The reference to the school next to the temple is of some interest. Banaras as a seat of learning retained its position in the medieval period as is attested by Sujān Rai Bhandari, as well as Bernier and Tavernier.[30]

From Banaras, Maḥmūd Balkhī, accompanied by the Sannyasis, travelled to the *ṣūba* of Bihar, arriving at Patna on 28 January 1626.[31] He did not stay there for long. However, before travelling further east, he had a unique experience which he records thus:

> At dawn I reached the bank of the river (Ganga), performed ablutions. In the meanwhile I saw a man coming from the Hajipur side walking briskly over the water. When I looked at him closely, I found he was Shah 'Ālam, whom previous to this I had met at some of the worshipping places of the Hindus. He was one of the sages of the men of lore (*'uqlā'i majānīn*) of that time. There was little coherence in his words and most of his utterances were filthy and abusive. He was yet quite firm in his own faith and practices. Contrary to the established practice, he recognized me at that hour and indulged in conversation. He caught hold of my ear and rubbing it vigorously said that one cannot walk on the water unless he becomes as dust. Beware the sparks of adversity that are flying about fiercely.[32] (Couplets)
>
> He also uttered some words in this regard and, bidding farewell, returned.[33]

[27] *Dabistān-i Mazāhib*, p. 200.

[28] Ibid., p. 203.

[29] *Banaras, the Sacred City*, Chapters XIX, XX; *Archaeological Survey, N.W.P.*, pp. 199–202, 206.

[30] *Khulāṣat-ut Tawārikh*, p. 42; *Travels in the Mogul Empire*, 1891, pp. 334–5; *Travels in India*, II, pp. 234–5.

[31] *Baḥru-l Asrār*, p. 23.

[32] Ibid., p. 26.

[33] Ibid., pp. 25–6.

It is of some interest to find a Muslim like Shāh 'Ālam frequenting Hindu temples and seeking to imitate Yogic practices; for walking on water was supposed to be an achievement of the Yogis.[34] Whether Maḥmūd Balkhī really saw him perform the act can of course be discussed only by the credulous.

The author travelled to Rajmahal by river. At that time Rajmahal seems to have been a flourishing centre for merchants who came from distant places such as Khurasan, Balkh, Iraq, Turkey, Syria, etc., with their merchandise.[35]

Maḥmūd Balkhī says that he heard the Bairagis praising the Deccan, specially Sri Lanka, and so decided to travel south through Orissa. Journeying through Burdwan he arrived at Midnapore,[36] where he found people going for the ensuing Jagannath Festival at Puri:

Countless Hindu men and women were surging from the hill and forest (far and near)[37] so that nearly 50,000 Hindu men and women had assembled at Midnapore. The fact of the matter is that in Khurdah, which is one of the *parganas* of Orissa and is at a distance of one month's journey from Midnapore, there is a temple known as Jagannath. One of the basic rites of the Hindus is that they must visit the place once in life. They believe that if they visit the place every year, the sins of their forefathers would be forgiven, if they are careless and indolent in this regard, they would invite the wrath of the Ten Avatars. Accordingly in the first 10 days of Ramazan, which is the period of paying the promised religious duties, the Hindus from distant and remote parts of Hindustan assemble and offer the rites of attendance and worship there.[38] At the time of journey to the above mentioned place, men and women get mixed up together, naked and reciting '*Hari bol*' travelling day and night. During the course of their travel they sleep and eat very little, and abstain from jesting and cheering conversation among themselves. In short, seeing their assemblage, my desire also became intense, since I had undertaken the entire travel with the object of observing God's wonders. On account of my desire, I had been inclined to join them for visiting that place. Now I resolved firmly to visit it (Jagannath). During the night when the caravan of the Hindus began to move forward I also joined the concourse reciting '*Hari-bol*' with head and feet

[34] *Khulāṣat-ut Tawārīkh*, p. 22.

[35] *Baḥru-l Asrār*, p. 28.

[36] Ibid., pp. 28–32.

[37] The same spirit survives. See W. W. Hunter, *Statistical Account of Bengal*, XIX, pp. 58–9.

[38] Maḥmūd Balkhī must have gone to Jagannath in AH 1035, in which year the month of Ramazān began on 27 May 1626. The Jagannath festival takes place in June/July so that our author is quite accurate here.

bare, and travelled with them entertaining myself with strange sights. After a journey of 32 days we arrived at the place just before the commencement of Ramazan. I saw a very wide and extensive quadrangle. It was thronged by such a large number of people, as is difficult to count and imagine. In the middle of that quadrangle stood the temple. (Couplets)

The height of the above named temple is 150 *zirā'* (yards) and the courtyard 60 *zirā'*.[39] Its ramparts have been built of stone so that the cells are all connected with each other. The Hindus observe some regulations there. First, the Muslims are not allowed to enter.[40] Second they adopt friendship among their various sects and have no inhibition in eating and drinking with each other.[41] Since at that time I had absolutely concealed my identity, the guards and doorkeepers did not object to my entrance, and permitted me to enter. With awakened heart and open eyes I enjoyed the sight of that place. I observed the buildings and whatever I had spent on the journey I regained there. (Couplet)

In short, the next day which happened to be the first day of Ramazan, the Brahmans and those who minister (at the temple) decorated the rat (*ratha*, the chariot) and the *deora* (idol), beat the drums and tolled the bells, so that people from that noise began to gather from all sides. It seemed as if it was the day of Resurrection. In short, the narration of their peculiar system, is that the attendants who have this duty among that misguided people, first prepare a high chariot made of wood, square shaped at every side, carried by ten wheels, whose circumference (diameter?) is 20 *zirā'*.[42] The length of the chariot is sixty *zirā'* and width fifty *zirā'*. On the top of it are raised large and elevated structures worth seeing. The height of the pinnacles would be more than 80 *arash* (40 *zirā'*) from the ground.[43] The idol, whose name Jagannath really is, and who is considered by the Hindus to be the 10th *avatār* is seated on the top of that structure and many curtains are drawn before the idol on that high spot. About 500 Brahmans throw coconuts (*juziha*) from their hands. A troupe consisting of about one hundred *kalawants*, and *natnis* (dancers) are engaged in singing, and drummers and kettle-drum beaters create a thunderous sound from all sides. At that time, they tie strong and heavy ropes to

[39] Sujān Rai says it was 150 hands high, 90 hands in width (*Khulāsaṭ-ut Tawārīkh*, p. 50).

[40] Hunter gives a list of communities which are forbidden to enter the temple. These include Muslims and Christians (*Statistical Account of Bengal*, XIX, p. 62).

[41] W. W. Hunter, *A History of Orissa*, I, p. 6.

[42] Hunter (*Statistical Account of Bengal*, XIX, p. 59) gives the number as 16 wheels, each 7 feet in diameter. The wheels Maḥmūd Balkhī describes are thus fewer but larger, unless *bist* (20) is a misreading for *hasht* (8). A circumference of 20 yards would be roughly equivalent to a 7 foot diameter. The Mughal yard was about 32 to 33 inches in length.

[43] Hunter (*Statistical Account of Bengal*, XIX, p. 59) says that the Rath was 45 feet high and 35 feet square. Maḥmūd Balkhī's Rath was much larger than this.

the chariot and all people pulling at these bring it to the tank where they believe Jagannath had his *rasoi* (cooking place). After reaching the above place and performing the usual rituals, they return for a great assembly and large feast. The said Rat (chariot) is broken and people collect parts of it as a sacred relic paying one rupee each.

One of the strange sights is that during the movement of the chariot there is a high cupola like a lofty gate(?). There is a group of self-sacrificing worshippers who disregarding any possession or wealth in the pursuit of worship, resolve to offer their own lives; they climb over the pinnacles and to the top of the said tower. When the chariot reaches near them, and the curtain keepers remove the curtain from the face of Jagannath, and all the Hindus who ascend that tower throw themselves all of a sudden under the wheel and so by this means go to Hell.[44] On that day, I was told nearly 2,000 persons, by throwing themselves down from that elevated place, obtained annihilation.[45] Those who are old and weak and cannot climb that tower, simply throw themselves under the Rat (chariot) so that the idol rides over them and kills them. On that day some two thousand died like this. Let it not be hidden that the temple is on the shore of the sea, so that the sea is near which can reach (overturn) that structure.[46]

Maḥmūd Balkhī's account of Jagannath is of great interest, notably his description of the Car Festival and details of the chariot. The ritual suicide under the chariot is described by many later authorities. This ritual seems to have originated on account of the general belief that Puri was the place that washes away sin.[47] A similar belief existed about Banaras, with the difference that people wished simply to die there in peace.[48]

From Jagannath, our author travelled to Konarak, of which he has given the following account:

Thus after having seen the wonders of that place (Jagannath), I proceeded to see Konarak[49] which is situated at a distance of 10 *kurōhs* (22½ miles) from the above-mentioned temple I reached there in the evening. I passed the night without trouble. Next day I saw the place for which I had stayed. According to the Hindus of that area, this was the first erection of the *deora* of Suraj, i.e. a temple where the Sun is worshipped. For the Hindus, the Sun is among the

[44] *Baḥru-l Asrār*, pp. 32–8. [45] Ibid. [46] Ibid.

[47] Abbé Dubois, *Hindu Manners and Customs*, reprint, 1959, p. 597; Hunter, *A History of Orissa*, I, p. 5; and *Statistical Account of Bengal*, XIX, p. 6.

[48] *Khulāṣat-ut Tawārīkh*, p. 42.

[49] Locally called Deul, the monument is 21 miles north-east of Puri and 42 miles south-east of Bhuvaneshwar. See Mohammad Hamid Kureshi, *Archaeological Survey of India* (New Imperial Series, Vol. LI), p. 285.

earlier *avatārs* so that Sun worship is now abandoned among the Hindus. It is called Konarak,[50] because it is situated near the Black Sea. A Mughal having a reputation of a strong archer, shot an arrow from middle of the building to the top; but it could not touch the top of the temple,[51] though a third of the building is said to be covered with sand. There is a marble pillar in one piece of different colours which is also buried in sand, whatever of it is visible being more than fifty *zirā'*.[52] The door of that (temple) is 10 *zirā'* high and five *zirā'* wide.[53] There is one piece of iron, over which three storeys of balustrades are placed. Its roof [rests on] twenty-two iron bars (*bālār-i āhinī*) each one being fifteen *zirā'* long with a thickness of the body of a man of average physique. Its walls are of sculptured carvings. On the top of it, is placed one piece of iron stone (ore) weighing approximately one thousand maunds.[54] I have repeatedly heard from the Europeans (Farangis) that there is no known hill containing stone (ore) in the neighbourhood.

Maḥmūd Balkhī's description of Konarak is perhaps the first account by any traveller, and is exceptionally detailed. A little earlier Abū'l Faẓl also gave a description of Konarak (based on official reports, apparently). He writes that near the Jagannath temple stands the temple of the Sun, the construction of which consumed the revenue of twelve years of the whole of Orissa.[55] He further writes that the wall surrounding the temple was 150 cubits high and 19 cubits thick. In front of the gate stood a pillar of black stone, fifty yards high.

Maḥmūd Balkhī's account of Konarak does not, however, give any information about the twenty-four wheeled chariots drawn by seven horses. Since our author says that one-third of the temple was sunk in sand, we may infer that he could not see the chariot and horses which are just above the foundation of the temple.

It is noteworthy that sun worship had been abandoned by the

[50] The literal meaning of Konarak is 'a place sacred to Purushuttama (God)'. Cf. *Sanskrit-English Dictionary*, ed. Monier Monier-Williams, reprint, p. 313.

[51] The Puri temple records indicate that the total height of the sun temple was 175 feet to the top of the steeple, and 225 feet to the top of the *dhwaja* or flag (*Archaeological Survey of India*, New Imperial Series, LI, p. 291).

[52] This pillar actually stands outside the principal entrance of the Jagannath temple, and this is how the *Ā'īn-i Akbarī*, tr. Jarrett, II, pp. 140–1, situates it. See Hunter, *A History of Orissa*, I, p. 127; also *Statistical Account of Bengal*, XIX, p. 58.

[53] This is corroborated by the estimate given in the *Archaeological Survey of India*, LI, p. 209.

[54] Five tons in *Archaeological Survey of India*, LI, p. 292.

[55] *Ā'īn-i Akbarī*, tr. Jarrett, II, pp. 140–1.

time of Maḥmūd Balkẖī's visit. The sun temple, however, seems to have been in good condition at that time, since when it has undoubtedly suffered much damage. Part of the tower, to a height of about 120 feet, was intact in 1822. It remained in position till 1837, but had entirely collapsed by 1869.[56] At the time of compilation of the archaeological survey by Hamid Kureshi it was only fifty feet high above the plinth.[57]

What Maḥmūd Balkẖī says of the big iron bars is of much value. A number of iron bars originally used in the building of Konarak lie near the temple. 'They are all solid and very heavy', weighing over five tons each, and measuring as much as thirty-five feet in length. This broadly accords with the length Maḥmūd Balkẖī gives, viz. 15 ẕirā'.

From Konarak our author travelled to Hyderabad on his way to Cape Comorin and Sri Lanka. He then sailed to south-east Asia but was ship-wrecked on the Coromandel coast and ultimately had to come to Cuttack where he met Baqir Kẖān, the Governor of Orissa.[58]

The remainder of Maḥmūd Balkẖī's account has, however, little of interest as far as Indian religious practices and monuments are concerned. While he intersperses his description with some sneers (faithfully reproduced in our translations), the fact remains that he seems to have been sincerely interested in Hinduism, and his descriptions are largely accurate and based on first-hand observation. The account is thus a welcome addition to the sources of social history of India in the seventeenth century.

[56] *Archaeological Survey of India*, LI, p. 292.

[57] Ibid.

[58] *Baḥru-l Asrār*, pp. 65–6. Baqir Kẖān was appointed Governor of Orissa towards the close of Jahāngīr's reign, and was removed by Shāh Jahān from this position in 1632. However, he seems to have regained imperial favour and died as Nāzim of Allahabad in 1638 with a *manṣab* of 4000/4000. Shāh Nawāz Kẖān, *Ma'āṣiru-l Umarā*, I, pp. 408–12; Athar Ali, *Apparatus of Empire*, p. 140.

7

An Aristocratic Surgeon of Mughal India: Muqarrab Khān

SYED ALI NADEEM REZAVI

Physicians did not lack recognition in the Mughal Empire, and their names are often listed in Mughal histories along with those of the learned and men of letters of the time.[1] In spite of this they were not regarded as part of the Mughal ruling aristocracy. It was therefore remarkable that Muqarrab Khān, a surgeon and physician, who was known for his skill in treating elephants as much as for treating men, should have attained the high *manṣab* of 5,000 *zāt* and 5,000 *sawār*, and been appointed governor of three provinces during Jahāngīr's reign.

The career of Shaikh Hasan Hassū, who was given the title Muqarrab Khān by Jahāngīr,[2] was quite eventful. He belonged to a family of *shaikhzādas*, that is of Indian Muslims.[3] He is first noticed when he assisted his father Bhīna (or Bahā, as in the *Tuzūk*), a surgeon of some repute,[4] in bleeding Akbar, when the emperor was afflicted with some injury in 1595–6.[5]

[1] Abū'l Fazl, *Ā'in-i Akbari*, I, ed. Blochmann, Calcutta, 1867–77, p. 543; Abdul Hamīd Lāhorī, *Bādshāhnāma*, ed., I, pt. i, p. 350 and *passim*.

[2] *Tuzūk-i Jahāngīrī*, ed. Saiyid Ahmad Khan, Ghazipur and Aligarh, 1863–4, p. 12; Khwāja Ni'matullah, *Tārīkh-i Khān Jahānī*, Dhaka, p. 667. It appears that Muqarrab Khān was popularly known as Abū'l Hasan. See J. J. Modi, *Dastur Kaikobad Mahyar's Petition and Laudatory Poem addressed to Jahangir and Shahjahan*, Bombay, 1930, verse 152, p. 13.

[3] The only reference to him in the *Zakhīrat-ul Khwānīn* is that his grandfather hailed from Panipat. From Muḥammad Ṣāliḥ's *Tabaqāt-i Shāhjahānī* (MS Department of History, AMU, f. 570) we learn, however, that he was from Sirhind.

[4] Abū'l Fazl mentions him in his list of physicians (*Ā'in*, I, p. 543).

[5] Abū'l Fazl, *Akbarnāma*, ed. Beveridge, III, pp. 1061–2; Mu'tamid Khān, *Iqbālnāma-i Jahāngīrī*, Nawal Kishore, 1870, II, p. 446.

Muqarrab K͟hān attained much greater recognition with the accession of Jahāngīr. In the very first year of the reign he was granted the title by which he is known, and was deputed to accompany Dāniyāl's children coming to the Court from Burhānpūr.[6]

In 1607 he was sent in an embassy to Goa.[7] Of this embassy, which proved abortive, Guerreiro says:

> The ambassador [Muqarrab K͟hān] was awaited at Goa by the Viceroy, Ruy Lourenço de Tauoro, who had also arrived, and had written to say that he might now come to Goa with all security. At the same time orders were given for one of our ships to bring him. But as he was at this time recalled by the King, he was unable to come. His duties as the Mogol's ambassador were therefore carried out by Fr. Pinheiro, who shared his office.[8]

It seems that at the time of his deputation to Goa in 1607, Muqarrab K͟hān was holding some position at Cambay.[9] It was during this mission that he tried to win over the Jesuits by expressing his love for their faith—he is alleged to have shown reverence to a painting of Jesus and Mary at Surat.[10] But it was perhaps more an aesthetic reaction than faith in Christ's divinity that occasioned his admiration. Muqarrab K͟hān also allowed the Jesuit father, Pinheiro, to treat his adopted son—later known as Masīh-i Kairānawi—with Christian relics.[11]

Some time before 1611, Muqarrab K͟hān had been appointed Governor (presumably *Mutaṣaddi*) of Cambay and then of Surat.[12]

[6] *Tuzūk*, I, 12.

[7] Account of Father Fernão Guerreiro, based on Father Pinheiro's letter written in November 1609. As for the object of this embassy, Guerreiro writes: 'The embassy had for its object nothing more than the maintenance of friendly relations with the (Portuguese) State, while the Ambassador (Muqarrab K͟hān) was instructed to bring back with him any rare and curious object he could procure in India for the Portuguese' (*Jahangir and the Jesuits, with an Account of The Travels of Benedict Goes and the Mission to Pegu and the Relations of Father Fernao Guerreiro, S.J.*, tr. C. H. Payne, London, 1930, pt. I, p. 44). Also see H. Maclagan, *The Jesuits and the Great Mogul*, London, 1932, p. 77.

[8] Payne (tr.), *Jahangir and the Jesuits*, pt. I, pp. 86–7.

[9] Ibid., p. 77.

[10] Ibid., p. 78: 'and so deeply was he impressed with the majority visible in their figures, that he said that it would be better not to have lived at all than to have lived without seeing so marvellous a work.'

[11] Ibid., p. 79.

[12] *Tuzūk*, I, p. 80; *Letters Received by the East India Company from its Servants in the East*, ed. W. Foster, I, pp. 23, 26, 33, 138 and 140. In 1607 or even earlier, his income was 'fifty thousand *pardaos*, besides a hundred and fifty thousand which he received from the King' (Payne (tr.), *Jahangir and the Jesuits*, I, p. 77).

From there he is reported to have sent European rareties as gifts to the Emperor.[13] Since the English had now arrived, he established contact with them as well. The English complained that he was demanding gifts for which he did not pay or else procured them at very low prices;[14] a complaint which seems to have persisted till the very end.[15] At one time the English Factors reported:

> As you have seen the Nabob [Muqarrab K͟hān] by the hand of one man to buy all the trifles amongst the common people of the ships so you shall do well to remember to give advice that no man bring any of their things to land, which will procure great troubles and delays to the main business...[16]

It seems that in the beginning Muqarrab K͟hān was more inclined towards the Portuguese. Moreover, Fr. Pinheiro, a Jesuit Father, had dealt skilfully with him, bribing him in such a manner that he might help the Portuguese as against the English.[17] Muqarrab K͟hān, after having initially been friendly towards the English agent William Hawkins in 1609, changed in manner. But much as he wanted to hinder him, he could not, as Hawkins claimed to possess a letter from the English King to the Great Mughal.[18] It is alleged that in league with the Jesuits, Muqarrab K͟hān even tried to have Hawkins poisoned or killed on the way, but the attempt proved abortive.[19] At Agra Jahāngīr accorded some favour to Hawkins and

[13] *Tuzūk*, I, p. 80; see also Jourdain, *Journal, 1608–17*, ed. Foster, Hakluyt Society, 2nd Series, no. XVI, Cambridge, 1905, pp. 180–2.

[14] Samuel Purchas, *Purchas his Pilgrims or Hakluytus Posthumus*, reprint Glasgow, 1905, IV, pp. 21, 23 and 24; *Letters Received*, I, pp. 23–4 and 33; ibid., II, pp. 135 and 138.

[15] The last entry in *English Factories in India 1624–29* (ed. Foster, p. 271) also ends with a complaint of delay in payment. See also ibid., pp. 151, 241.

[16] *Letters Received*, III, p. 31.

[17] Account of Fr. Guerreiro in Payne (tr.), *Jahangir and the Jesuits*, pp. 85–6; also see Hawkins in *Early Travels in India*, ed. Foster, p. 84.

[18] Hawkins writes that this reluctance initially stemmed from the non-payment for goods acquired by Muqarrab K͟hān from the English. It was further strengthened by Portuguese scheming; Muqarrab K͟hān had agreed to grant a licence to Hawkins to proceed towards Agra, but 'the Father (Pinheiro) put into Mocreb Chan his head, that it was not good to let me passe: for that I would complaine of him unto the King. Thus he plotted with Mocreb Chan to overthrow my journey, which he could not doe, because I came from a King: but he said, that he would not let me have any force to goe with me' (*Purchas*, III, p. 9.)

[19] *Purchas*, III, pp. 9–10; The Portuguese too report a misfortune which befell the English (Payne (tr.), *Jahāngīr and the Jesuits*, p. 86). This was but wishful thinking on the part of the Jesuits when they talked of Hawkins slaughtered by robbers on the way to Agra.

even made him a 'captain of four hundred horse'.[20] Hawkins felt that Muqarrab K͟hān's machinations pursued him even at Agra.[21]

In March 1610 Muqarrab K͟hān himself arrived at the Court from Gujarat. But soon after, he fell from grace owing to a serious accusation being brought against him of having kidnapped a *banīya* girl and presented her to one of his attendants.[22] His *manṣab* was reduced to half.[23] There is unfortunately no information about his actual *manṣab* before reduction. Muqarrab K͟hān did not however remain under a cloud for long and seems to have been restored to the Emperor's confidence soon afterwards. Hawkins now tried to press him to clear his previous debts. But in the process he seems to have annoyed K͟hwāja 'Abul Hasan 'the Chiefe Vizier', who, along with Muqarrab K͟hān, effectively obstructed Hawkins. Hawkins thought that Jahāngīr's decision to withdraw the privileges offered to the English was due to this intrigue.[24]

It was only after a war had ensued between the Portuguese and the Mughals that Muqarrab K͟hān began to seek the friendship of the English. He was pleased when he heard that the English had sunk a Portuguese ship and damaged another.[25] Sir Henry Middleton and Nicholas Downton inform us that in late 1611, Muqarrab K͟hān, as Governor of Cambay, came to visit Middleton in his ship anchored off Swālly, near Surat, and stayed there for a night. He even promised the English some concessions, though he was unable to keep his word. He was presented a letter from King James I which pleased him very much, and promised Middleton that he would allow the setting up of a factory.[26] In return he asked for a treaty and assurance of English aid in any fighting with the Portuguese.[27] The Portuguese, not surprisingly, resented these

[20] *Purchas*, III, p. 14. [21] Ibid.

[22] Ibid., pp. 17–18; Jāhangīr too mentions this incident and puts the blame for the girl's death on one of Muqarrab K͟hān's servants, for which he 'had him put to death, and reduced Muqarrab K͟hān's *manṣab* by one half...' (*Tuzūk*, p. 83).

[23] *Tuzūk*, p. 83.

[24] *Purchas*, III, pp. 19–20. Muqarrab K͟hān had written a letter to his Emperor against the English merchants.

[25] *Letters Received*, I, p. 138; III, p. 64.

[26] Account of Sir H. Middleton in *Purchas*, III, p. 179; see also Jourdain, *Journal, 1608–17* pp. 180–2.

[27] *Purchas*, IV, p. 219: 'that if I [Nicholas Downton] would assist them [the Mughals] against the Portugals, the Nabob would do us all the favour that in his power lyeth....' See also *Purchas*, IV, pp. 220, 222 and 258.

negotiations and warned Muqarrab K͟hān to desist,[28] at which he rapidly changed his mind. On 27 January 1612 he reiterated his offer to help the English to establish a factory, but within two or three days he asked them to leave the port.[29] From Middleton's letter dated 18 May 1612, addressed to the Mughal Emperor, one can judge the annoyance the English factors now felt at Muqarrab K͟hān and his 'unjust dealinge'.[30]

Muqarrab K͟hān seems to have gone to Goa, some time in early 1612, to buy paintings for the Emperor. In April 1612 Jahāngīr mentions his return.[31] The English factors too mention his visit to Goa at this time.[32] He was a suitable choice for the mission, since he once again succeeded in persuading the Portuguese that he was attracted to their religion. Indeed he was reported to have embraced Catholicism. Nicholas Withington, in one of his despatches of 17 November 1613, says that:

> After this Mocrobacann proceeded on his journey for Goa, where (as the Portingals say and swear) he according to his desire was christened, saying he felt his conscience very light and jocund after his baptism.[33]

Maclagan too refers to this 'conversion' but says that 'the new convert was an "imperfect Christian" and the authorities at Goa treated him with some circumspection.'[34] He also refers to a letter which had been written by Muqarrab K͟hān on 3 April 1615 wherein the name 'Jesu' was superscribed.[35]

On his return from the mission to Goa Muqarrab K͟hān brought rareties (paintings?) which highly pleased Jahāngīr.[36] He seems by now to have been completely exonerated from the charges and was

[28] *Letters Received*, I, pp. 175–6; *Purchas*, III, p. 271.

[29] *Purchas*, III, pp. 184–5, also pp. 265–6.

[30] Jourdain, *Journal, 1608–17*, pp. 218–24.

[31] *Tuzūk*, pp. 104–5.

[32] *Letters Received*, III, p. 298 *n*.

[33] Ibid. The story of conversion is repeated by Bocarro.

[34] H. Maclagan, *The Jesuits and the Great Mogul*, London, 1932, p. 78.

[35] Ibid.

[36] *Tuzūk*, pp. 104–5: 'According to orders he went with diligence to Goa, and remaining there for some time, took at the price the Franks asked for them the rareties he met with at the port, without looking at the face of money at all. When he returned from the aforesaid port to the court, he produced before me one by one the things he had brought.'

soon appointed Governor of the *ṣūba* of Delhi.[37] It was in the same year that he was given very rapid promotions. In the 7th Regnal Year, he was granted three enhancements in rank, raising his *manṣab* from 2,000/1,000 to 2,500/1,500,[38] and then to 3,000/2,000.[39] He was also honoured with the grant of standard and kettledrums.[40]

One of the most important incidents in the life of Muqarrab Khān also occurred in 1612 during his tenure at *ṣūba* Delhi. Soon after his appointment we find him treating the Emperor, who was reportedly suffering from *khūn-pārā* (congestion of blood). Upon his physicians' advice, Jahāngīr was bled, and about a *ser* (approx. 1¼lb avdp) of blood taken from his left arm. The operation was successfully carried out by Muqarrab Khān.[41]

Muqarrab Khān thus remained a great favourite of his Emperor, who always treated him generously and easily forgave his faults. Jahāngīr's attitude towards him is illustrated by an incident which took place in 1613 when the Portuguese organized a raid on the port of Surat and sacked four ships.[42] Muqarrab Khān who held Surat in his charge (*havāla*), as customer or *Mutaṣaddī* was consoled by Jahāngīr by the award of a horse, elephant and robe of honour. He was then apparently at the Court.[43]

In retaliation for the Portuguese action Muqarrab Khān got St Xavier and other Jesuits arrested at Surat in 1614, and closed their churches.[44]

In spite of this hostility between Muqarrab Khān and the Portuguese, the English continued to bear a grudge against him since he was still not letting them have direct access to the

[37] *Tuzūk*, p. 109. Incidentally this is one of the few instances when Jahāngīr mentions him without compliments as 'my closest friend', 'my confidant'.

[38] Ibid., p. 106.

[39] Ibid., p. 112. On p. 105 of *Tuzūk*, Jahāngīr records his *manṣab* as 3000/2000, but this seems to be a slip since on the very next page, while recording actual promotions, he records it correctly as 2000/1000.

[40] Ibid., p. 112.

[41] Ibid., p. 110.

[42] Ibid., p. 125.

[43] Ibid. This shows that Muqarrab Khān was at Agra and not at Surat. This is confirmed by *Letters Received*, I, pp. 277–81. It was in 1614 that Muqarrab Khān was ordered to proceed to Surat. Kerridge says that Muqarrab Khān was also the governor of Cambay at this time. See *Letters Received*, II, pp. 103–4.

[44] *Letters Received*, II, pp. 96, 107.

Emperor.[45] When he heard of the growing hostility between the English and the Portuguese (in 1614–15), he seems to have become friendlier towards the English;[46] he naturally believed that a conflict between the two European powers could only benefit the Mughals.[47] In any case he was forced to side with the English through his fear of Portuguese naval raids.[48] Jahāngīr gave him a free hand to deal with the Europeans, even forwarding James I's letter to him to reply to on the Emperor's behalf.[49] The English factors, aware of his influence with the Emperor,[50] perhaps expected too much from him, and therefore felt that he was not really supporting them.[51] They even complain of the high rates that he was charging (5 instead of 3½ per cent) as customs.[52] We find that in 1615, it was with some reluctance that he let the English carry their gifts directly to Jahāngīr.[53]

This permission and the fact that he was passing on to them information against the Portuguese modified somewhat the English

[45] Ibid., p. 176; III, pp. 37, 39, etc.; 'Master Aldworth strived to persuade me [Nich. Downton] that Mocrib Chan the Nabob was our friend, and that now was the best time by reason of their Warres (with Portugals) for us to obtaine good trade and all Privileges that in reason we could demand.... I liking all their hopefull words, yet ever wishing some other in his place, and that Mocrib Chan had beene further away, of whom I rested still in doubt, that we should have no free trade but according to his accustomed manner...' (*Purchas*, IV, pp. 217–18).

[46] *Purchas*, IV, pp. 224–5.

[47] Ibid., pp. 225–6.

[48] Ibid., p. 243; 'The cause of their request [to the English to stay on at Surat], was their feare lest the Vice-Roy [of the Portuguese] after my (Downton's) departure should come against Surat with all his forces.' Thomas Elkington also writes of Muqarrab Khān's anxiety to befriend the English. Ibid.

[49] *Letters Received*, II, p. 104: 'and though I urged that Mocrob Chan could give no answer to our king's letter, yet prevailed nothing....'

[50] Ibid., pp. 103–4, 157, 185; III, p. 23, points out that the king was using him as an instrument against the English.

[51] Ibid., II, pp. 138, 149, 151, 178, 239–40; III, pp. 5, 22, 23, 37, 39, 43 and 44.

[52] Ibid., p. 5.

[53] Ibid., p. 22. English suspicions regarding Muqarrab Khān and the Portuguese appear to be justified in the light of a Treaty of Peace signed by Muqarrab Khān and the Portuguese Gocalo Pinto da Fonseca on 7 June 1615, which declared that the Mughals and the Portuguese 'will not engage in any trade' with English and Dutch merchants, nor would they be sheltered in ports, or supplied with provisions. See *Indian Historical Records Commission*, Vol. IX, pp. 78–80 and S. A. I. Tirmizi, *Mughal Documents (1526–1627)*, New Delhi, 1989, pp. 97–8.

attitude towards him.[54] The general complaint against him for non-payment for gifts nevertheless continued to the very end.[55]

Jahāngīr's favours, however, continued. Muqarrab Khān was given further *manṣab* enhancements: in 1616 he was promoted to the rank of 5,000/2,500.[56] In 1617 his rank was raised again to 5,000/5,000,[57] and he was appointed *sūbahdār* of Gujarat.[58] Thus within a short span Muqarrab Khān had attained the very prestigious rank of 5,000/5,000 which only a few could reach. Moreover, he was given charge of one of the important *ṣūba*s of the Mughal Empire, which he held for a year or two.

Muqarrab Khān's appointment as Governor of Gujarat was criticised by his contemporaries. Khān-i 'Āzam is reported by the English factors to have considered it unsuitable;[59] this criticism is also voiced by Lāhorī, who says that Jahāngīr was unable to recognize talent and was indiscreet in selecting people.[60]

After his term as Governor of Gujarat, Muqarrab Khān was sent to Bihar in 1618,[61] though initially he appeared reluctant to go there. He delayed going to Patna and came to the Court,[62] perhaps to plead against his transfer; but it was not revoked and he ultimately took up his post there.

[54] *Letters Received*, II, pp. 51–2, 325; Nicholas Downton: 'The twelfth [February, 1615] Lacandas came downe, informing me from the Nabob (he being so assured by the Jesuits, with whom he always kept faire weather for his better securitie, if we should be put to the worse) that there were sixe or eight [Portuguese] Frigates gone to the Northwards, with four or five Fireboats to be let drive among us in the night; and therefore wished carefully to looke out, for that it should be when we should least expect. I allowed his kindnesse, was glad of his carefull regard....' *Purchas*, IV, p. 241; see also pp. 262–3.

[55] *English Factories, 1624–29*, pp. 151, 241 and 271.

[56] *Tuzūk*, p. 149. [57] Ibid., p. 163.

[58] Ibid.; also Thomas Roe, *The Embassy of Sir Thomas Roe, 1615–19*, ed. Foster, London, 1926, p. 424.

[59] *English Factories, 1622–23*, p. 282.

[60] Abdul Hamīd Lāhorī, *Bādshāhnāma*, ed. K. Ahmad and A. Rahim, A.S.B., Calcutta, 1867, Vol. I, pt. i, p. 159.

[61] *Tuzūk*, p. 244; Shāh Nawāz Khān, *Ma'āsir-ul Umara*, ed. Molvi Ashraf Ali, Vol. III, pt. i, p. 381; *English Factories*, 1618–21, p. 9, note Muqarrab Khān as 'our then governor Muckrob Chan', implying that by February he had been transferred.

[62] 'Before this, an order had been given that Muqarrab Khān, having been appointed to Bihar, should hasten off there. He came to the court in order to pay his respects before he repaired to his destination...' *Tuzūk*, p. 271.

At Patna Muqarrab Khān is reported to have helped construct some Jesuit churches and to have kept a priest, maintaining his links with the Portuguese and so enriching himself.[63]

It was during this time that the Emperor visited Kairānā, where Muqarrab Khān had established a garden which was reputed for the variety of fruits grown there. Jahāngīr visited this garden in 1619, when he went there with the Imperial ladies.[64] He seems to have been so impressed that in 1620 he made another entry in his Memoirs of having gone to Kairānā a second time.[65]

Muqarrab Khān remained in Bihar till 1622 when he was given the Governorship of the province of Agra for one year.[66] Robert Hughes, an English factor at Patna, while recording the replacement of Muqarrab Khān from Bihar by Sultān Pervez, says that Muqarrab Khān upon the end of his term despatched Rs 300,000 to Agra by means of bills—an amount sufficiently large to disturb the exchange between the two places.[67]

We have little information about Muqarrab Khān after 1623 in the Persian sources. According to the *Ma'āṣiru-l Umarā* he was now appointed second *bakhshi* of the Empire.[68] Factory Records show that he also held charge of the port of Surat in that year.[69]

In 1628 Muqarrab Khān was retired from active service by Shāhjahān, obviously because of the trust he had enjoyed at his

[63] Maclagan, *The Jesuits and the Grand Mogul*, pp. 78–9. Maclagan quotes Father Simon Figueredo's letter of 20 December 1620, where the Father says that Muqarrab Khān kept a priest 'with no other object than that of attracting Portuguese trade, from which he could enrich himself.' But this in no way hindered his friendship with the English. For we are informed that he even helped the English factor Hughes to find a house on rent in the heart of the city 'on a rent of Rs 6/12 per month' (N. N. Ray, *The Annals of the Early English Settlement in Bihar*, Calcutta, 1927, p. 24.)

[64] 'Truly it is a very fine and enjoyable garden' (*Tuzūk*, p. 283).

[65] Ibid., p. 324.

[66] Ibid., p. 375; Mu'tamad Khān, *Iqbālnāma-i Jahāngīrī*, ed. Abdul Hai and Ahmad Ali, Calcutta, 1865, Vol. III, p. 178; *Ma'āsir-ul Umara*, III, p. 381. Jahāngīr in *Tuzūk* (p. 394) only mentions that 'Having conferred on Muqarrab Khān, who is one of the old officials, the government and administration of Agra, I gave him his leave.'

[67] *English Factories, 1618–21*, pp. 236, 248. On p. 248, Hughes writes to the President and Council at Surat: 'Money received from Agra and invested. Accounts cleared with Muqarrab Khān....'

[68] 'Was appointed as the Second *Bakhshi* of the Empire and thus came closer to Jahāngīr' (*Ma'āsir-ul Umara*, III, p. 381).

[69] 'The reporte here is that the King hath given the government of Surrat to Mocrob Chaun' (*English Factories, 1622–23*, p. 282).

father's court.[70] Farīd Bhakkari informs us that he spent the rest of his time in tending his gardens and orchards.[71] The main source of income for him was from his *watan* Kairānā, which was granted to him by Shāhjahān as *suyūrghāl.* The income from this place, we are told, amounted to one lakh of rupees.[72] In 1635 he is also mentioned as the *tuyūldār* (*jāgīrdār*) of Sambhal by Lāhorī.[73]

Muqarrab Khān was by hereditary profession a surgeon, and it was owing to this that he seems to have won Jahāngīr's favour initially. Even after he had attained high *manṣabs*, he continued to pursue this profession. Muqarrab Khān's skill in the field of medicine was so great that he was praised by Farīd Bhakkari as the Avicenna and Galen of the age.[74] This was of course exaggerated praise, but even Lāhorī admits that Muqarrab Khān was incomparable in the field of surgery (*jarrāhī*).[75] He is also reputed to have been interested in treating elephants' disorders.[76] Two of his works, *Ā'in-i Āshkār* and *Ā'in-us Shifa'*, based on the *Tibb-i Sikandari*, survive to this day. The first relates to symptoms and diseases,[77] while the second deals with drugs, their preparation, properties, temperament, degrees of efficacy and tested cures.[78]

Muqarrab Khān's activities were not confined to the administrative, diplomatic and medical fields alone. He seems to have taken much interest in horticulture, hunting, architecture and collecting all kinds of curiosities and rareties.

Thus in 1614–15 when he presented a list of items which he wanted to procure for the Emperor to the English factors he included 'pictures in cloth', canines of several varieties like 'mastiffs, greyhounds, spaniels and other small dogs'.[79] We also know that a

[70] Lāhorī, I, i, p. 159. The prejudices of contemporaries against him are well reflected through Lāhorī's words. See also Shaikh Farīd Bhakkari, *Zakhīratul Khawānīn*, ed. Moinul Haq, Karachi, 1970, II, pp. 271–3; *Ma'āsir-ul Umara*, III, p. 381.

[71] *Zakhīratul Khawānīn*, II, pp. 271–3; *Ma'āsir-ul Umara*, III, p. 381.

[72] Lāhorī, I, ii, p. 350.

[73] Ibid., p. 76.

[74] *Zakhīratul Khawānīn*, II, pp. 271–2; *Ma'āsir-ul Umara*, III, p. 380.

[75] Lāhorī, I, ii, p. 350; see also Muhammad Sādiq, *Tabaqāt-i Shāhjahānī*, MS Maulana Azad Library, ff. 570–71.

[76] Lāhorī, I, ii, p. 350.

[77] MS Bankipur Library, Patna.

[78] MS Central State Library, Hyderabad; cf. A. Rahman, M. A. Alvi et al. (ed.), *Science and Technology in Medieval India—a Bibliography of Source Materials in Sanskrit, Arabic and Persian*, New Delhi, 1982.

[79] *Letters Received*, II, p. 173; also, Memorandum of Downton in *The Voyage of Nicholas Downton to the East Indies, 1614–15*, p. 187.

rare bird, the Turkey-cock (*meleagris galhparo*) which was brought by the Portuguese from Goa was presented to the Emperor by Muqarrab K͟hān in 1612.[80] Jahāngīr also notes that in 1616 Muqarrab K͟hān had made a present to him of a small African elephant which greatly pleased the Emperor.[81] The ability to please the King in this manner stood him so well that his portrait adorned the wall of the Dīwānk͟hāna in Lahore along with the portraits of other great nobles like K͟hān-i Jahān, Sharīf K͟hān, Mahābat K͟hān and others.[82]

It appears that Muqarrab K͟hān was quite successful as a merchant as well. Apart from procuring gifts for the Emperor, he carried on private trade. His commercial links with both Portuguese and English merchants are time and again alluded to in the Factory Records. In 1611, when he visited an English ship along with K͟hwāja Nizām, a prominent merchant of Gujarat, he is alleged to have 'busied himselfe in buying of Knives, Glasses or any other toyes he found'.[83] Middleton also tells us of the commercial transactions which he conducted along with Muqarrab K͟hān and K͟hwāja Nizām.

> I went to him to his tent, where after friendly salutation and complements past, wee fell to treat of businesse; and agreed for prices of all our Lead, Quicksilver, and Vermilion, and for their goods likewise in liew thereof.[84]

This K͟hwāja Nizām who appears to have been a business partner of Muqarrab K͟hān was reportedly such an influential merchant that no other merchant dared to trade with the English 'without his prevention and leave'; and he was thus able to dictate terms to the English merchants.[85]

Probably it was due to the commercial acumen of Muqarrab K͟hān that all the business concerning the English factors in Gujarat was handed over by the Emperor to him:

[80] *Tuzūk*, pp. 104–5; also see M. A. Alvi and A. Rahman, *Jahangir, the Naturalist*, New Delhi, 1968, pp. 63–4; and A. Jan Qaisar, *The Indian Response to European Technology*, (*A.D. 1498–1707*), New Delhi, 1982, p. 152.

[81] *Tuzūk*, p. 158.

[82] Narrative of William Finch as given in *Purchas*, IV, p. 54.

[83] *Purchas*, III, pp. 179 and 262–3.

[84] Ibid., pp. 180 and 265–6. Apart from these commodities, we find Muqarrab K͟hān trading in various kinds of cloth. See, for example, *Purchas*, IV, pp. 224–5.

[85] *Purchas*, III, pp. 180–1; IV, pp. 219–20.

...All business concerning us and our trade is referred unto him, and as he adviseth so things here will pass, and what he granteth there will be confirmed here....[86]

In his commercial transactions, Muqarrab Khān made full use of his position; we find him forcing the English to sell their goods at lower prices.[87] Further, it appears that he owned some ships and carried on private trade.[88] We are told that among his contemporaries, Muqarrab Khān 'hath more adventures at sea than any of this country.'[89]

Muqarrab Khān was also interested in European technology. In 1612, he asked the English factors to provide him a model of a 'Chaine-Pumpe', which, it seems, was presented to him.[90] He had even wanted to 'experience' the use of window panes, a wish which unfortunately could not be fulfilled by the English factors due to the non-availability of a glacier.[91] Then in 1621 he is said to have purchased a looking-glass at the high price of Rs 300.[92]

Muqarrab Khān also emulated European fashions in dress. In 1615 he asked to be presented with an English suit which was given to him at Surat. The English suspected that his desire to have this suit was just to show off to the women of his harem.[93] The *Tuzūk* records that he also received a hat from the Europeans.[94]

Muqarrab Khān was known for his love of orchards and gardens. He had established his family seat at Kairānā, a *pargana* in *sarkār* Sahāranpūr, Muẓaffarnagar district, to which he ultimately retired. It is situated partly in the fertile low-lying areas of the Jumna and partly on a sloping bank.[95] It was here that Muqarrab

[86] *Letters Received*, II, p. 157.

[87] See, for example, *Purchas*, IV, pp. 21, 23, 24; *Letters Received*, II, p. 138.

[88] *Purchas*, III, p. 176; IV, pp. 224–5; *English Factories*, 1618–21, p. 19.

[89] *Letters Received*, I, p. 307; *Purchas*, III, p. 2.

[90] *Purchas*, III, pp. 263–4; A. Jan Qaisar, 'Merchant Shipping in India during the 17th Century', *IESHR*, V, no. 2, June 1968, p. 198, *n*. 1.

[91] *English Factories*, 1618–21, p. 11.

[92] Ibid., p. 246. On p. 327, there is a reference to a 'looking-glasse' sold. We are however not told of the identity of the buyer.

[93] Farewell's account in *Voyage of Downton*, p. 150.

[94] *Tuzūk*, p. 115.

[95] Edwin T. Atkinson, *Statistical Description and Historical Account of the North-Western Provinces of India*, III, pt. ii, Allahabad, 1876, p. 685; H. R. Nevill, *Muzaffarnagar, A Gazetteer, being Volume III of the District Gazetteers of the United Provinces of Agra and Oudh*, Allahabad, 1903, pp. 267–8.

Khān laid out a complex of buildings with a very large orchard, of which the *barā'darī* and tank survive.[96] He also built a *dargāh* over the tomb of Shāh Sharaf Bū'Ali Qalandar in Kairānā, according to his contemporary Farīd Bhakkari.[97]

His gardens at Kairānā where he planted fruits, especially mangoes, brought from all parts of the country became famous.[98] The mangoes from his orchards could be got even two months after the mango season was over in India.[99] Unfortunately we do not know about the varieties of mangoes or other fruits that he planted, nor whether he made use of grafting techniques, which his friends the Portuguese had introduced to produce the first grafted mango, the Alfonso. However, the trees in his orchards continued to fruit well after the mango season was over elsewhere.

As Governor of Gujarat, Muqarrab Khān renovated old buildings and built *jharoka*s at Ahmadabad.[100]

In his last years Muqarrab Khān spent his life peaceably in his harem of 1,000 women, tending the mausoleum of Shāh Sharaf Bū Qalandar.[101] He died aged about 90 in AH 1056/AD 1646.[102]

Muqarrab Khān left behind three sons and a daughter. One of the sons, Riẓqullah, is known to have continued in his father's profession of physician and attained the rank of 800 during Shāhjahān's reign.[103] In 1649 a sum of Rs 1,000 was also fixed in his name by the Emperor.[104] A brother, Shaikh 'Abdur Rahīm, had acted as his *nā'ib* when Muqarrab Khān was at Cambay in 1611.[105]

[96] Atkinson, *North-Western Provinces*, p. 685; Nevill, *Muzaffarnagar*, p. 268; A. Fuhrer, *The Monumental Antiquities and Inscriptions in the North-Western Provinces and Oudh*, Varanasi, 1969, p. 13.

[97] *Zakhīratul Khawānīn*, II, p. 272.

[98] Ibid., pp. 271–3; *Ma'āsir-ul Umara*, III, pp. 381–2. According to the *Tājul Ma'āsir*, the mangoes of Kairānā were long celebrated in Delhi (cf. Atkinson, *North-Western Provinces*, p. 686; Nevill, *Muzaffarnagar*, p. 268).

[99] *Tuzūk*, p. 283.

[100] Ibid., p. 162.

[101] Rizqullah built this saint's tomb some eight years before Muqarrab Khān's death. See Nevill, *Muzaffarnagar*, p. 267.

[102] Lāhorī, II, ii, p. 613. Though the author of *Tabaqāt-i Shāhjahānī* (f. 570) gives AH 1050/AD 1640 as the year of his death.

[103] *Ma'āsir-ul Umara*, III, p. 382. Aurangzeb gave him the title Khān, and he ultimately died in AD 1668. See Atkinson, *North-Western Provinces*, p. 589.

[104] Muhammad Wāris, *Bādshāhnāma*, MS Rampur (transcript, Department of History Library, AMU), I, p. 71.

[105] Jourdain, *Jounal, 1608–1617*, p. 173; Lāhorī, I, ii, p. 351; *Purchas*, III, p. 3.

'Abdur Rahīm's son, Shaikh Qāṣim, was an expert surgeon, having been tutored by Muqarrab Khān himself. He was also well-versed in mathematics.[106] Of his other relatives, mention is made of a son-in-law who is said to have been 'a very ingenious young man', helping Muqarrab Khān in his diplomatic and administrative missions.[107]

Muqarrab Khān's was a colourful life: he was physician, nobleman, man of culture, diplomat, with many of the virtues and vices of the Mughal nobility. His career is representative of Jahāngīr's policy of bringing in new elements into the nobility: the *Shaikhzādas* (Indian Muslims) were those who particularly benefited from his favours.[108] But Muqarrab Khān possessed certain qualities that Jahāngīr particularly liked: he was accomplished, cultured, perhaps a man of skill and taste—and perhaps a witty conversationalist. Men like Muqarrab Khān could not as easily claim the attention of a cold and calculating intellect like that of Shāhjahān's.

[106] Lāhori, I, ii, pp. 350–1.
[107] *Purchas*, IV, p. 245.
[108] See M. Athar Ali, *The Apparatus of Empire*, Delhi, 1985, pp. xx–xxi.

8

Agriculture and Revenue Rates in the Mathura Region (1724–42)

S. P. GUPTA

No study has yet been attempted of local crop-patterns and revenue-rates in any area of the Mughal Empire, except for Rajasthan. However, documents from the first half of the eighteenth century preserved at Bikaner, make it possible for us to offer such a study for Mathura.

Pargana 'Shri Mathurājī', i.e. Mathura, *sarkār* and *ṣūbā* Akbarābād (Agra), was assigned to Sawāī Jai Singh in *tankhwāh jāgīr*, which he apparently continued to hold from the 1720s till his death (1744) with some intervals. Accordingly, his government maintained detailed accounts of income and expenditure for *pargana* Mathura. These are available in *aṛhsatta*s, which are now kept at the Rajasthan State Archives, Bikaner. The period covered in the *aṛhsatta*s is from 1723 to 1744, and although a continuous series is not available and there are considerable gaps, the details for six different years for the same *pargana* enable us to have an impression of the direction of change.

The number of *mauza*s (villages) in *pargana* Mathura was fifty-five. Of these, twenty-three villages were held by Jai Singh in his own *khālisa* (lands reserved for himself and not sub-assigned); the remainder were assigned either to *patshahi-manṣabdar*s or to other sub-assignees. Fortunately for our study, the number of villages held in *khālisa* did not change over the years. It would not be unreasonable to presume that the crop-pattern and revenue-rates that existed in the *khālisa* areas represented conditions in the Mathura region generally, though minor variations cannot, of course, be ruled out.

The *aṛhsatta*s of *pargana* Mathura contain information on the following points among other things: Total revenue demand on the gross cropped area; proportion of the demand from *kharif* and *rabi* harvests; and cash demand on area under each of the *zabti* and *jinsi* crops. Both the *zabti* and *jinsi* crops were primarily assessed according to *zabt* (i.e. by measurement). Incidentally, on some *jinsi* crops, the demand was assessed not in cash, but in kind which was commuted into cash by applying a schedule of prices. The system ordinarily applied was most probably *kankut*.[1] A detailed account of the rate of payment per *bigha* for individual crops is given in the *arhsattas*. In certain cases, particularly in times of scarcity, *batai* (actual crop-sharing) was applied. In this case, the proportion of the rate of demand generally seems to have been one half of the produce.[2]

Kharif was the major harvest in the area, as may be seen from Table 1:

TABLE 1

Percentage of Area under *Kharif* and *Rabi*

Year	*Kharif*	*Rabi*
1724	80	20
1730	78	22
1732	80	20
1735	58	42
1741	68	32
1742	69	31

The *kharif* harvest was the more important not only because the area sown is larger; the revenue realized in different years was also larger.[3] The disproportion between the *kharif* and *rabi* is most marked between the years 1724 and 1732, when the area under *kharif* seems to have been four times the area sown under *rabi*. However, it is reduced in the successive years except for 1735, when the area covered in *rabi* amounted to as much as 42 per cent of the total.

The position in modern times with respect to the relative area

[1] For the definition of *kankut* see Irfan Habib, *The Agrarian System of Mughal India*, pp. 199–200.

[2] *Arhsatta pargana* Shri Mathuraji vs 1799/1742.

[3] *Arhsattas pargana* Mathura for different years.

under *rabi* and *kharif* is entirely different. In Mathura *tahsil*, for example, during the period 1897–8 to 1906–7 (*fasli* 1305–10), the area under *rabi* crops averaged not less than 41 per cent of the gross cropped area.[4] The much lower extent of *rabi* in the eighteenth century, therefore, stands in need of explanation. Partly, it may be due to the expansion of canal irrigation in the later half of the nineteenth century, this mainly affecting *rabi* crops. In 1910–11, the area irrigated by canals was about 29 per cent of the total cropped area.[5] Secondly, the demand for wheat as an export crop in the late nineteenth and early twentieth century may also have resulted in expansion of *rabi* cropping, wheat being a crop of that harvest.

The statistics of revenue-rates on individual crops throw a good deal of light on the relative importance of the crops. We have examined the percentage of areas under each crop (Table 2) along with the percentage of the revenue realized from them (Table 3). In working out these percentages, crops with less than one per cent whether in terms of area or revenue, have been ignored. However, the total percentage for such crops has been given in the category 'miscellaneous'. Although the proportion of different crops estimated according to revenue yield or area, is different in many respects, the overall picture of the crop-pattern as well as of the major changes during the period under review appears to have remained the same.

The principal *kharif* crops were *bajra*, *jowar* and *moth*, occupying on an average over 85 per cent of the entire area cultivated in this harvest. *Kharif* cash crops like cotton (*van*), though not grown largely, was sown in almost all parts of the area (Table 2). These crops did not, in any case, cover more than 3 per cent of the total area. However, *til* (sesame) and sugar-cane[6] covered 20 per cent and 6 per cent of the area respectively in 1730. Thereafter, the cultivation of these two crops became insignificant. The other *kharif* crops such as rice (*dhan*), hemp (*sunn*) and *mash* are of little importance. It would seem that of the *kharif* crops, cotton has shown a remarkable expansion in area since the seventeenth century. In 1897–8 to 1906–7,[7] cotton accounted for 14.16 per

4 D. L. Drake-Brockman, *Muttra, A Gazetteer*, VII, Appendix Table VI.

5 Ibid., Table V.

6 The word used for sugar-cane in our document is *gada* or *sarha*.

7 Drake-Brockman, *Muttra*.

TABLE 2

Percentage Area under *Kharif/Rabi* for Different Crops

	KHARIF										
	Zabti									*Jinsi*	
	Cotton	Rice	*Til*	Sugar-cane	*Dhan*	*Naj (Jins)*	*Jowar*	*Bajra*	*Moth*	*Urd*	Miscellaneous
1724	1.97	—	—	—	—	94	—	—	—	—	4
1730	2.54	—	14	2	—	69	31	11	20	6	12.46
1732	—	—	—	—	3	95	—	—	—	—	2
1735	1	—	—	—	—	93	—	—	—	—	6
1741	—	—	—	—	—	97	—	—	—	—	3
1742	—	—	—	—	—	92	—	—	—	—	8

	RABI								
	Gram	Wheat	Barley	*Kakri Kharbooza*	*Gojai (Gojra)*	*Baijhri*	*Brinjal*	*Tarbooz*	Miscellaneous
1724	36	33	7	1	—	—	—	—	23
1730	25	21	34	—	—	—	—	—	20
1732	57	9	15	10	—	4	—	—	5
1735	66	11	4	—	—	8	—	—	11
1741	62	15	4	8	—	4	3	2	2
1742	2	18	30	25	4	—	—	12	9

TABLE 3

Percentage of Revenue Derived from Different Crops (*Rabi*)

	Gram	Wheat	Barley	*Khar-booza/ Kakri*	*Tar-booz*	*Methi*	Brinjal	*Chena (Arzan)*	Tobacco	Onion	*Ajwain*	*Gojar/ Gojra*	*Baijhri*	Miscel-laneous
1724[a]	24	39	8	17	6	1	1	1	1	—	—	—	—	2
1730	14	25	37	12	—	4	2	—	—	1	—	3	1	2
1732	40	12	19	16	—	—	2	—	—	—	1	—	5	5
1735	46	17	5	6	—	1	4	—	—	—	2[b]	—	10	9
1741	45	22	6	13	2	—	3	—	1	—	—	1	6	1
1742	2	22	34	23	9	—	4	1	—	—	—	5	—	—

[a] In this year the figures are subclassified under two heads: *jinsi bigha* and *batai jinsi*. Under *batai* the revenue realized for gram, wheat and *sarson* is 87 per cent, 3 per cent and 2 per cent respectively. For *bhoos* the revenue realized is 8 per cent. The total comes to one hundred.

[b] *Ajwain* and onion are combined here, having the same rate of Rs 5 per *bigha*.

cent of the area under *kharif* in Mathura *tahsil*, and cotton raised with *arhar*, 21.50 per cent; the respective percentages of total area were 8.32 and 12.63. In the early eighteenth century, the area under cotton ranged from only 1 to 2.54 per cent of the total area under *kharif* crops, and on average, only 1.11 per cent of the total cropped area. On the other hand, *moth*, which was an important *kharif* crop, was no longer deemed significant enough to be recorded early in this century. For the rest, *jowar* dominated the *kharif* crops early in the eighteenth century as well as in the early twentieth century.

In *rabi*, the most important crops were gram, wheat and barley. Of the three, the most distinct position was occupied by gram. The area sown under gram rose from 36 per cent in 1724 to 66 and 62 per cent in 1735 and 1741 respectively. However, 1742 was a year of scarcity, and the area under gram fell by 2 per cent. The overall area under wheat was comparatively small; it amounted to 33 per cent in 1724, generally declining in subsequent years. The proportion of barley does not remain uniform. The minimum limit is 4 and the maximum 34 per cent. The maximum area sown under barley seems to have been at the cost of gram.

Various mixed crops known as *gojro* or *gojai* (wheat and barley mixed), *gochani* (wheat and gram) and *baijhar* (a mixed crop of wheat, barley gram and peas) were also sown. Of them only *baijhri* is worth noticing, which covered 4 to 8 per cent of the area in *rabi* between 1732 and 1741.

The other *rabi* crops are insignificant except for *kakri-kharbooza* (cucumber and melon) and *tarbooz* (watermelon). In the year of scarcity, i.e. 1742, these crops covered 25 and 12 per cent respectively of the total area.

The most remarkable change in *rabi* cropping since the eighteenth century seems to have been the expansion in the cultivation of wheat. In our period, wheat on average covered 16 per cent of the total area under *rabi* crops; around the beginning of this century, it covered 26.79 per cent. In terms of total area the expansion is still more marked. In 1724–42, wheat was sown in 3.95 per cent of the total cropped area, which increased in the period 1897–8 to 1906–7, to 11.05 per cent (in Mathura tahsil),[8] a relative expansion of nearly three times. Barley also improved its position. But gram

[8] Ibid.

declined in its share of area under *rabi* (falling from 49 to about 34 per cent),[9] although its share in the total cropped area seems to have remained stable (13.28 per cent in 1724–42; about 13.5 per cent in the early nineteenth century).

One of the most striking features of the division of area sown under each crop is that in both harvests, cash crops occupied a rather insignificant position. Though tobacco, cotton, and *ajwain* were sown in this region, the area under them was not large. *Til* was sown only in one year, when, however, it occupied a large area. It is not clear why it was not normally sown.

The area sown under the *jinsi* crops is much larger than that of the *zabt* crops in the two harvests. Table 4 shows the percentage of the area under two heads, *zabt* and *jins*.

TABLE 4

Area under *Zabt* and *Jins*

Year	*Kharif*		*Rabi*	
	Zabt	*Jins*	*Zabt*	*Jins*
1724	6	94	—	—
1730	31	69	16	84
1732	5	95	14	86
1735	7	93	11	89
1741	3	97	14	86
1742	8	92	44	56

The *zabt* crops included cash crops. In 1730, the high percentage of the *zabt* area was because of an increase in cultivation of *til* and sugar-cane. Otherwise the *zabt* area does not exceed 8 per cent of the total. Another interesting point which emerges from this Table is the increase of *zabti* crops in the *rabi* harvest, which does not indicate any sharp rise and fall in different years except in 1742.

Once we have established the relative position of the areas sown under different crops over a number of years of the first half of the

[9] Gram cultivated alone was on 24.54 per cent of the area and when raised in combination with barley, 18.36 per cent. The formula I have adopted here is to add half the proportion to the total of barley and the remaining half to the gram. The total comes to about 34 per cent.

eighteenth century, we can compare it with those collected from modern statistics[10] to establish any further changes that might have taken place in the relative position of various crops during the intervening period. As stated earlier, due to the effective application of the *zabt* system, we have the details of rates per *bigha* for the various *kharif* and *rabi* crops (Table 5). Along with the revenue rates, a lump sum amount on the whole group of villages was also realized from *zamindar*s as *bilmuqta*, which varied from 1 to 5 per cent of the total revenue.

Table 3 strongly suggests that the rate of revenue demand per *bigha* for the various crops showed a remarkable continuity throughout the years for which *aṛhsatta*s are available, except in the case of some *jinsi* crops in *kharif* and *rabi*. Differences in the rate of demand depended on variable factors such as the quality of the produce, productivity of the soil, and prices. In our region, the rates sometimes differed because of the quality of soil. For example, the rate of demand on *khadar*[11] (low or alluvial lands) land was higher than on *banjar* land; in 1742, the rate of demand on wheat and *gojai* (wheat and barley mixed) was Rs 5 and 4 per *bigha* in *khadar* and *banjar* land respectively, while for barley it was Rs 4.75 and Rs 3.75 respectively. Another factor responsible for the variation, inferred from our records, is that different *dastur*s were applied to different categories or castes of peasants. For example, in *kharif*, for the *jinsi* crops, the *pahi*s[12] (outside cultivators) and *chaudhuri* and *qanungo* were charged land-revenue at lower rates than the *gaventi* or *gawai* (resident cultivators or *khudkasht*). The explanation for this difference, first, may be that *pahi*s were invited specifically to extend cultivation; and most probably the inferior quality lands were allotted to them. Their role is more significant and effective at the time of scarcity as may be seen in 1742.[13] The *chaudhuri* and *qanungo* enjoyed the privilege of paying lower rates, being officials. The maximum demand, therefore, fell upon the *gaventi* cultivating the *polach* land (most fertile land).

In both harvests, however, cash crops show a uniform rate of demand.

The revenue rates for some crops may be compared with the

[10] Drake-Brockman, *Muttra*.

[11] On the *khadar* land barley and wheat are grown with or without irrigation.

[12] *Aṛhsatta*s Mathura 1798/1741; 1787/1730 and 1789/1732.

[13] Ibid., 1799/1742.

TABLE 5

Rate of Revenue per Crop per Bigha (*Kharif*)
(Rupees)

Year	To-bacco	*Van* (Cotton)	*Sunn* (Hemp)	*Sali* (Rice)	*Maka*	*Naj* (*Jins*)	*Jowar*	*Moth*	*Bajra*	*Til*	Sugar-cane	Vege-tables	*Ariya*	*Brinjal*	*Dhan*	*Kaguni*	*Urd*	*Madhwa*
1724	5.00	3.00	3.00	3.00	2.00	1.00	—	—	—	—	—	4.50	1.50	—	—	—	—	—
						1.50												
						1.56												
						1.62												
						1.75												
1730	—	3.00	3.00	3.00	2.50	1.65	1.75	1.10	1.62	1.50	5.00	4.50	1.50	2.25	3.00	2.00	1.25	—
							1.87	1.34		2.00				3.25				
								1.40		2.50								
								1.62		3.00								
								1.94										
1732	—	3.00	3.00	—	—	1.37	—	—	—	—	—	4.50	1.50	—	3.00	2.00	—	2.00
						1.50												
						1.56												
						1.62												
						1.75												
						1.87												

Table 5 continued

Year	To-bacco	*Van* (Cotton)	*Sunn* (Hemp)	*Sali* (Rice)	*Maka*	*Naj* (*Jins*)	*Jowar*	*Moth*	*Bajra*	*Til*	Sugar-cane	Vege-tables	*Ariya*	*Brinjal*	*Dhan*	*Kaguni*	*Urd*	*Madhwa*
1735	5.00	3.00	3.00	—	2.50	1.56	—	—	—	—	—	4.50	1.50	2.25	2.50	2.00	—	—
						1.62									3.00			
						1.75												
						1.87												
1741	—	3.00	2.00	—	—	1.62	—	—	—	—	5.00	4.50	—	—	3.00	—	—	—
			2.50			1.87												
			3.00			0.75												
						1.06												
						1.25												
						1.50												
						1.62												
1742	—	3.00	—	—	—	1.31	2.50	—	1.50	—	—	—	—	—	3.00	—	—	—
									1.57									

Table 5 continued

RABI

Year	To-bacco	Gram	Wheat	Barley	*Cheena (Arzan)*	Brin-jal	Onion	*Methi*	*Tar-booz*	*Kakri*	*Gajar*	*Aj-wain*	*Khar-booza*	*Gojra (Gojai)*	*Bai-jhri*	*Ghan*	*Cholai*	*Go-chani*
1724	5.00	2.00	1.75	2.87	1.50	3.25	5.00	4.50	2.50	4.00	2.00	5.00	—	—	—	—	—	—
		1.75	3.25	3.75					3.00									
		2.00	3.75															
		2.12	4.00															
			3.00															
1730	5.00	1.62	3.50	3.00	1.50	3.00	5.00	4.50	—	—	2.00	—	4.50	3.25	3.25	—	—	—
		1.75	3.75	3.25										3.87				
		2.00	4.00	3.75														
1732	5.00	1.25	4.00	3.25	2.00	3.25	5.00	4.50	2.12	4.50	2.00	5.00	4.50	3.87	3.25	3.00	—	—
		2.00		3.75														
1735	5.00	2.00	4.00	3.75	1.75	2.97	5.00	4.50	—	—	2.00	5.00	4.50	—	2.25	—	2.00	3.87
					2.00										3.00			
															3.25			
1741	5.00	1.87	3.75	3.75	1.25	3.25	5.00	4.50	2.12	4.25	—	5.00	4.50	3.87	3.25	—	—	—
		2.00	4.00		1.50													
1742	—	2.00	5.00	4.75	1.35	3.25	—	4.50	2.12	4.00	2.00	—	4.00	5.00	—	—	—	—
			4.00	3.75									3.50	4.00				
													2.12					

dasturs given in the *A'in-i Akbari* (Table 6) for the *dastur* circle of Agra which included the *pargana* of Mathura. The *A'in*'s *dam* and *jital* are converted into rupees (one rupee being equivalent to 40 *dams*) and *bigha-i Ilahi* into *bigha-i daftari*, which was two-thirds of *bigha-i Ilahi*.[14] It can be seen from the comparison that for gram, wheat and barley, the rates were 2.38, 3.17, and 4.07 times those of the *A'in* for an interval of nearly a century and half.

TABLE 6

Revenue Rates per *Bīgha* of Different Crops: *A'in* and Early Seventeenth Century (rupees)

Crops	*A'in* *Dastūr* circle Agra (A)	Mathura Documents Mathura (B)	Ratio (B):(A)
Kharif			
Cotton	1.64	3.00	1.82
Sunn	0.55	3.00	5.45
Sali	0.87	3.00	3.44
Jowar	0.84	1.87	2.22
Moth	0.55	1.40	2.54
Sugar-cane	2.76	5.00	1.81
Vegetables	1.59	4.50	2.83
Urd	0.75	1.25	1.66
Bajra	—	—	—
Rabi			
Wheat	1.26	4.00	3.17
Gram	0.84	2.00	2.38
Barley	0.92	3.75	4.07
Cheena (*Arzan*)	0.46	1.75	3.80
Onion	1.59	5.00	3.14
Tarbooz	2.10	2.12	1.00
Ajwain	1.59	5.00	3.14
Kharbooza	0.29	4.50	15.51

[14] *A'in-i Akbari*, ed. Blochmann, I, pp. 356–63.

This rise in revenue demand can also be detected in cash crops such as cotton, *ajwain*, *sunn*, sugar-cane and *arzan* (*cheena*) the rates on which were respectively 1.82, 3.14, 5.45, 1.81 and 3.80 times those given in the *A'in*. This rise can be explained as part of the general rise in agricultural prices during the intervening period. Incidentally, some of the prices of *jinsi* crops are recorded in our *arhsattas*, giving a fair idea of the proportionate rise in prices compared to prices in the *A'in* given for Agra in rupees per maund (*man-i Shahjahani*).

Crop	Agra[15]	Mathura		
		1693[16]	1724[17a]	1742[17b]
Wheat	0.40	0.83	1.66	2.00
Gram	0.27	—	1.54	—
Barley	0.27	—	—	1.60
Sarson	0.40	0.83	2.66	—

In a normal year like 1724, the prices at Mathura were respectively 4, 5.7 and 5.92 times those of wheat, gram and barley given in the *A'in*. If we adjust the rise in the rates to that in prices of these crops, we can conclude that there was no large real change in the rate of revenue demand from the *A'in*'s period to our period.

An important problem for consideration is whether the revenue demand on individual crops underwent any change between the time of the *A'in* and the early eighteenth century. For this purpose I have indexed the revenue rates from both sources, with the rate on wheat in either as 100. Table 7 sets out the result.

It is singular that the valuation set on cotton in the *A'in* is so much higher than the indexed rate in the eighteenth century. It is interesting that cotton was rated in value per acre in Agra and Aligarh in 1870–1 and 1872–3[18] at about the same level (66.67 and

[15] *A'in*, I, pp. 60–1.

[16] *Nirakh bazar qasba* Mathuraji vs 1750/1693.

[17a,b] *Arhsattas Pargana* Shri Mathura vs 1781/1724 and 1799/1742.

[18] Atkinson, *Statistical, Descriptive and Historical Account of the N.W. Provinces of India*, VII, pp. 455–6, Allahabad, 1875. Also see Vol. IX for Aligarh (Kol). Cf. Shireen Moosvi, 'The Magnitude of the Land Revenue Demand and the Income of the Mughal Ruling Class under Akbar', *Medieval India—A Miscellany*, IV, p. 95.

TABLE 7

Relative Revenue Rates of Crops per *Bīgha*
(wheat = 100)

Crops	*Dastur*-circle Agra (*A'in*)	Mathura (early 18th c.)	Agra (1870–1)	Kol (Aligarh) (1872–3)
Kharif				
Van (cotton)	130.15	75	66.67	78.57
Sunn (hemp)	43.65	75	—	—
Sali (rice)	69.65	75	—	—
Jowar	66.67	46.75	41.14	42.86
Moth	43.65	35	—	—
Sugar-cane	219.05	125	197.56	217.86
Vegetables	126.9	112.5	—	—
Urd	59.52	32.25	—	—
Bajra	—	47	—	41.61
Rabi				
Wheat	100	100	100	100
Gram	66.67	50	40.65	48.57
Barley	73.12	93.75	70.24	65.32
Cheena (*arzan*)	36.51	43.75	—	—
Onion	126.19	125	—	—
Tarbooz	166.67	53	—	—
Ajwain	126.19	125	—	—
Kharbooza	23.6	125.5	—	—

78.57) in terms of wheat, as in the early eighteenth century (75 per cent). Sugar-cane shows a low indexed rate in the early eighteenth century, but the *c.* 1870 assessments in Agra and Aligarh (Koil) were closer (197.56 and 217.86) to the *A'in*'s rate. Barley is exceptionally highly rated (93.75 per cent) in the early eighteenth century, compared to both the *A'in*'s (73.12 per cent), and the 1870 assessments (70.24 and 65.32 per cent for Agra and Aligarh). The rates on *tarbooz* and *kharbooza* are diametrically opposite to those in the *A'in*; modern assessments are not available. The indexed rates of other crops seem to have remained approximately the same between 1595 (the *A'in*), and the early eighteenth century.

The data drawn from the Mathura documents indicate that neither the cropping pattern nor the relative value placed on the yield of different crops has remained the same over long periods. The change between the early eighteenth and early twentieth centuries has been especially marked. There has been a remarkable growth in *rabi* cropping; and a dramatic expansion in the cultivation of cotton and wheat. Clearly, the canals and railways of the latter half of the nineteenth century had much to do with this expansion of cultivation in two crops so prominently intended for the market. The well-known hypothesis about the commercialization of agriculture in the latter half of the nineteenth century receives clear corroboration from such early but firm statistics.

9

The Ruler and the Nobility in Marwar during the Reign of Jaswant Singh

B. L. BHADANI

James Tod in his celebrated interpretation of the history of Rajasthan tenaciously held to the view that the medieval Rajput polity was strikingly analogous to the feudal system of Europe.[1] Tod endeavoured to show that Rajput society was hierarchical and, hence, the relationship between the *pattawat* and the Raja was that of vassal and lord, as in European feudalism. This relationship was based on a contract of mutual support and fidelity.[2] Tod emphasized the hierarchical and clannish organization of Rajput vassalage, by which, according to him, a sub-vassal could neglect the sovereign (Raja) in favour of the latter's vassal from whom the sub-vassal got his own land grant.[3]

Tod discovered two distinct groups of tenureholders: the *grasiya thakur* or 'lord', and the *bhumia*. The *grasiya* held land grants given by the prince or Raja. It was purely a service tenure since the holder had to maintain regular contingents as fixed by the Raja. Although these *patta*s or fiefs could be renewed,[4] they were neither lifelong nor hereditary.[5] On the other hand, *bhumia* tenure was not a service grant, but was hereditary.

Since the *pattawat*s considered themselves kinsmen of the Raja and thus in a sense his equals, they did not accept any interference in or resumption of their grants. About the beginning of the nineteenth century, many protests by *pattawat*s about resumption

[1] James Tod, *Annals and Antiquities of Rajasthan*, I, reprint, New Delhi, 1978, pp. 109–10.

[2] Ibid., p. 127.

[3] Ibid., p. 128.

[4] Ibid., p. 133.

[5] Ibid., p. 136.

of their *patta*s were made to the British Government. The main contention was that such confiscation violated the earlier practice;[6] they argued that the Raja had no right to resume the grants because he himself belonged to the same stock of Rajputs. One *pattawat* of Marwar protested against this 'innovation' and addressed a petition in 1821 to the British Resident in the following words.[7]

> Sri Maharaja and ourselves are of one stock, all Rahtores. He is our head, we his servants; but now anger has seized him, and we are dispossessed of our country. Of the estates our patrimony and our dwelling, some have been made *Khalisa*...

Some *pattawat*s further claimed:

> ...before the face of his [the Raja's] ancestors, our own ancestors have slain and been slain; and in performing services to the [Mughal] kings, they made the state of Jodhpur what it is. Wherever Marwar was concerned, there our fathers were to be found, and with their lives preserved the land. Sometimes our head was minor; even then by the wisdom of our fathers and their services, the land was kept firm under our feet, and thus has it descended from generation to generation.

Similar sentiments were expressed by the chief of Deogarh and his sub-*pattawat* towards the Maharana of Mewar: 'When Deogarh was established, at the same time were our allotments; as his patrimony, so is our patrimony.' The claim was that 'Our rights and privilege in his family are the same as his in the family of the Presence.'[8]

From the foregoing statements two significant points emerge. First, the *pattawat*s were claiming hereditary rights in their *patta*-areas. Secondly, the *pattawat*s considered themselves to be the ruler's kinsmen, so that the monarchy was what U. N. Ghoshal said of pre-thirteenth century North Indian states, a 'clan-monarchy'.[9]

Lyall differs only in emphasis from Tod: he too lays much stress

[6] Tod, *Annals*, pp. 159–62. See Daniel Thorner, 'Feudalism in India', in *Feudalism in History*, ed. Rustom Coulborn, London, 1956, p. 139.

[7] These petitions, translated into English by Tod, are given in the Appendices (see Appendices 1 to 20, pp. 159–71). Tod himself supported the representation of the *pattawat*s and impressed upon the British Government the desirability of protecting the cherished rights of the *pattawat*s. See R.P. Vyas, *Role of Nobility in Marwar*, New Delhi, 1969, p. 64.

[8] Tod, *Annals*, Appendix II, pp. 160–1.

[9] U. N. Ghoshal, *The Hindu Revenue System*, Calcutta, 1972, pp. 316–17.

on the blood ties between the chieftain (*pattawat*) and the ruler.[10] According to him, 'pure blood' is the origin of the tenure of *pattawat*s in western Rajputana.[11]

These views need close examination, a process which is made possible by the considerable body of documentary evidence coming to us from the seventeenth century.

II

First of all, we find that the *patta* (assignment of *pattawats*) was in essence a service tenure and by its very nature transferable.[12] Sometimes transfers took place after one year or even less; in others the *patta*s continued for a much longer time. At any rate, it was a common practice for villages in *patta*s to be frequently transferred from one *pattawat* to another[13] or to the *khalisa* of the Raja.[14]

The *pattawat* was entitled to collect the land revenue and other taxes from the territory assigned to him by this document issued by the ruler. The revenues of the *patta* were in fact granted in lieu of a cash salary; hence it was a revenue assignment proper, in Moreland's terminology,[15] and not a land grant. A certain amount was determined to be the income of each *patta*, and termed *rekh* in Marwar.[16] If it fell short of the fixed salary, the balance due was treated as *talab* (lit. pay claim)[17] which was either paid in cash[18] or through additional assignments.[19] Sometimes half the salary was

[10] Sir Alfred C. Lyall, *Asiatic Studies*, First Series, London, 1899, pp. 244–6.

[11] Ibid.; cf. Thorner, *Feudalism in India*, p. 142.

[12] The word *tagir* or *tagirat* (Pers. *taghir* or *taghayyur*) means transfer and occurs frequently in assignment orders, as in those reproduced in Nainsi's *Khyat*, ed. Badri Prasad Sakriya, Jodhpur, 1962, II, pp. 146–8; and *Jodhpur Hakumat-ri-Bahi*, ed. Satish Chandra, Raghubir Sinh and G.D. Sharma, New Delhi, 1976, pp. 201, 210. Cf. G.D. Sharma, *Rajput Polity* (New Delhi, 1977), p. 122.

[13] In one example, Rathor Umarsi held two villages in his *patta* in 1664; but after a year these villages were transferred and another village, Khetawas, was assigned to him instead (*Hakumat Bahi*, p. 132).

[14] Ibid., p. 128.

[15] W. H. Moreland, *The Agrarian System of Moslem India*, Delhi, 1968, pp. 209–14.

[16] See my article, 'Revenue Estimation and Realization in Mughal Empire—A case study of Marwar', *Islamic Culture*, LXIV (No. 1), 1990, pp. 69–81.

[17] *Hakumat Bahi*, p. 137.

[18] Ibid.

[19] *Phutkar Khyat*, f. 156(a), Kaviraja Sangrah, Granth No. 6, Part 'B', Natnagar Shodh Sansthan, Sitamau.

paid in cash, while for the other half villages were assigned.[20]

Generally, a whole village (*darobast*)[21] was assigned to one *pattawat*, but we find joint *patta*s in the same village being assigned to two brothers. In the latter case the amount of *rekh* was divided between them and they had to serve the state jointly.[22]

The *pattawat*s were obliged to pay *peshkash* (offering) to the ruler in Marwar,[23] on occasions such as when a *patta* was resumed and then reassigned.[24] When a son succeeded to his father's *patta* he too had to pay a *peshkash*,[25] fixed by the Raja in kind or in cash.[26] It is difficult to establish any relationship between the *rekh* and the *peshkash*; the *peshkash* could be half the *rekh*; sometimes it was equal to the *rekh* or even more.[27] But *peshkash*, unlike *rekh*, was not an annual claim.

The fiscal rights of the *pattawat*s and those of Mughal *jagirdar*s were quite similar. The *pattawat*s were authorised to collect land revenue and other taxes according to the terms and conditions prescribed in the *patta*. Besides this, they could collect *ghasmari* (grazing tax), *mal* and *tolbantai* (weighing tax) over and above the land revenue. Sometimes the *pattawat* was given the right to collect *dan* (transit-tax) and income from fairs. Instead of being assigned villages, a *pattawat* could occasionally be authorised to collect some taxes from particular villages and might even be assigned the tax on wells and ploughs in the *patta*.[28]

Since the *patta* was a service tenure, it was obligatory on the part of the *pattawat*s to maintain cavalry. The military obligation of a *pattawat* was specifically entered against the *rekh* or amount stated

[20] Ibid., f. 155(a).

[21] Nainsi's *Khyat*, I, p. 281.

[22] *Hakumat Bahi*, p. 150.

[23] *Phalodi Bahi*, vs 1701 (folios are not mentioned), R.S.A. Bikaner; *Patta-Bahi* of vs 1719, *Jodhpur Records*, Basta No. 51/71; *Hakumat Bahi*, pp. 128, 130 and 134.

[24] The *patta* of Rathor Ram Chand Gopal Das was resumed in 1663. Later on it was reassigned to the same *pattawat* after receipt of a *peshkash* of Rs 250 (Cf. *Hakumat-Bahi*, p. 126).

[25] Ibid., p. 147.

[26] In one case the *pattawat* was asked to pay *peshkash* in cash; but in another the *peshkash* was fixed at two camels (Ibid., pp. 126 and 128).

[27] G. D. Sharma contends that the amount of *peshkash* was never more than the *rekh* (*Rajput Polity*, p. 120). But there are numerous examples to the contrary; see *Hakumat Bahi*, p. 141; *Patta Bahi*, vs 1766.

[28] *Hakumat-Bahi*, pp. 134 and 202.

in money as the estimated income of the *patta*.[29] The level of military obligation probably bore some relationship to the size of the *rekh*, such an obligation being expressed in terms of numbers of horsemen to be maintained. In Appendices I and II we give the *rekh* and the required number of cavalry to be maintained as given in certain *patta*s of *pargana*s of Sanchor and others.

The Appendices suggest that a *rekh* of Rs 1,000 used to be assigned to a *pattawat* for the maintenance of one horse; this rate seems to be standard, occurring in 45 of the 65 *patta*s. In two cases it comes to Rs 2,000 and 1,333 per horse, while in 17 *patta*s it is less than Rs 1,000. It may be that where the *rekh* per horse is high, it was a concession. On the other hand, where the *rekh* per horse is low, the expectation might have been that the *pattawat* would not provide horses of the requisite quality or would not have adequate remounts. But without more detailed knowledge, any explanation of the deviation from the standard of one horse per Rs 1,000 of *rekh* would remain speculative.

III

It may be useful to compare the contents of the actual *jāgīr*-assignment orders of the Mughal emperors with those of the Rathor rulers.[30] The assignment orders of both Mughals and Rathors mention practically similar terms and conditions. All local officials are informed about an assignment, identifying the specific territory and the assignee.[31] Both orders clearly stated that only land revenue and other authorised taxes could be realized by the assignee.[32]

Whenever a territory was assigned in *jāgīr* to a Mughal *jāgīrdār* or in *patta* to a *pattawat*, the estimated income was also mentioned. It was known as *jama'* or *jama'dami* in the Mughal Empire and *rekh*

[29] Ibid., p. 152.

[30] A format of the *patta* survives in the *Phutkar Khyat* (Part 'B', Kaviraja Sangrah, Granthak No. 6, Sitamau). It records how the *patta*s of the *chakar*s (servants) should be written. The translation of the document is given in Appendix III.

[31] For Mughal assignment orders, see *Selected Documents of Shah Jahan's Reign*, ed. Yusuf Hussain Khan, Hyderabad, 1950; Cf. M. Athar Ali, *The Mughal Nobility under Aurangzeb*, Delhi, 1968, p. 76. For Rathor assignment orders see *Granth* No. 785, ff. 57(a) and (b), Sitamau, and *Jodhpur Records*, Basta No. 76/2.

[32] Cf. Athar Ali, *Mughal Nobility*, p. 81; and transcription of a Rathor assignment order in G. D. Sharma, *Rajput Polity* (Appendix 7:1), p. 217.

in the Rathor dominions. In both cases, when the entire salary was given in the form of a revenue assignment, the estimated income was considered equal to the pay of the *jāgīrdār* or *pattawat*.[33] But there was one difference, albeit minor: where the Mughal assignment orders mentioned the actual rank and sanctioned pay-claim, the orders for *pattawat* assignments left out the rank (nothing comparable to the *mansab* was granted by the raja) and stated the amount of salary in a roundabout way; listing each village with its *rekh* figures. It can be inferred that the total *rekh* figures were equal to the pay claims of the *pattawat*. While the Mughal orders give the *zāt* and *sawār* ranks, the *patta* documents record the number of mounted retainers the *pattawat*s were obliged to supply for service.

This comparison strengthens the belief that the *jāgīr* and *patta* assignment orders were essentially similar to each other with just trifling differences. This undermines the assertion that *patta*s were some kind of perpetual tenure. Further evidence to this effect is furnished by some Persian sources. It is recorded in the *Waqai-i Ajmer* that Maharaja Jaswant Singh had only a few villages in each *pargana* in the *khalisa*, the rest of the villages having been assigned by him in *patta*s to his officials for their pay.[34] The *Mi'rat-i Ahmadi* tells us that in 1690–1 when Marwar was under the occupation of the Mughals, Shuja'at Khan, put in charge of Marwar, gave *patta*s in lieu of *jāgīr* to many Rajputs and *pattawat*s according to the established practice of their ancestors.[35]

IV

Besides the transferable *patta*s, there were some hereditary villages which were known as *watan* (*utan* in Rajasthani)[36] as well as *rajthan*

[33] Cf. *Selected Documents of Shah Jahan's Reign*, pp. 79–84. For *rekh* see *Hakumat Bahi*, 126; *Granth* No. 78, ff. 57(a) and (b), Sitamau.

[34] *Waqai-i Ajmer*, Aligarh transcript, ff. 84, 114; Irfan Habib, *The Agrarian System of Mughal India*, Bombay, 1963, p. 186.

[35] Ali Muhammad Khan, *Mir'at-i Ahmadi*, ed. Nawab Ali, I, p. 325. Cf. Irfan Habib, *Agrarian System*, p. 184.

[36] In a copy of a Rajasthani manuscript of the reign of Maharaja Jaswant Singh, we have a record of the *watan*s and their holders (*Marwar Mahe Rathor Rajput Rawtan-ra-Utan*, for which see *A Descriptive Catalogue of the Rajasthani Manuscripts*, ed. V. B. Trivedi, revised ed. Sukumar Sen, Calcutta, 1957, No. C. 60, Part I, ff., 1(a)–4(b).)

(seat of royalty).[37] These assignments were not normally resumable and were regarded by custom as hereditary; for example, the total villages of *tappa* Mahewah of Jodhpur listed as being in the *watan* of Jagmal of the Mahewacha—a Rathor subclan[38]—are again listed in the *patta* of Bharmal, son of Jagmal.[39] This means that the *watan* was really a hereditary *patta*; and provision of cavalry against it remained obligatory. Failure to do so could entail resumption of the *watan*-villages,[40] for though succession by a son was assured,[41] the Raja held at least the nominal right of choosing the successor.[42]

Before Maldeo (1532), the system of assignment was based on the concept of *bhai-bant* ('sharing among brothers').[43] Maldeo asserted his supremacy over his clansmen (*bhai-bandh*) and treated them as clan-retainers (*bhai-bandh chakar*). The use of the Turko-Persian word *chakar*, meaning servant, indicated the subordinate position of the assignee.[44] During his time, *patta*s were given to those family members and other kinsmen who accepted his suzerainty. They were assigned some villages as *patta*s in perpetuity.[45] These villages were developed by the grantees as their 'home domain', and they often constructed small forts in particular places for their families.

The holders of *watan* villages were also assigned ordinary *patta*

[37] The term *rajthan* is frequently used synonymously for *watan* in Nainsi and other contemporary sources; see Nainsi's *Khyat*, II, p. 154. These villages with the lapse of time came to be called *thikana* and their holders, *thikanadars*; but we do not find the term *thikana* or *thikanadar* in any 17th-century document. Sharma (*Rajput Polity*, pp. 123–6) is therefore not very correct when he uses these terms in his account of the earlier period; nor when he equates them with *bhum*-tenures, which were quite different in nature.

[38] *Marwar-Mahe Rathor Rajput Rawatan-ra-Utan*, f. 2(a).

[39] *Hakumat Bahi*, pp. 152–3.

[40] *Hakumat Bahi*, pp. 152–3.

[41] *Patta-Bahi*, vs 1714, Jodhpur Records, Basta No. 51/7, R.S.A. Bikaner.

[42] Nainsi's *Khyat*, II, p. 157.

[43] Mutha Nainsi, *Marwar-ra-pargana-ri Vigat*, ed. Narain Singh Bhati (Jodhpur, 1968), Vol. I, pp. 36–40. The *Vigat* gives a detailed list of the brothers and sons among whom the territory was distributed. Pokaran and Phalodi were assigned to Rao Satal and Bika. See Nainsi, *Khyat*, Vol. III, p. 105. Cf. Sharma, *Rajput Polity*, p. 5, for the custom of *bhai-bant*.

[44] *Vigat*, II, p. 51.

[45] Rao Maldeo granted a *patta* of village Lavera in Jodhpur to Bhati Niba, son of Anand, and he confirmed this village as his *rajthan* (home domain). This village continued in his family's possession till at least the time of Maharaja Jaswant Singh (Nainsi, *Khyat*, II, pp. 154–7).

villages if their pay-claim could not be satisfied with the *rekh* of their *watan*-villages.[46]

A similar category was that of *kadimi* villages, which were 'ancient' (Persian, *qadim*) assignments, held for a long time in the past without transfer. It seems that generally these assignments, made by previous rulers of Marwar, continued to be recognized. A ruler could, of course, enlarge the *kadimi-patta*, by granting further villages through fresh *patta*s or villages.[47] While we cannot say with certainty that every *patta* issued by a previous ruler was continued by every succeeding ruler, the 'ancient' *patta*s did tend to become exempt from transfer. Holders of some of these *patta*s could also acquire *bhomichara* rights (the Rajput version of *zamindarī*)[48] over these villages. A late eighteenth-century source asserts that *kadimi-pattawat*s had *bhomichara* rights in their villages.[49]

The *watan*-villages and *kadimi-patta*s can thus be seen to be similar in nature to the *watan-jagir*s granted to territorial chiefs by the Mughals. The *jama*' of the *watan-jagir* was adjusted against the assignee's salary. It too, while hereditary, was subject to confirmation by the Emperor after the death of each holder.[50]

V

The rulers of Marwar were, in the eyes of the Mughal Government, the *jagirdar*s of Marwar, holding the *jagir* in *watan*. It largely rested with the Marwar rulers as to how they administered their territory and how they subassigned it. The Marwar rulers, therefore, freely subassigned or granted rights to the land revenue and other taxes to their subjects, but especially to their clansmen. This was done, as we have seen, by the system of *patta*s.

It can be deduced from our information that in assigning a *patta*

[46] *Hakumat Bahi*, p. 234.

[47] Kishan Rathor got one village from a preceding Raja of Jodhpur. The *patta* was recognized by Jaswant Singh and he was also granted the additional villages of *tappa* Osiyan of Jodhpur in *patta* in 1660 (*Hakumat-Bahi*, p. 126).

[48] See my article, 'The Allodial Proprietors (?)—The Bhumias of Marwar', *Indian Historical Review*, VI, Nos. 1–2, pp. 141–53.

[49] *Vigat*, II, Appendix 1(a), pp. 400–5. The names and clans of such *pattawat*s are recorded.

[50] For *watan-jagir* see Irfan Habib, *Agrarian System of Mughal India*, p. 184; and Athar Ali, *Mughal Nobility*, pp. 79–80.

the Rathor rulers were chiefly guided by considerations of clan and blood ties. Merit and competence were a secondary consideration.

The various Rathor sub-clans had over 85 per cent of the total assigned revenue-income during the time of Maharaja Jaswant Singh. Table I sets out the proportion of revenue income possessed by certain prominent sub-clans of the Rathors:

TABLE I

Proportion of Revenue Income possessed by the *Pattawat*s of Rathor clans and Others[51]

Sub-clan	*Rekh*	% of Total *Rekh*
Jodha	6,48,000	18.10
Mertiyas	5,43,300	15.17
Champawats	5,02,800	14.04
Kumpawats	4,66,800	13.04
Udawats	3,23,811	9.04
Jaitawat	1,42,000	3.97
Others (including non-Rathors)	9,54,057	26.64
TOTAL	35,80,768	100.00

All the members of the six Rathor sub-clans given in Table I were reputedly descended from the sons and brothers of Rao Jodha, the legendary founder of Jodhpur. Being direct descendants of Rao Jodha, the Jodha sub-clan, to which the Maharaja also belonged, claimed the lion's share in the revenue resources. Next came the Mertiyas, descendants of Rao Duda, son of Rao Jodha, holding over 16 per cent of revenue resources.

An identical picture emerges from the evidence of the *patta*s (with villages) listed in the *Phalodi Bahi* of 1701/1644,[52] although generally the dominance of each sub-clan varied from *pargana* to *pargana*: one clan would have prominence in one *pargana* while in another it had a subordinate position or no *patta*s at all.

The position of non-Rathors among the *pattawat*s is of some interest, since it would show how far, if at all, the Marwar rulers

[51] This table is based on the *Hakumat Bahi*.

[52] Cf. Sharma, *Rajput Polity*, pp. 128–30.

attempted to counterbalance the dominance of the Rathor nobility by admitting other Rajput clans. Table II below shows that the latter accounted for 14.77 per cent of the *rekh* of *patta*s granted by Jaswant Singh as recorded in the *Hakumat Bahi.*

TABLE II

Share of non-Rathor Rajputs in the revenue income

Clan	*Pattawat's rekh*	% of total
Kachhwahas	1,50,050	4.19
Chauhans	1,39,150	3.88
Bhati	1,22,007	3.41
Parihar	40,600	1.13
Gor	28,000	0.78
Panwar	13,400	0.37
Others	35,850	1.00
TOTAL	5,29,057	14.77

The Kachhwahas, who, as Table II shows, were the most prominent of the non-Rathor clans, were mainly granted *patta*s outside Marwar, these being placed in the additional ordinary *jagir*s the Maharaja held against his high *mansab*. The Bhatis, on the other hand, held all their *patta*s within Marwar.

These statistics do not support the view that the Rathor rulers granted *patta*s only to blood relations, but they do indicate that non-Rathors had a relatively minor share of the total area under the control of the ruler of Marwar.

Of non-Rajput castes, only five or six castes or communities were given *patta*s, namely, the Muhtas (Baniyas), Muslims, Charans, Brahmans and Raibaris.[53]

The relationship of *pattawat*s to *bhumia*s varied somewhat from that of the *zamindar*s and *jagirdar*s of the Mughal empire; in *pargana* Jalor for instance, the *bhumia*s and *pattawat*s belonged to the same clan in the majority of the villages. But it nevertheless seems that the *pattawat*s and *bhumia*s remained distinct, though it

[53] *Hakumat Bahi*, pp. 231–3.

was possible for a *pattawat* to be a *bhumia* as well, just as a Mughal *jagirdar* could also be a *zamindar*.[54]

Our finding, then, is that during the seventeenth century the *patta* system tended to become practically a replica of the Mughal *jagir* system, though its origins lay in the distribution of territorial acquisitions by rulers among their clansmen. The relationship between the *pattawat* and the Raja was not therefore that of a vassal and lord in Europe as suggested by Tod. We cannot also call the Rathor polity a full-fledged 'clan monarchy' because, as we have seen, the Rathor rulers tried to counterbalance the Rathor nobility by admitting other Rajput clans into their *pattawat*-nobility.

[54] Bhadani, 'Allodial Proprietors', p. 153.

APPENDIX I

	Pattawats	Clan and sub-clan	*Rekh* at which *patta* is assigned (in rupees)	Number of horses	*Rekh* per horse
1.	Rathor Dhan Raj	Champawat	4,000	4	1,000
2.	Rathor Badri Das	„	3,500	4	875
3.	Rathor Bagh	„	3,000	3	1,000
4.	Rathor Nahar Khan	„	4,000	4	1,000
5.	Rathor Rup Singh	„	3,000	3	1,000
6.	Rathor Kalyan Das	„	4,000	4	1,000
7.	Rathor Ram Chand	„	1,000	1	1,000
8.	Rathor Jaswant	„	3,000	3	1,000
9.	Rathor Roop Singh	„	700	1	700
10.	Rathor Beni Das	„	400	1	400
11.	Rathor Badri Das	„	2,000	1	2,000
12.	Rathor Fateh Singh	Kumpawat	10,000	10	1,000
13.	Rathor Rugh Nath	„	12,000	12	1,000
14.	Rathor Ram Chand	„	16,000	16	1,000
15.	Rathor Vithal Das	„	13,000	13	1,000
16.	Rathor Himat Singh	„	1,500	2	750
17.	Rathor Dan Singh	„	6,000	6	1,000
18.	Rathor Mohkam Singh	„	2,500	3	833.33
19.	Rathor Pratap Singh	„	4,000	4	1,000
20.	Rathor Udai Singh	„	3,000	3	1,000
21.	Pirag Das	Ida	1,000	1	1,000
22.	Narsingh Das	Ida	2,500	3	833.33
23.	Kishan Das	„	900	1	900
24.	Ugaro	„	800	1	800
25.	Mandan	„	800	1	800
26.	Hem Raj	„	700	1	700
27.	Sanwal Jaswant	„	500	1	500
28.	Jai Singh	„	900	1	900
29.	Bharmal	„	500	1	500
30.	Bhopat	Mangliya	4,000	4	1,000
31.	Kesodasot	„	4,000	4	1,000
32.	Pirag Das	„	2,000	2	1,000
33.	Balu Bhopat	„	2,000	2	1,000
34.	Som Das	Hul	800	1	800
35.	Pitho	„	800	1	800
36.	Duda	„	400	1	400
37.	Rugho Das	„	400	1	400
38.	Bhani Das	„	700	1	700
39.	Pirag Das	Gor	20,000	20	1,000

Source: *Patta-bahi* of *c.* 1660 (*Jodhpur Records*, *Basta* No. 7/51).

APPENDIX II

	Pattawats	Clan	*Rekh*	Number of horses	*Rekh* per horse
1.	Viramde	Chauhan	14,000[a]	4	1,000
2.	Kesari Singh	"	4,000	3	1,333.33
3.	Budsingh	"	4,000	4	1,000
4.	Prithviraj	"	4,000	4	1,000
5.	Jait Singh	"	2,000	2	1,000
6.	Prithviraj	"	2,000	2	1,000
7.	Jalaun Singh	"	2,000	2	1,000
8.	Bane Singh	"	1,000	1	1,000
9.	Kusal Singh	"	4,000	4	1,000
10.	Mal Singh	"	2,000	2	1,000
11.	Madho	"	1,000	1	1,000
12.	Than Singh	"	1,000	1	1,000
13.	Kani Ram	"	1,000	1	1,000
14.	Siv Singh	"	4,000	4	1,000
15.	Sagtidan	"	4,000	4	1,000
16.	Anand Singh	"	1,000	1	1,000
17.	Rai Singh	"	1,000	1	1,000
18.	Bhojraj	"	2,000	2	1,000
19.	Man Singh	"	1,000	1	1,000
20.	Gajiya	"	1,000	1	1,000
21.	Umo	"	1,000	1	1,000
22.	Nawal Singh	Rathor	1,000	1	1,000
23.	Man Singh	"	1,000	1	1,000
24.	Sangram Singh	"	1,000	1	1,000
25.	Sawai Rawat Singh	"	1,000	1	1,000
26.	Ratan Singh	"	4,000	4	1,000

[a] Rs 14,000 seems to be incorrect, and should perhaps be Rs 4,000.

APPENDIX III

Model Text of a Patta

The *Patta*s of the Servants are written in the following way:*

By the order of His Highness Shri Maharajadhiraj Maharaj Shri Ajit Singh—(the name and caste of the person to whom the *patta* is given are to be recorded here).* He is employed by [the Maharaja's] benevolence and will to perform service (*chakri*). Where (the Raja) will send him he will go, without any excuse (*ujar*—Arabic '*uzr*). In carrying out duty he will not make any new claim and will not talk [complain ?] to anybody (?). The order of the *panch* will be followed (?). He will get his retainers (*asami*) and horses branded.

1 *Airaki* [*Iraqi* – Persian]	1 *Taji* [*Tazi* – Arabian]	1 *Turki*

DOCUMENT

Aurangzeb's *Farmān* to Rasikdās on Problems of Revenue Administration, 1665

SHIREEN MOOSVI

The seventeenth century, as it advances, becomes rich in official as well as unofficial documents; yet there is a peculiar handicap. From Akbar's reign, in spite of the relative paucity of documents, we are nevertheless fortunate in having memoranda and reports on revenue administration from Todar Mal and Fatḥullāh Shīrāzī, and a general set of Imperial regulations (*dastūr-ul 'amal*).[1] Such documents have not survived from subsequent reigns. Aurangzeb's *farmān* on general matters of revenue administration, issued to a revenue official, Rasikdās, therefore assumes great importance, being the first document of its kind coming to us after a gap of some seventy years.

The *farmān*, issued in the 8th regnal year of Aurangzeb (1665), sheds light on the agrarian situation at the time and gives us an impression of agrarian distress which is consistent with the evidence from Bernier. It also attempts remedies whose prescription is ascribed to the Emperor. For this purpose it describes the current practices of revenue administration, offering welcome light on the deficiencies which it seeks to rectify.

The credit for bringing the *farmān* to light goes to Sir Jadunath Sarkar who published its text,[2] as well as a translation into English.[3]

[1] Abū'l Faẓl, *Akbarnāma*, III, ed. Ahmad Ali, Calcutta, 1873–87, pp. 381–3; 457–9. For the original version of Todar Mal's memorandum see Br. Lib. MS Add. 27247, ff. 31b–32b.

[2] *Journal of the Asiatic Society of Bengal*, June 1906, pp. 249–55.

[3] J. Sarkar, *Mughal Administration*, Calcutta, 1924, pp. 213–29.

Moreland,[4] and then Irfan Habib,[5] explained some of its technical terms and brought out its importance for analysing the agrarian conditions during Aurangzeb's reign.

Unfortunately, the text that Sarkar published was not collated with other available MSS and was based on only one MS, by no means the best of the surviving copies of the document. Many transcriptional errors, some of them serious, remained undetected by Sarkar. In his translation, he was led into many errors by the defects of his text; but there are other slips as well, especially in the rendering of technical terms. For instance, he renders *sāl-i kāmil-o muttaṣil*, not as 'year of full realization and the year previous (to the current)' but as the 'past year and the year preceding it'. The *'amal-i jarīb* and *kankūṭ* (two distinct methods of assessment of land-revenue based on measurement)[6] simply become 'actual valuation of crop'. Again, *jins-i kāmil* is translated as 'full crop' and not as high grade or cash crop. The term *dastūr-ul 'amal* though very clearly used for cash revenue-rates, is rendered as 'revenue guide'. In clause 8 he misread *ṣarf-i sikka* (discount on mintage)[7] as *ṣirf sikka*, *ṣirf* taken to mean 'only', and the whole sense of the clause is lost. This list of Sarkar's errors, which is not exhaustive, suggests that a fresh translation is necessary to enable one to understand the *farmān* properly.

The translation that follows is based on a text collated with nine available copies of the *farmān*: viz.,

A: I.O. 1146 (Ethe' 2185)
B: I.O. 1566 (Ethe' 2186)
C: I.O. 4014, ff, 8a–11b.
D: Br.Lib.Add. 19503, ff. 62a–63b.
E. Br.Lib.Or. 1735, ff. 162b–64b, 129a–32b.
F: Bodleian Pers. e-1 (I, 1385)
G: Berlin Royal Library, Pertsch's Cat. 15(23), ff. 267a–72a.
H: *Nigārnāma-i Munshī* (Nawal Kishor ed.), pp. 123–4 and 99–102.

[4] *The Agrarian System of Moslem India*, Cambridge, 1929, pp. 132–8.

[5] *The Agrarian System of Mughal India*, Bombay, 1963, pp. 222 and *n*., etc.

[6] For the significance of these terms see ibid., pp. 193, 200.

[7] See Irfan Habib, 'Currency System of the Mughal Empire', *Medieval India Quarterly*, IV, 1961, p. 5n.

I: Text as printed by Sarkar in *Journal of the Asiatic Society of Bengal*, N.S., II, 1906, pp. 249–55.

Of these, seven MSS are apparently copies of the *farmān* as issued to Rasikdās; in D his name is replaced by that of Mīr Muḥammad Mu'izz, *dīwān-i khāliṣa ṣūba* Bihar. This led Irfan Habib to suggest that it was not a *farmān* issued to an individual, but a circular meant for all the *dīwāns* of the *khāliṣa*.[8] In that case, being a general order for at least the areas under the *khāliṣa*, it acquires much greater importance than it would have had if it was merely issued to an individual. However, clause 7, which deals with the specific case of an area that was in a particular prince's *jāgīr* earlier, suggests that it was first issued in response to certain problems raised by Rasikdās; then, perhaps, in view of its general significance, it was circulated to others. The fact that it is preserved in so many MS copies also indicates that the *farmān* was deemed to contain regulations of relevance in general administration.

In Sarkar's printed text, Rasikdās's name is followed by the designation *karorī* (revenue-collector); no other MS carries this designation. Moreover, it is evident from the internal evidence in the *farmān* itself that it was addressed to a higher official, of the status of *dīwān*.[9]

The date of the *farmān* appears from the reference to the 8th regnal year of Aurangzeb in the Preamble, the year being styled as that of the commencement of implementation of the regulations contained in the *farmān*. The year corresponded to 18 March 1665–6 (March 1666); but the *farmān* was to come into effect from the beginning of the kharif harvest within that year, and this (meaning August) could only fall within AD 1665.

The translation is based on the text provided in version A. Variations from other versions are noted only if they are of any substance. Obvious spelling mistakes are not noted.

The translation is followed by a glossary of the technical terms used in the *farmān*. The terms are given in the translation in their original form. For well-known technical terms the meaning is given in brackets in the translated text.

[8] *Agrarian System of Mughal India*, p. 222 and *n*.

[9] Moreland, *Agrarian System*, p. 133 and *n*.

TRANSLATION

Copy of the farmān *of the Emperor Aurangzeb*[10]

Let the *kifāyat-sha'ār*[11] (skilled in financial prudence), *Muṭī'-ul Islām* (obedient to Islam) Rasikdās,[12] be hopeful of Imperial favour, and know that, whereas the entire elevated attention and desires of the Emperor are devoted to the increase in the population and cultivation of the Empire and the welfare of the whole *ri'āyā* (peasantry) and the entire people, who are the wonderful creation of the Creator; now, therefore, an explanation having been desired of the actualities of *'amal* (revenue-collection) of *parganas* of the *k͟hāliṣa* and *tuyūldārs*,[13] it has been submitted to His Majesty by the Imperial functionaries, that during the current year, the *umanā'* (pl. of *amīn*, assessment officers) of the *parganas* of the Imperial dominions assess the *jama'* (revenue demand) of most of the villages of the *parganas* at the beginning of the year, keeping in view the *ḥāṣil* (revenue-realization) of the *sāl-i kāmil* (year of maximum revenue-collection) and of the previous year and the cultivable area and the condition of the peasantry's capability and other peculiarities. And if the peasants of certain villages are not agreeable to this mode of collection, they assess the *jama'* at the harvest time by the method of *jarīb* or *kankūṭ*. And in some of the villages, where they know the peasants and cultivators to be in distressed circumstances and with inadequate resources, they practise *g͟halla-bak͟hshī* (crop-sharing) at the rate of a half or one-third or two-fifths (of the produce) or more or less. At the close of the year the *ṭawāmīr* (registers) of *jama'-i naqdī* (*jama'* stated in cash), (drawn up) in conformity with the regulations and actual practice, with his (the *Dīwān*'s) own *taṣdīq* (confirmatory endorsement) and the *qubūl* (acceptance) of the *karorīs* and the *dastk͟haṭ* (signatures) of the *chaudhrīs* and *qānūngos*, are sent to the Imperial Office. But the Imperial Office does not receive the record of the

[10] D reads 'Copy of the *farmān* of Emperor Aurangzeb 'Alamgīr issued to Mīr Muḥammad Mu'izz *dīwān-i k͟hāliṣa ṣūba* Bihar by way of a *dastūr-ul 'amal*'; B adds ''Alamgīr G͟hāzī' after 'Emperor Aurangzeb'.

[11] A title commonly used for officers of the revenue ministry by the Mughal administration.

[12] D reads '*Sa'ādat Mā'āb* (receptacle of bliss), *Wizārat Panāh* (officer of ministerial status) *Kifāyat Dastgāh* (master of financial prudence) Mīr Muḥammad Mu'izz'.

[13] E omits *tuyūldārs*.

ārāẓī (measured area) of each *pargana*, specifying the cultivated land and details of the *rabi*ʻ and *kharīf* crops, showing (1) how much (land) was (under) the *jins-i kāmil* (high-grade crops) and *jins-i nāqiṣ* (inferior crops) during the previous year, and whether there has been any change, i.e. an increase or a fall during the current year compared to the previous year, and (2) the number of *muzāri*ʻs (cultivators) classified as *mustājirs* (revenue-farmers), *ri*ʻ*āyā* (peasants), etc., whereby the condition of each *maḥal* and the competence of the *mutaṣaddīs* (officials) of that place, who, upon the occurrence of a short-fall in the *ḥāṣil* (revenue-collection) of that *maḥal*, after the assessment of the *jama*ʻ, grant a reduction from the total *jama*ʻ, making a pretext of deficient rains, or the calamity of frost or the cheapness of grain or something else, might become known, in conformity with the reality. If, informing themselves of the actual condition of the cultivators and cultivation in each village, they (the officials) proceed to (assess and) collect revenue (ʻ*amal-numāyand*) on the basis of (such) detailed knowledge, and endeavour to get the cultivable land cultivated and to enlarge the cultivation of *jins-i kāmil* (high-grade crops), the (villages of) *parganas* will be inhabited and cultivated, the peasantry will be well-off and there will be an increase in the *maḥṣūl* (revenue, produce). And in this situation if any (natural) calamity occurs, no great loss will take place in the *ḥāṣil* (revenue collection), owing to the abundance of cultivation.

(Accordingly) the World-subduing, Universe-governing order is (hereby) issued to the effect that he should inform himself of the actualities of each village of the *parganas* attached to his *dīwānī* and *amīnī* (office of *dīwān* and *amīn*), namely, how much is the (area of) cultivable *ārāẓī* (land) within it (his jurisdiction), how much out of it is cultivated, how much uncultivated, the extent of land under *jins-i kāmil* each year, and the cause of the said *ārāẓī* remaining uncultivated. He should further find out what were the *dastūrs* (rates) of the levy of *maḥsūl* (revenue) in the blessed reign of *Ḥaẓarat ʻArsh Āshiyānī* (Akbar) during the *dīwānī* of Rāja Todar Mal; and whether the *sā'ir* taxes are according to the old regulations, or have been fixed at a higher (rate) since the year of the beginning of this august reign; how many villages are inhabited and how many are desolate and what is the cause of their desolation. After obtaining information on these matters, he should strive for progressively populating the desolate villages and getting the cultivable land cultivated, with a just *qual* (pledged revenue-rate), appropriate *qarār* (agreement), and increasing (the cultivation of) the *jins-i kāmil*. Wherever there is a well that is out of repair, he should repair it and also dig new ones. He should make assessment of *jama'* in such a manner that the whole peasantry receives its due and the *māl-i wājib* (authorised land-revenue) is realized in time, and not a single peasant is subjected to oppression. He should, every year, prepare records containing the number of cultivators of each village and the *ārāẓī* (area), cultivated and uncultivated, irrigated by wells and dependent on rain only; and *kāmil* and *nāqiṣ* crops, and the extent of success in getting the cultivable land cultivated, and increasing the (area under) *kāmil* crops and populating the villages that have been desolate for years. He should then submit (to the Imperial Office), the details of enhancement, if any, between that which has (now) been fixed and the previous *dastūr-ul 'amal*, together with the amount that has been collected in the whole year.

This regulation and rule of procedure is to be deemed to be in effect from the beginning of the *kharīf* of the Īlān Īl, the 8th year from His Majesty's accession, and he should act in conformity thereto, and also instruct the *'āmil*s of *maḥal*s and *jāgīrdār*s to work in the manner here prescribed:

1. That he is not to allow the *chaudhrī*s and *'āmil*s to see him in private and should direct that they be in attendance at the *dīwānī* (office); he should (on the other hand) admit the *reza-ri'āyā* (small peasants) and the poor, who come for making submissions as to their condition, into private as well as public audience and make them familiar with himself so that they might not need any other person's mediation in representing their needs.

2. That he should direct the *'āmil*s that they should at the beginning of the year find out the (number of) cultivators with the number of ploughs and extent of *ārāẓī* (area), village by village. If the peasants are well off, they should arrange that all of them, according to their condition, try to increase (the area under) sowing and so, in comparison with last year, bring about an enlargement in the area cultivated and, while shifting from the inferior crops (*jins-i adnā*) to high grade (*jins-i a'lā*), not leave waste any cultivable land, so far as they can. If any one from amongst the cultivators (*kārinda*s) has fled, they (*'āmil*s) should find out the reason thereof and try hard in the matter of his return

to his native place. Similarly, they should use praiseworthy endeavour and much effort at soothing and conciliation, to gather cultivators from all sides and directions. As for *banjar* (cultivable waste) land, they should impose such *dastūrs* (revenue-rates) on it as to enable it to be brought under cultivation.

3. That he should direct the *amīns* of the *parganas* that they should every year discover the actual conditions (*maujūdāt*) of cultivation, village by village, peasant-wise (*āsāmīwār*), and, after minute scrutiny, assess the *jama'*, keeping in view the financial interest (*kifāyat*) of the government and the welfare of the peasantry, and submit the *daul* (register) of *jama'* to the Imperial Office without delay.

4. That, after the assessment of *jama'*, he should so settle that, in conformity with the settled procedure, the instalments (for payment) of *māl-i wājib* (land-revenue) that[14] are established in each *pargana*. In this respect, he should direct that they (*'āmils*) should start the realization of *maḥṣūl* in time, they should demand (the payment) according to the fixed time; and he should himself take weekly reports (of the collection). He should direct that nothing should be left (uncollected) out of the settled instalment. In case some part of the first instalment is left uncollected, it should be realized with the second instalment, and by the third instalment the full payment, without any arrears, be made.

5. That he should fix suitable instalments for the *bāqī* (arrears) of the (previous) years, according to the condition and capability of the peasants. He should instruct the *karorīs* that (these instalments) should be realized according to agreement, and he should keep himself informed of the progress of the revenue collection. There should not be any delay due to the fraudulent practices and negligence of the *'āmils*.

6. That, whenever he himself goes out to obtain information about the true condition of the *parganas*, in each village which he passes through, he should observe the state of cultivation, *rai'* (crop yields),[15] the capacity of the cultivators and the amount of the *jama'*. If (he finds that) in the distribution of the *jama'* fairness and proper calculation has been followed in respect of each individual

[14] So in the text; but the word *ki* (that) should be omitted.

[15] D, G, and H read '*rub'*' (one-fourth) and the rest '*rafa'*' (dismissal): these are obvious misreadings for '*rai'*' (crop-yields).

payer, well and good; but if the *chaudhrī*, or *muqaddam* or *patwārī* is involved in oppression he should, comforting the cultivator, let him have his due; and take away the *gunjāyash* (gain) from the dominant ones (*mutaghallibān*). He should, devoting himself to a detailed, truthful inquiry into the assessment of the present year and the distribution of its *maujūdāt* (assets), report in detail (to the Imperial Office), so that the true state of efficiency of the *amīn*s and the good management of that *Wizārat Panāh* (i.e. incumbent of office in revenue department; in this case, the addressee) be observed.

7. That he should maintain the *nānkār* and *in'ām* (revenue-free grant) according to the revenue regulations of the *khāliṣa* administration. He should discover whatever the *'āmil*s of the Prince have increased, so that, keeping in view such past matters as how much is left in arrears and what deductions have been obtained, on account of scarcity (of rain) or calamity, by that set of people (recipients of *nānkār* and *in'ām*) from the beginning of the assignment (*tankhwāh*) of the *jāgīr*, he should recover (the excess paid in *nānkār* and *in'ām*). And for the future he should settle that whenever they restore the *pargana*s to their original state and the fact is reported to the Imperial court, each would receive concessions in accordance with the amount of services rendered by him.

8. That he should arrange that in the *foṭakhāna* (treasury) the treasurers (*foṭadār*s) should (only) accept the auspicious *'ālamgīrī sikka*s (newly-coined money of Aurangzeb). In the event of the non-availability of this kind of rupee, they should accept the *Shāhjahānī chalnī* (current) coins[16] that are current in the market and collect the fee (*abwāb*) of *ṣarf-i sikka* (mintage). But they must never accept for the Treasury under-weight rupees that are not current in the market. However, if they find that by rejecting the defective coins, revenue collection (*taḥṣīl*) may be delayed, they should, taking right and just discount from the peasantry, make the exchange (of the defective coins into good) in the presence (of the payers).

9. That, if, God forbid!, any natural calamity occurs in a locality (*maḥal*), he should strongly direct the *amīn*s and *'āmil*s that they should watch over the *maujūdāt* (assets) of the cultivation with every care, and, finding out (the extent of loss) peasant-wise, they

[16] H adds '*khazāna*' (coins of the earlier reigns) after '*chalnī*'.

should make an assessment according to the *hast-o-būd* by means of detailed scrutiny. In no case should they make a collective deduction on account of calamity (*āfāt-i sarbasta*), whose distribution would be in the hands of the *chaudhrī*s, *qānūngo*s, *muqaddam*s or *paṭwārī*s, so that the small peasants (*reza ri'āyā*), receiving their due, remain safe from injury and loss, and the dominant ones are not able to oppress them.

10. That he should stringently direct the *amīn*s, *'āmil*s, *chaudhrī*s, *qānūngo*s and *muqaddam*s in the matter of extinction of *malba*, elimination of such expenses that are in addition to the *māl* (land revenue) and the prohibited cesses, that are the cause of the distress of the peasantry. He should take bonds from them, that they would never make any increase in the *malba*[17] and (indulge in) extraction of the cesses forbidden and remitted by the Imperial court. He should always keep himself informed; if anyone still commits such acts and persists in them despite prohibition and censure, he (the *Dīwān*) should report the matter to the Imperial court, so that he (the culprit) be dismissed from service and some one else be appointed in his place.

11. That, for translating the Hindwī papers into Persian,[18] he should discover the amounts of *bāchh*, *behrīmāl*, *ikhrājāt* (village expenses), and *rusūmāt* (perquisites), paid by each peasant (*āsāmī*). Having brought into the accounts of the Treasury, everything that comes out of the peasant's house, on all accounts, he should record the balance, appropriated by the *amīn*, the *'āmil*, the *zamīndār*s, etc., name by name. So far as possible, he should collect and translate the *kāghaz-i khām* (*paṭwārī*'s papers) of all the villages of the *pargana*. If, due to the absence of the *paṭwārī* or for some other reason, papers from a few villages are not obtained, he should, for that part, enter in the register the average, struck on the basis of the appropriation (*barāmad*) of all the villages. After the preparation of the register, the *Dīwān* should inspect it. If it has been drawn up in conformity with the rules (*dastūr*) he should accept it, and recover the amount misappropriated by the *'āmil*, in accordance with (?) the regulations, and (also) whatever the *chaudhrī*, the *qānūngo*, the *muqaddam* and the *paṭwārī* have appropriated in excess of the established perquisites (*rusūm*).

17 The correct reading '*malba*' is provided by D and H.

18 In H some superfluous words are added that are not supported by any of the MSS.

12. That he should write (the name of) everyone from amongst the *amīns*, *karorīs* and *foṭadārs*,[19] who has served with uprightness and devotion and, having acted in every matter in conformity with the rules that have been laid down here, has worked laudably, so that he should get the reward for his prudence and honesty. If anyone has acted in a contrary fashion, he (the *Dīwān*) should report the fact to the Imperial court, so that he may be dismissed from service and discharged from duty, and, being called to account, receive punishment for his improper conduct.

13. That he should insist upon the receipt of the register in time. At the *maḥal* where he has himself taken residence, he should daily secure the *roznāmcha* (daily account) of the collection of the land revenue (*māl*) and the cesses (*sā'ir*) and the price list; and from other *parganas*, the *roznāmcha* of the collection of *māl* and *maujūdāt* every fortnight, and the *aṛhsatta*[20] of the account (*taḥwīl*, lit. money in custody of) the *foṭadārs*, the *jama' wāṣil-bāqī*, every month, and the register of *jama'*, *mujmil*, and *jama'bandī* and the income and expenditure (*jama'-o-kharch*) account of the *foṭadār*, every harvest. He should inspect and call to account whomever has appropriated anything in excess of the due amount, and send the report to the Imperial Office. He should not delay (the collection of) the papers of the *kharīf* till the *rabī'* and of the *rabī'* till the *kharīf*.

14. That he should strictly take papers from the *amīn*, the *'āmil* or the *foṭadār*, who has been dismissed from service, and should settle his account. He should recover through audit the appropriations recoverable (*abwāb-i bāzyāftī*) in conformity with the rules of the *dīwānī*. He should send the paper with the record of the realization of the audited appropriations (*abwāb-i badarnawīsī*) to the Imperial *kachehrī* (office), so that he (the dismissed official) may obtain from that office (the certificate of) 'accounts cleared' (*az muḥāsiba farāgh*).

15. That he should compile the papers of the *dīwanī* each harvest, in conformity with the established rules, and send these to the Imperial Office, under his own seal and endorsement.

[19] D reads '*jāgīrdārs*' in place of '*foṭadārs*'.

[20] H reads '*athhata*'; I has '*tatma*' and G '*shubh*'.

GLOSSARY

Abwāb-i bāzyāftī	*Abwāb* (lit. gates), taxes, cesses; *bāzyāftī*, resumption; hence cesses due to be collected or malappropriations that are due to be recovered (Wilson's *Glossary*, s.v.)
Āfat-i sarbasta	*Āfat*, calamity; *sarbasta* (lit. closed at the head), aggregate; hence lump sum deduction on account of calamity.
'Amal	(Lit. practice) collection of revenue, also term of office or assignment.
'Amal-i jarīb	For *'amal* see prec.; *jarīb*, measuring rope; hence assessment of land-revenue by measurement. Cf. Irfan Habib, *Agrarian System*, p. 200.
Aṛhsatta	Abstracts of revenue accounts. Cf. S. P. Gupta, *The Agrarian System of Eastern Rajasthan*, Delhi, 1986, pp. 317–18. See also *Memoirs on Sind*, ed. R. H. Thomas, 1855, p. 730 (*atsatha*).
Āsāmī-wār	*Āsāmī* (lit. named individual), individual peasant; *wār*, Persian suffix equivalent of English suffix '-wise'; hence (assessing revenue on) each peasant separately.
Behrī Māl	*Behrī*, levy on each share (*bahra*); *māl*, land-revenue; hence amount demanded from each peasant, comprising, or over and above, the authorised revenue and other cesses (Wilson, *Glossary*, s.v.; cf. Habib, *Agrarian System*, p. 126 and *n*).
Bāqī	Balance, arrears.
Dastūr or *dastūr-ul 'amal*	*Dastūr*, regulation, rule; *'amal*, revenue collection. Hence revenue regulations, revenue-rates.
Ghalla bakhshī	*Ghalla*, produce; *bakhshī*, a portion; hence crop-sharing. Cf. Habib, *Agrarian System*, p. 197.
Gunjāyash	(Lit. profit) gains.
Haṣt-o-būd	*Hast*, is; *būd*, was. A method of assessment based on summary estimation of total produce (Wilson, *Glossary*, s.v., Cf. Habib, *Agrarian System*, p. 198 and *n*.)
Ikhrājāt-i deh	Village expenses paid out of revenue collection. Cf. Habib, *Agrarian System*, p. 243 and *n*.

Jama'-o-kharch	Collection and expenditure. See also *arhsatta.*
Jama' wāṣil bāqī	A statement of total assessment of revenue (*jama'*), amount realized (*wāṣil*), and the balance outstanding (*bāqī*) (Yāsīn's Glossary, Add. 6603, f.58b, and Wilson, *Glossary*, s.v.)
Jins-i kāmil, Jins-i a'lā	High grade crops, cash crops (Yāsīn's Glossary, Patna, f.66a).
Jins-i nāqiṣ, Jins-i adnā	Inferior crops, ibid.
Kankūṭ	Method of assessing revenue, based on measurement of land and estimation of yield. Cf. *Agrarian System*, p. 175.
Malba	Cesses above authorised revenue, collected ostensibly for village expenses. Cf. Habib, *Agrarian System*, pp. 126–7, 243 and *n*.
Nānkār	Allowance paid to *zamīndār* out of the revenue collection or by allotment of tax-exempt land for services rendered in collecting land-revenue. Cf. *Agrarian System*, p. 146 and *n*.
Reza ri'āyā	Small peasants.
Sāl-i Kāmil	Abbreviated form of *sāl-i ḥāṣil-i kāmil*, year when the revenue realized was the maximum.
Ṣarf-i Sikka	Discount on account of mintage.
Sarishta-i wuṣūl-i abwāb-i badarnawīsī	*Sarishta*, register; *wuṣūl*, receipt; *badarnawīsī*, audit. Hence audited register of collection of unauthorised appropriations.
Tiyūldār	*Tiyūl*, area whose revenues were assigned by the Emperor. Hence holder of *tiyūl* or *jāgīr*, which are synonyms.

Reviews

Hiroshi Fukazawa, *The Medieval Deccan: Peasants, Social Systems and States, Sixteenth to Eighteenth Centuries*, Oxford University Press, Delhi, 1991, pp. xiv + 252. Rs 250.

The late Hiroshi Fukazawa (d. 1986) represented the post-World War II generation of Japanese historians who turned to India and asked fundamental questions about its social and economic history. Fukazawa began characteristically by research into the origins and early development of the modern Indian textile industry, where imperialism and nationalism had such a major confrontation. From here he passed on to pre-colonial history, learning Persian and Marathi and sifting massive evidence in these languages to analyse the agrarian and social history of Maharashtra before the British conquest. His major studies were scattered in different journals, especially the *Hitotsubashi Journal of Economics*, and some were printed in Japanese only. Not surprisingly, these studies were largely inaccessible to Indian scholars; and it is a treat for us to have them collected together in the present volume, for which we should be grateful to Professors Noboru Karashima and H. Kotani.

Readers will immediately notice with what care and caution Fukazawa approaches his materials, and how he sheds irrelevancies to reach the essence of the matter. The very first study is a pioneering—and classic—survey of local administration under the 'Ādil Shāhs. But the major part of Fukazawa's studies concerns the Maharashtra of the Peshwas (eighteenth century). I would particularly recommend his study (Chapter 8) of the village community in Maharashtra, in which he preferred the classical view to that of Wiser (now so much in fashion), by a lose scrutiny of Marathi documents. The other two studies of seminal importance are of the Maratha State and the caste system (Chapter 4) and the land system and the peasantry under the Peshwas (Chapter 7); but almost nothing is superfluous in the entire volume.

Fukazawa's early death deprived Indian historians of a colleague from whose reflective and painstaking work so much more was still expected. Many of us also lost an ever courteous and indulgent friend.

IRFAN HABIB

M. A. Farooqi, *The Economic Policy of the Sultans of Delhi*, Konark Publishers, Delhi, 1991, pp. xiv + 152. Rs 105.

A study of the economic measures of the Delhi Sultans becomes possible because the available sources contain tolerably sufficient information on the subject. The theme has already received the attention of modern historians. The merit of the present monograph is that it is exclusively devoted to this significant aspect of the history of the period and, while making references to the original sources, has also drawn on previous scholarly contributions made in the field.

The first chapter presents the economic situation on the eve of the Ghorid conquest, basing itself almost entirely on the works of R. S. Sharma and B. N. S. Yadav and others. Farooqi calls the period 'feudal' and talks of the presence of serfdom, almost without any qualification.

Farooqi discusses the economic measures of the Sultans, placing them in the context of the economic conditions and tracing their consequences for the economy. In the second chapter she discusses the economic impact of the Ghorid conquest, following rather too closely the framework of Muhammad Habib and K. A. Nizami's contributions to *A Comprehensive History of India*, Vol. V, as modified by the work of Irfan Habib. The same framework is followed in the rest of the three chapters as well, though there is a welcome effort to go again to the original sources. The appendix on 'coinage' is a good effort, but it would have been still more useful if Farooqi had been a little more analytical and had discussed minting with reference to the economy, viz., the need for more currency owing to realization of land revenue in cash, or to the need for gold and silver coins for large transactions following upon growth in trade.

The analysis offered at times defies logic: it is difficult to understand how the abundance of cultivable land (all within the control of the Sultans) could result in 'checking relentless exploitation of the peasantry' (p. 132). It would certainly result, as it did, in closer control over the peasants who, though 'free born', were not free to leave the land.

One can perhaps legitimately object to the wording of the title. There was certainly no single 'economic policy' of the Sultans, but policies, or rather, simple economic measures. One also wishes a little more care had been taken in revising the thesis for the press. The book still refers to itself as a 'thesis' (pp. v and 2).

The book is a useful volume for postgraduate students, who can find most of the information conveniently available in one place, by an author who is well-versed in Persian sources as well as modern work.

SHIREEN MOOSVI

Dirk H. A. Kolff, *Naukar, Rajput and Sepoy—The Ethnohistory of the Military Labour Market in Hindustan, 1450–1850*, Cambridge University Press, Cambridge, 1990, pp. 217. Price not stated.

Abū'l Faẓl in the *Ā'īn-i Akbarī* gives us an official census (with returns from each *pargana*) of armed retainers of *zamīndārs* (excluding the Mughal army proper), the totals for the whole Empire coming to 3,84,558 cavalry and 42,77,057 infantry, i.e. over 4.5 million armed men. Adding another million, as estimated by Moreland, for the Peninsula we would have some 5.5 million armed men. If we allow for some 19 million others as dependent members of the families of these armed men, and follow S. Moosvi in her estimate of the Indian population *c.* 1595 at 145 millions, we may well have to conclude that some 15 to 20 per cent of the population was dependent wholly or partly on the pursuit of arms. This lends weight to Kolff's emphasis on the importance of the 'military labour market' in pre-British India. He examines in what is a most interesting book the social and political basis of this soldiery. He shows how among this mass of 'armed peasants' (Kolff's expression), there was a tendency to Sanskritize and turn into Rajputs—a movement from the Little into the Great Tradition. The recruitment base of the Mughal professional cavalry—the crucial arm of the sixteenth- and seventeenth-century Mughal army—is less well studied, or, rather, not taken up at all. But that may legitimately be held to be outside the area of Kolff's main concern. Kolff's use of source materials is largely restricted to printed sources, though among these he forages widely and insightfully. There is no doubt that the inquiry pursued by him would have gained considerably from use of documentary evidence in Persian, Rajasthani and Marathi; but such evidence is likely to support, rather than throw doubt on, Kolff's main theses.

I should have liked Kolff to develop his own important suggestions in the section on 'the modern doctrine of caste' (pp. 181–92), where he deals with rural demilitarization, on the one hand, and the dominance of Brahman sepoys in the Bengal Army, on the other. The first process emanated from the very nature of British rule, which converted *zamindars* from armed magnates into landlords. The 'military labour market' of pre-colonial India contracted and disappeared because of this fundamental change. Kolff here underlines one of the major 'discontinuities' brought about by colonialism in its early phases, discontinuities which some historians in India and abroad are nowadays rather prone to overlook.

IRFAN HABIB

Brajadulal Chattopadhyaya, *Aspects of Rural Settlements and Rural Society in Early Medieval India*, S. G. Deuskar Lectures, Centre for Studies in Social Sciences/K. P. Bagchi & Co., Calcutta, 1990, pp. 131. Price not stated.

What happened to Indian society between the fifth and twelfth centuries has been dominated by the theory of Indian feudalism proposed by D. D. Kosambi, and elaborated and much reinforced by R. S. Sharma. Of many aspects of this theory Professor Chattopadhyaya has been an important critic. In the present monograph Chattopadhyaya has undertaken an inquiry into the internal structure of the village, to which, despite their concerns with the agrarian roots of feudalism, Kosambi and Sharma could not pay much attention, beyond propounding a theory of Brahman dominance. Chattopadhyaya assembles the epigraphic evidence for three regions, Bengal, South-eastern Marwar and southern Karnataka, treating each separately, and comes out with a picture of stratified peasantry and private property rights. He does not entirely dismiss the village community, but is not prepared to apply any stereotyped form of it to his period. He may perhaps be less than fair in suggesting that all the earlier scholars assumed a uniform or egalitarian village, but he has certainly offered us a considerable amount of systematically arranged, well-criticised material from a large body of inscriptions (of whose limitations Chattopadhyaya is himself very conscious), for which one must be very grateful. He has put in welcome details on a vast canvas, of which much, alas, still remains blank.

SHIREEN MOOSVI

John S. Deyell, *Living without Silver: The Monetary History of Early Medieval India*, Oxford University Press, Delhi, 1990, pp. xix + 369, 11 maps, 32 plates. Rs 325.

Deyell's work encompasses a seemingly dark period in North Indian coinage history, spanning the time between the emergence of the Gurjara-Pratiharas and the establishment of the Sultanate (750–1250). There has been a need to bring all the scattered materials together and classify it in a well-ordered manner. He is right to insist that in considering both the quantitative aspects and the spread of coins, hoard reports rather than museum catalogues should be the primary source. He has certainly given us an excellent work of reference for the various pre-Sultanate dynastic and regional coinages, supported by a comprehensive bibliography.

The only reservation the reviewer has is in respect of Deyell's anxiety to show that the earlier interpretations of this period as one where commerce and money-exchanges declined were wrong-headed, and that he has brought up new material to dispose of such interpretations. The basic tables on which this 'revisionist' challenge is based will be found on pp. 35 and 36. Lest readers be led into accepting the quantities shown in these tables at their face value, it is necessary to note that (a) all coins are here treated as equal units without distinction of metal (gold, silver, billon, copper), and of weight; and (b) all hoards are treated as equal, irrespective of the number of coins contained in each. Since copper dominated the period 750–1200 to the practical exclusion of gold and silver, it is not surprising that Deyell gets the result he was looking for. The careful reader should remember that in the late sixteenth century the gold *muhr* was worth about 680 times its weight in coined copper; and the silver rupee about 70 times. To forget this, and to treat all coined pieces as representing the same level of commercial transaction lacks justification. On the face of it, the relative absence of gold and silver coins would suggest that large transactions were on the decline. There could be other ways (bills, commercial paper) in which the needs of large transactions could be met. But Deyell has come up with no evidence that bill-money existed on a scale commensurate with such needs. Until such evidence comes to light, the judgement of Kosambi, R. S. Sharma, L. Gopal and B. N. S. Yadava about a commercial decline in early medieval India must continue to command respect.

This reviewer's difference of opinion with Deyell's basic thesis notwithstanding, he has no hesitation in recommending the book as a necessary acquisition for any library concerned with Medieval India or Indian numismatic history. One hopes that Deyell will continue to pursue his searching inquiries into Indian coinages, and their implications for history.

IRFAN HABIB

K. N. Chaudhuri, *Asia before Europe: Economy and Civilization of the Indian Ocean from the Rise of Islam to 1750*, Cambridge University Press, 1990, pp. xviii + 477, 17 maps, 81 illustrations. £50.

In his preface and introduction Chaudhuri makes clear his ambition to attempt a descriptive and analytical work on a Braudelian scale. With such a public declaration to start with, Chaudhuri has to claim possession of theoretical baggage that ordinary souls are not blessed with, *viz.*, 'the linguistic logic of Wittgenstein, the semiology of Saussure, Jacobson, and Hjelmslev, Chomsky's different theories on generative grammars, the outline of Cantor's set theory and Godel's Incomplete Theorem', together with the discovery of how, in view of 'the structuralism of Levi-Strauss and the logic of Boolean algebra', 'abstract reasoning could become a powerful instrument of applied research' (p. 8). If one is still not aware of what it takes to fuse these theories and obtain a historical analysis, one is furnished with a Glossary of Theoretical Terms (not of terms in use in Asian civilizations, as an uninitiated reader may have expected). Here we are told that the Incomplete Theorem means that 'The consistency proof for the system S can be carried out only by means of modes of inference that are not formalized in the system S itself' (p. 425). This apparently is crucial for understanding Asian history. More: 'differentiation, structural' does not mean what it means generally to economic historians, but is 'The process of reasoning through which a concept, a word or a structure which is seen as a single entity or an integral can be further partitioned' (p. 424).

This too presumably forms a fundamental principle for Chaudhuri's neo-Braudelian methodology. Despite the respectable size of the book, however, one gets the feeling that such a mass of theory is just too heavy for the relatively light body of fact that Chaudhuri can collect, on all kinds of aspects of life, from diet and animals, to towns and technology. Putting China in the Indian Ocean area for one thing seems, indeed, rather arbitrary (for which see Glossary, *s.v.* 'Arbitrary'). As for India, the claim that *al-Hind* was the 'Arabic term for the Indian Ocean regions including the Indian sub-continent *and Iran*' (index, p. 465) offers one instance of how, in spite of obvious deficiencies in his knowledge of Arabic and Persian, Chaudhuri can yet make confident assertions about evidence from sources in these languages (and in Turkish and Chinese).

I was naturally interested in how Chaudhuri has used the information for medieval India. I found that not only is his source-base very small (and largely secondary), but also that it has not been accurately represented. For example—

1. 'The pious Muslim historian, who would die in severe self-inflicted poverty...' (p. 83). Baranī's poverty in his last days was the result of his dismissal and imprisonment, not 'self-inflicted'. (See Baranī himself, *Tārīkh-i Fīrūz-Shāhī*, Bib. Ind., p. 466. Chaudhuri does not cite the Persian text anywhere).

2. There is no authority for the statement that 'the Turkish Sultans of Delhi were *constantly* reminded by their warrior followers that *the Turks lived by plunder*' (p. 275). Chaudhuri cites no source for this statement, nor does he give any reference for a passage from Baranī (*op.cit.*, 51–2, which is, however, devoid of this statement) that he proceeds to paraphrase.

3. On p. 76 Abū'l Faẓl is quoted as stating that revenues had to be remitted when prices fell, but Inalcik, 'Rice Cultivation in the Roman Empire', is cited in the reference (on p. 393, ref. 3.13). The correct page number from the translation is given in the preceding note (3.12), where it is made to substantiate a statement about Jaipur, which did not then exist, and where too the name of the translator is wrongly given as Jarrett, instead of H. Beveridge.

4. On pp. 218–19, Abū'l Faẓl's difficult chapter on the 'Maintenance of Livelihood' (*Rawāī-i Rozī*) is cited, without indication of the text or translation or volume thereof (p. 407, ref. 8.2; it should be 'trans. Jarrett, rev. Sarkar, Vol. II'). But there is nothing in Abū'l Faẓl's chapter about restoring 'the pristine quality of a lost livelihood' (Chaudhuri's words); in fact, Abū'l Faẓl simply presents with much rhetoric his version of the theory of the Original Social Contract as a justification for the Mughal monarchy, an argument which does not emerge well in Jarrett's translation.

5. With reference to Abū'l Faẓl's statistics, Chaudhuri speaks of 'the fiscal and statistical templates, drawn up by the Chief Diwan's office *in Delhi*'

(p. 232). Surely he should have known that Delhi was not Akbar's capital. Nor does the *Ā'īn-i Akbarī* offer any evidence that 'the tabulation of resources, (and) the differential fertility of soil', were 'encoded and documented' for different localities ('disaggregated units of space'!). Characteristically, when we turn to the reference for this on p. 408, we have 'Abu'l Fazl's historical account in *Ain-i Akbari* [ed.? transl.?], II, 55–8.' The pages suit neither the Jarrett-Sarkar translation, nor Blochmann's ed.

6. 'The four significant industrial regions of India specialising in the manufacture of cotton fabrics were the Panjab, Gujarat, the Coromandel Coast and Bengal' (p. 307: repeated from Chaudhuri's own *Trading World of Asia*, p. 243). The specification of the Panjab as a major region of cotton manufacture, as against Sind, Awadh, Malwa, Khandesh, the Delhi–Agra area, etc. has little merit, and the evidence of the map on p. 311, with textile products quantified, is merely impressionistic, there being no reference to sources on which it is based.

7. 'The technique of casting large cannon from bronze or iron was evidently quickly mastered by the Asian metallurgists, once the use of artillery had become well established' (p. 328). Contrast this with the statement on p. 331: 'At what period Indian smiths mastered the art of casting iron objects is not known for certain.' Indeed, it is not certain whether they ever learnt to cast large iron objects, notwithstanding the single reference to iron-casting in Orissa in Hamilton, who might have been misled on the point: large iron anchors need not have been cast, just as the celebrated Mehrauli iron-pillar was not cast.

When Chaudhuri spoke of reading Braudel during a holiday in Spain, and of then reflecting sombrely on his own 'computerised research' for his *Trading World of Asia* (1978) one tended to wonder maliciously whether he really needed computers when the simple additions and indexing required for his tables could have been done with ordinary calculators. Similarly when, for his present book, the claimed novelty is not computerization but theory, one wonders whether he should have gone to all this trouble for the simple results presented in his Conclusion. The phase in the 'life-cycle' for Indian Ocean civilizations that he places 'from the rise of Islam to about 1750' can be supported more from conventional history, i.e. from the spread of a Perso-Arabic ('Islamic') culture covering or influencing much of the shores of the Indian Ocean, than from the alleged lack of alteration in 'the average value of certain ratios', viz. 'ratios between population and cultivable land, between the level of technology and the rate of innovation, between expected standards of living and the possibilities of improvement, between the state's capacity to regulate economic life and the autonomy of social groups' (pp. 382–3). There is no proof that these 'ratios' were any different during the period [illegible] BC–AD 622 than during 622–1750. So why not start the 'life-cycle' around 500 BC? Except for the rather quaint use of the term 'state capitalism' [illegible] commerce generated by state taxation, I see no new discovery in [illegible] description of the economies of the late Medieval Asian empires summ[illegible] in the last paragraph of the book (pp. 386–7). But one should still be grateful for a recognition here of 'nineteenth century colonialism and Western economic imperialism'. This at least marks a shift, however slight, from the position of 'the establishment of the Right' (see p. 5).

The book is well printed and well illustrated. If Chaudhuri could possibly have rectified the 'ratios' between claims and content, and between irrelevant theory and relevant facts, by eliminating much unnecessary reflection, autobiography and verbiage, the book could have been a readable one, and some valuable insights might have been rescued. He would still have needed to be more careful about his sources, however.

IRFAN HABIB

Douglas Streusand, *The Formation of the Mughal Empire*, Oxford University Press, Delhi, 1989, pp. 206. Rs 175.

Streusand professedly aims at explaining the nature of empire-formation under Akbar during the earlier period of his reign, 1556–82. The period has been well worked on by historians, though there is always an expanding domain of sources which can justify a fresh effort. Streusand, however, has had no access to the new material. The documents at Allahabad, Aligarh and Vrindavan are apparently not known to him, and he dismisses those at Bikaner for the strange reason that Rajasthan was not in 'the heart of the Mughal Empire'. The *Munshāt-i Namkīn*, a massive collection with many documents of much importance belonging to the period of Akbar's reign he studies, is not even listed in his bibliography. As far as the narrative sources are concerned, Streusand has not used any MSS, even when these are necessary to clarify doubtful readings. He does not seem aware of the earlier version of the *Akbarnama* and has not used *Tarikh-i-Alfi*.

Strangely, even Monserrate's *Commentaries* and Jesuit letters have not been used. Streusand's familiarity with recent work is equally limited. He does not seem aware of a large number of papers published within the last thirty years, eg. by Irfan Habib on *manṣabs* and local administration, A. Hasan on silver influx, by the reviewer on Akbar's religious views, or Shireen Moosvi on revenue rates and *suyurghal*.

What Streusand lacks in access to sources and modern work, he makes up by supreme confidence in his own effort. He begins by a survey of work on the subject in which most of the work done so far is put down under 'present-minded (!) interpretation', and historians are classified according to their religion and domicile. The accuracy here is remarkable in that Irfan Habib is classed among historians writing 'primarily on Mughal decline' and of Iqtidar Alam Khan it is said that he 'follows the Hindu communalist perspective'!

Streusand's easy assumption of ignorance on other people's part (see p. 7, lines 5–7 and fn 19, both in comments on Iqtidar Alam Khan) often crosses the bounds of propriety. Not infrequently, as in the case of Akbar's measures with regard to the *jizya*, it is he who is guilty of ignorance. The *jizya* was abolished twice, in 1564 and 1579, not once. Badāūnī II, p. 210, speaks of the re-imposition of the *jizya* at the instance of Abdu-n Nabi in AH 983/1575–6 AD, and this presupposes both a prior and subsequent remission. Streusand's insistence that there was only one remission (pp. 114–15) and his strictures on Iqtidar Alam Khan again in this connexion (p. 115, n. 20), suggest that he himself has not read Badāūnī's text with any care.

On the very important matter of administrative construction, Streusand has little to offer. *Nasaq* appears as *nāsaq* (pp. 70–1 and so indexed), and its sense is misunderstood, being absolutely different from the one given by Irfan Habib whom he cites as his authority here The *zabt* system is not even discussed. On the *manṣab* his statement is all too brief. The continued use of the term *Dīn-i-Ilāhī* (pp. 148 ff.) for Akbar's religious views, despite its incorrectness and capacity to cause misunderstanding, does not help clarity.

A confused unbalanced narrative leads to a confused conclusion: 'One may envision the Mughal empire as a hybrid, Islamic—in the broadest sense—at the centre; Indian in the provinces' (p. 181). Whatever does this mean? It is just flourish, with no substance. The same thing may be said of the whole book.

M. ATHAR ALI

Ishwar Prakash Gupta, *Agra: The Imperial Capital (16th & 17th Centuries): Urban Glimpses of Mughal India*, Discovery, Delhi, pp. ix + 133. Rs 100.

This short monograph on the Mughal metropolis, Agra, is evidently drawn from the author's Ph.D. thesis, 'Urban Life in North India during the Seventeenth Century', which he wrote at Aligarh in the early 1960s. Most of the material presented in this volume has already been published by him in the form of stray articles during the preceding two decades, some of which are listed in the bibliography attached to this volume.

I. P. Gupta's central contribution to the history of Agra is represented by his description of its physical dimensions as well as civil life during the sixteenth and seventeenth centuries in chapters 1, 2, 3 and 5. His attempt in chapter 2 at tracing the growth of the urban settlement at Agra down to Shahjahan's reign is no doubt commendable. The map of Agra appended to that chapter especially deserves commendation. But for a student of history, the real importance of I. P. Gupta's work seems to lie in its being an attempt at pointing to the availability of a considerable body of source material on the theme, which still awaits proper analysis.

In his brief Foreword, Professor Satish Chandra tends towards a rather optimistic view of I. P. Gupta's own contribution. According to him, the study challenges the notion of the commercial decline of Agra after the shifting of the Mughal capital to Shahjahanabad and 'gives the quietus to the notion put forward by the Frenchman, François Bernier, that the cities in India were little more than armed camps.' One is tempted to point out that there is hardly any attempt in I. P. Gupta's monograph to come to grips with this significant question. Suggestions that Agra continued to prosper even after the capital shifted to Shahjahanabad are of course repeatedly made by him, but he has not produced any reliable evidence in support of this seemingly plausible contention. As a matter of fact, the evidence marshalled by Gupta does not go beyond testifying to the growing prosperity of Agra till Shahjahan's time. None of the important sources relied upon by him for his description of Agra's commercial prosperity is valid for the eighteenth century. Thus, disagreeing respectfully with Professor Satish Chandra's assessment, one might suggest that the question as to what extent François Bernier's notion that the population of cities in Mughal India largely consisted of camp followers of the king, was applicable to Agra, could be answered with any measure of certainty only after the available source material pertaining to the late seventeenth and eighteenth centuries (left largely unexplored by I. P. Gupta) is analysed properly by someone having easier access to the Persian records. Besides archaeological records, travellers' accounts and Persian chronicles, this source material should also include traditions about the names of localities, private papers of leading land-owning and mercantile families, early British records of the Agra Commissionary preserved in the U.P. Record Office (Allahabad) and elsewhere, as well as the corpus of Urdu literary writings of the eighteenth century.

The most serious weakness of I. P. Gupta's research seems to stem from his inability to consult the original Persian texts of the Mughal chronicles cited by him. His exclusive reliance on English translations of these texts has sometimes led to grave errors. For example, on p. 58, Gupta mentions the establishment of *Shaitanpura*, a separate quarter for prostitutes 'outside the town' (which he assumes to be Agra) on the authority of the *Ā'īn-i Akbarī* and Badāunī's *Muntakhab-ut Tawārīkh*. This is a serious slip resulting primarily from his inability to consult the original Persian texts of these books. In reality, there is no mention of *Shaitanpura* in the *Ā'īn-i Akbarī*. The passage cited from Blochmann's English translation of the first volume of the *Ā'īn-i Akbarī* actually contains the English translation of the very passage of Badauni I. P. Gupta quotes in the same footnote as additional evidence. Moreover, from Badāunī's account, it is evident that *Shaitanpura* was built by Akbar not at the outskirts of Agra but at those of Fatehpur Sikri; and this, of course, makes the entire evidence irrelevant for Agra. A similar confusion also exists in Gupta's narrative on *Jogi Pura*, *Dharam Pura* and *Khair Pura* established by Akbar. These localities were established according to Badāunī, in AH 991/AD 1583–4, not at Agra, but at Fatehpur Sikri.

To end this review on a positive note, it would perhaps be worthwhile to mention a rather likeable deficiency in I. P. Gupta's argument throughout the volume. He betrays a general tendency of sympathy with the Mughal administration attributing to it a policy of 'public welfare'. In the present academic climate where one is sometimes dismayed to find even serious scholars referring to Turkish/Mughal rule as 'the Muslim yoke' (see for instance K. V. Soundara Rajan's *Junagadh*, published by the Director General, Archaeological Survey of India, New Delhi, 1985), Gupta's rather naïve and not wholly justifiable commendation of the Mughal administration comes as a pleasant relief.

IQTIDAR ALAM KHAN

Ashin Das Gupta and M. N. Pearson ed., *India and the Indian Ocean, 1500–1800*, Oxford University Press, Calcutta, 1987, pp. XI + 363 + one map. Rs 240.

In spite of the fact that the book is a collection of essays it does not fall into the usual genre of collectanea. It is entirely devoted to a single theme: trade in the Indian Ocean and Indian overseas trade during the sixteenth to the eighteenth centuries. Trade with East Africa and even Chinese trade in the South China Sea is dealt with.

The first two essays contributed by the two editors set out the 'subject' and the 'story'. Pearson, discussing the 'subject', describes the scope, surveys the work previously done and also helpfully explains the geographical limits of the Indian Ocean. Ashin Das Gupta lucidly sums up the 'story' during the three centuries, outlining the main arguments of the individual contributions. The four following essays then deal separately with each of the four centuries beginning with the fifteenth century. The remaining nine essays are devoted to different important related aspects such as the trade of Ceylon and Indonesia, the Dutch East India Company, etc.

The vantage point in almost all the essays remains Indian Ocean trade, and one of the editors says that the attempt is not to replace Eurocentrism by Indocentrism. Yet in most of the essays, while the Indian and Asian merchants and trade have been accorded attention, the European Companies are fairly near the centre of focus. The inferences are generally couched in a cautious style: e.g., 'The English and Dutch contribution to the generally prosperous trade of the Indian Ocean in the seventeenth century was to reinforce this expanding commerce' (p. 39).

A great merit of the book consists in the exhaustive bibliographies appended to each essay which are indeed most useful.

Since the book achieves so much it is with some reluctance that I record my grievances. The preface arouses high expectations by stating that the objective is to 'link the study of Indian history with that of the Indian Ocean'. One thus turns to the essay on 'India and Indian ocean in the sixteenth century' expecting to find a discussion on the implications of the establishment of the Mughal Empire for the trade of the Indian ocean. Alas, Pearson finds satisfaction in holding on to his earlier view that since sea trade did not contribute significantly to the revenues of the Mughal Empire it was of little consequence for the Empire. But is the converse, that the Mughal Empire was not important to Indian Ocean trade, equally true? Was the introduction of a uniform currency and taxation system, uniform units of weights and measures, protection of links between the hinterland and the ports, the expansion of demand for bullion and luxuries, of no significance for the trade? This complete delinking of major facts of Indian history from developments in Indian Ocean trade becomes all the more glaring in the essay by Bruce Watson, who still cannot find out 'why Indian merchants appear to have lost their preeminence in India's maritime trade by the second half of the eighteenth century' (p. 313). He has apparently not yet heard of Plassey, Buxar and Lord Clive.

Mercifully Ashin Das Gupta's essay on the eighteenth century addresses itself to the problems of the decline of the Mughal Empire and is an exception in this regard.

SHIREEN MOOSVI

Paul Jackson, S.J., *The Way of a Sufi: Sharafuddin Maneri*, Idarah-i-Adabiyat-i-Delhi, Delhi, 1987, pp. 278.

The work comprises, besides an introduction and two appendices at the end, three parts, consisting of two, one and three chapters respectively. Each chapter is based on a careful scrutiny of the evidence available in different contemporary and near-contemporary sources on the life and teachings of Shaikh Sharafuddin Maneri, a leading Firdausi Sufi saint of the fourteenth century. Miscellaneous sources such as Sanskrit inscriptions, legends about the early Muslim warrior saints in Bihar and the eye-witness account left by the Tibetan monk Dharmasvamin have been critically utilized in the reconstruction of the historical background to the Shaikh's life and work in Bihar. It is, no doubt, for the first time that the author draws our attention to the fact that the early Muslim conquerors of India did not destroy Hindu or Buddhist centres of learning on the basis of Dharmasvamin's account. Dharmasvamin found during Sultan Iltutmish's reign more than eighty Buddhist *viharas* in and around Nalanda, where teachers imparted knowledge to their followers. This is valuable inasmuch as it dispels the erroneous view that Nalanda was destroyed by Bhakhtiyar Khalji around AD 1200.

Chapter II, on the birth, education and transformation of the Shaikh from an orthodox *'ālim* (scholar) into a devout Sufi saint is interesting insofar as it provides fresh information about the rapid development of Sonargaon into an important centre of Islamic learning and culture under the fostering care of Sultan Shamsuddin Fīrūz Shāh. Here we get insights into the process of urbanization in a territory conquered and brought under the rule of the Sultans towards the close of the thirteenth century. Shaikh Sharafu'ddin, according to the chronology worked out by Paul Jackson, stayed in Sonargaon during the years 1305 to 1322 for his studies of Islamic sciences under the supervision of Maulana Sharafu'ddin Tau'ma and Balkhi *'ulamā* (scholars) there. The author's analysis of life and conditions in Bengal is based on authentic information available in the collections of discourses of Shaikh Sharafu'ddin Maneri.

Chapter III in Part II is related to the life and missionary work after Shaikh Sharafu'ddin Maneri's conversion to Sufism. Like the chapters in Part I, it also extends our understanding of the approach taken by sufi saints belonging to different *silsilahs* to the State. Like the Suhrawardi saints, Shaikh Sharaf u'ddin Maneri did not consider friendly relations with the ruler as something harmful to spiritual life. He had good relations with Sultan Muhammad bin Tughluq (d. AD 1351). On the latter's death, the Shaikh severed his relations with the Sultans of Delhi, yet he showed love and regard for Sultan Sikandar Shah of Bengal through correspondence with him. Besides details about Shaikh Sharaf u'ddin Maneri's life of dedication to the service of mankind and love of God, equally important is the information utilised by the author about Sultan Muhammad bin Tughluq's interest in metaphysical philosophy. It contrasts with the information available in other contemporary and later sources about the Sultan's hostility towards Sufis. The Sultan appears to have studied the *Maktubat-i-Sa'di* (a collection of one hundred epistles), written by the Shaikh on spiritual matters and was impressed by the philosophical thought contained therein. It is to be pointed out that in some of the epistles the Shaikh makes comments on Sultan Muhammad bin Tughluq's style of government and behaviour along with an exposition of Islamic beliefs and of Sufism. The Sultan was inspired into requesting him to write a treatise on Sufi philosophy for his perusal. The Shaikh did not agree, writing in reply: 'You, my brother, had desired that I should write something especially for you concerning the knowledge of the Sufis. Realize, my brother, that the knowledge of this group is extremely precious and exalted, and cannot be contained in letters and words....'

The remaining three chapters that comprise Part III are invaluable as they explain the essence of the spiritual philosophy of Shaikh Sharaf u'ddin Maneri. In the preparation of these chapters the author has carefully analysed the material contained in the Shaikh's own epistles and collections of his discourses. Undoubtedly, the author provides authoritative scholarship with illuminating analysis of the historical role of one of the great spiritual Sufi thinkers in medieval times.

Appendix B contains the translation of the utterances of the Shaikh during the last days of his life. It is also valuable insofar as it contains the names of disciples belonging to different strata who attended the Shaikh at the time of his death. The presence of Fatuha, the cook and the supervisor of the kitchen, points to the interaction between the great tradition, represented by the religious élite, and the little tradition to which the unlettered *murīds* of a great Sufi saint belonged.

It may be pointed out that the author has not employed a uniform method to refer to his sources. At some places the sources (generally secondary) are referred to in the footnotes on the page but the contemporary Persian works are mentioned in brackets at the end of the quotation in the text. At times only the page numbers are given and it is difficult to know which one of the sources is meant. It is to be hoped that the author will apply a uniform system in the second edition. I also wish the author had devoted some space in his work to the intellectual legacy of Shaikh Sharaf u'ddin Maneri. The Shaikh was not only a man of great spiritual power who wrote with facility but also a thinker, with a vast knowledge of Islamic sciences and religious literature, produced both in Arabic and Persian. The collections of his epistles and discourses contain references to Islamic classics, showing the range of his scholarly pursuits. Besides the works of and on Imam Abul Qasim Qushairi, Shaikh Bayazid Bistami, Imam Ghazzali, Shaikh Ain-ul Quzzat, Shaikh Shihab u'ddin Suhrawardi (the author of *Awarif-ul Ma'arif*), *Mathnavi-i Maulana Rumi*, he had studied literature on the *Hikmat-ul-Ishraq* and the Mutizilite philosophy as well. He judged every doctrine and philosophy in the light of the Quran's teachings. As regards Ibn al-Arabi's doctrine of *Wahdat-ul Wujud* (Unity in essence of the creator and the created), it gained popularity among certain sections of the Muslim religious élite and some of them had been misled into thinking that man could become part of God through spiritual progress. Though Shaikh Sharaf u'ddin Maneri seems to have been overwhelmed by the greatness of Ibn-al Arabi, he did not fully agree with him on the relationship between man and God. Discussing this problem, he observed that a sensible man would always be able to distinguish between the created and the Creator, 'in the sense that he perceives that they all come from him.' Likewise, the Shaikh disagreed with Ibn-al Arabi over whether sainthood (*wilayat*) had precedence over prophethood. Shaikh Sharaf u'ddin Maneri declared that one breath of the Prophet's was more blessed than the entire life of a saint.

The writings of the Shaikh himself and other contemporary literary sources yield enormous evidence about the intellectual trends, currents and cross-currents in Indo-Muslim society during the fourteenth century. As the Shaikh either responded to or reacted against certain currents, they need a somewhat detailed reappraisal. I hope my suggestions will be considered when the second edition of this excellent work is published.

IQTIDAR HUSAIN SIDDIQI

R. Nath (trans.), *Monuments of Delhi: A Historical Study*, English version of Sir Syed Ahmad Khan's *Athar al-Sanadid*, Indian Institute of Islamic Studies, New Delhi, 1979, pp. 100, with illustrations and inscriptions. Rs 180.

Like nations and peoples, towns and cities develop their own distinctive urban culture and social traditions over time. Every city and town has certain social and economic functions, but the role played by a metropolitan city in shaping people's culture and setting social norms is especially important. The fate of a civilization is ultimately reflected in the fate of its great cities. Delhi, which had been the seat of great imperial dynasties from the beginning of the thirteenth century to the decline of the Mughals in the eighteenth century has a fascinating history. A scientific study of the surviving monuments of medieval Delhi could give us socio-cultural insights that cannot otherwise be obtained.

Palaces, fortresses, pleasure gardens and water reservoirs added considerably to the grandeur of Delhi. This grandeur also created a marked sense of pride in Delhi's residents, from the early medieval period down to the eighteenth century. 'Isāmī, the fourteenth-century poet and compiler of the *Futūḥ-us-Salātīn*, looked down upon the residents of towns and cities in the neighbourhood of Delhi and considered them rustics not worthy of residing in Delhi. The famous eighteenth-century Urdu poet, Mir Taqi Mir, betrays the same feelings in his autobiographical work, *Zikr-i-Mir*, and over and over again in his *ghazals*.

With the establishment of British authority, the development of Indo-Muslim architecture came to an end. Even the future of important buildings became dark lending a sense of urgency to the task of compiling a description of Delhi's monuments, so that their memory could be cherished.

Sangin Beg, son of Ali Akbar Beg, seems to have been the first scholar to undertake the preparation of a work on buildings of historical significance in Delhi. In 1819 he produced a book in Persian entitled *Sair-ul-Manāzil*, where he mentioned the important buildings and also reproduced inscriptions found there. The *muhallas* or quarters where the buildings were located were described, as were the shops and workshops owned by artisans and different craftsmen in each *muhalla*, shedding valuable light on various economic activities. (Dr Naim Ahmad has published an Urdu translation of *Sai'r-ul-Manāzil*, Adabi Academy, Aligarh, 1980).

In 1846, Syed Ahmad Khan published his now famous work, *Āṣār-ul-Sanādīd*, divided into several parts, each containing a detailed account of the monuments erected in different parts of Delhi during different periods, as well as notices of scholars, Sufis, poets and artists of the city. Though written in ornate rhyming Urdu, it was thought to be an outstanding work of its kind. European archaeologists also found it a work of absorbing interest and considered it the basic authority for the study of the development of Indo-Muslim architectural styles in Delhi. To decipher the inscriptions on the building, he raised himself to the top of the Qutb Minar in a stringed contraption, although he was a man with a substantial frame.

In view of its importance, Col. Saxon, a member of the Royal Asiatic Society of Great Britain and the Board of Directors of the East India Company, asked A. A. Robert, the District Magistrate and Collector of Delhi, to get it translated into English. Syed Ahmad Khan was made an honorary member of the Archaeological Society of Delhi in 1852. It was at this time that Robert persuaded him to revise the archaeological portion and publish it in simple prose as rhyme was difficult to translate into English. Hence the publication of the second revised edition in 1854.

The second edition of the *Āṣār-ul-Sanādīd* relates only to the buildings and pleasure gardens; with some additions. For instance, there was a detailed account of the famous Jantar Mantar observatory erected by Sawai Jai Singh in 1724, based on Jai Singh's *Zich-i-Muḥammad-Shahi*. This MS copy is now in the Maulana Azad Library, AMU, and contains Sir Syed's autograph with the date on which he had purchased it. In general Sir Syed referred to his sources of information in his description of each monument. Every part of the work reveals the author's command over the vast historical literature produced in India during the medieval period. Some of the works he utilised do not seem to have survived the 1857 Revolt.

R. Nath has earned the gratitude of students of art history by rendering the Urdu classic into English, which can be utilised even by researchers not familiar with Urdu. It is, however, to be regretted that the translation is confined to Syed Ahmed's Urdu text leaving the inscriptions in different languages and scripts untouched. Let us hope that an English translation of these inscriptions along with an index will be included in the second edition of his translation.

IQTIDAR HUSAIN SIDDIQI

Contributors

ATHAR ALI	National Fellow of the Indian Council of Historical Research; former Professor of History, Aligarh Muslim University
B. L. BHADANI	Reader in History, Aligarh Muslim University
S. P. GUPTA	Professor of History, Aligarh Muslim University
IRFAN HABIB	Professor of History, Aligarh Muslim University
IQBAL HUSAIN	Professor of History, Aligarh Muslim University
IQTIDAR ALAM KHAN	Professor of History, Aligarh Muslim University
SHIREEN MOOSVI	Professor of History, Aligarh Muslim University
SYED ALI NADEEM REZAVI	Lecturer in History, Aligarh Muslim University
IQTIDAR HUSAIN SIDDIQUI	Professor of History, Aligarh Muslim University
ABHA SINGH	Lecturer in History, Indira Gandhi National Open University, New Delhi